B HARTFORD   Gubernick, Lisa
              Rebecca.

              Squandered
              fortune

$24.95

DATE		
FEB 5 1991		
MAR 2 1 1991		
APR 8 - 1991		
MAY 7 1991		
JUL 1 4 1992		

D1058425

SQUANDERED FORTUNE

Lieutenant Hartford (1942). He ran his ship aground twice.
(Courtesy of The Hartford Family Foundation)

SQUANDERED FORTUNE

The Life and Times of HUNTINGTON HARTFORD

Lisa Rebecca Gubernick

G. P. PUTNAM'S SONS NEW YORK

FOR PAUL

Published by G. P. Putnam's Sons,
200 Madison Avenue, New York, NY 10016.
Published simultaneously in Canada

Lines from ''Gerontion'' are quoted from *Collected Poems 1909–1962*
by T. S. Eliot, copyright 1936 by Harcourt Brace Jovanovich, Inc.,
copyright © 1964, 1963 by T. S. Eliot.
Reprinted by permission of the publisher.

The text of this book is set in Times Roman.

Library of Congress Cataloging-in-Publication Data

Gubernick, Lisa Rebecca.
Squandered fortune: the life and times of Huntington Hartford /
Lisa Rebecca Gubernick.
p. cm.
Includes index.
ISBN 0-399-13572-3
1. Hartford, Huntington, 1911- . 2. Millionaires—United
States—Biography. 3. Art patrons—United States—Biography.
4. United States—Social life and customs—20th century. 5. Upper
classes—United States—History—20th century. I. Title.
HG172.H37G83   1991   90-36068 CIP
973.9′092—dc20
[B]

Printed in the United States of America
1 2 3 4 5 6 7 8 9 10

History has many cunning passages, contrived corridors
And issues, deceives with whispering ambitions,
Guides us by vanities. Think now
She gives when our attention is distracted
And what she gives, gives with such supple confusions
That the giving famishes the craving. Gives too late
What's not believed in, or if still believed,
In memory only, reconsidered passion. Gives too soon
Into weak hands, what's thought can be dispensed with . . .

T. S. ELIOT, "Gerontion"

CONTENTS

I

❖

BEGINNINGS
From the A&P
to Bellevue Avenue

Hunt with Henrietta Hartford, who was left in full charge
of her adolescent son.
(New York Daily News Photo)

1

I T WAS a hot August afternoon, and a mangy German shepherd paced the front courtyard of the townhouse on East Thirtieth Street. At first, a watchdog seemed unnecessary for the brownstone-lined street. But as I walked down the block from Park Avenue to Lexington, passing a derelict in one doorway and a hooker in the next, the need for some sort of sentry became more evident.

I lingered on the safe side of the rusting iron gates bordering the yard, then called up to an open window. A withered blonde peered out and asked what I wanted. I shouted that I had an appointment with the master of the house. Before long, the blonde reappeared at the front door. She wore Betsey Johnson black jersey and fishnets, a mean scar welted across her throat and chest. She grabbed the dog by the collar and I crossed the strip of Astroturf, caked with pigeon droppings, that carpeted the path to the front door.

"He's just woken up," she announced. "You'll have to wait."

Inside, the paint was peeling, the furniture threadbare. The few remnants of wealth were littered with decay. Two squat Roman columns flanked the entrance to the front door, framing a marble torso of a Roman youth. A black rubber trash bin, a planter for a wilting philodendron, was balanced on his neck.

On the second floor, the patrician planes of a bronze bust of a young man glowed in the afternoon light; its base was obscured by a cluster of pill bottles and a ponytailed Barbie doll. Atop a dusty piano was a portrait of an overrouged woman draped in a green gauze gown. The back was inscribed, in feathery script, "Henrietta Hartford."

The two floors were a scrimmage of artifacts from the many projects built by her son, George Huntington Hartford II, the man I was waiting to see. They were small shrines of his broken dreams.

Just past the foyer sat a model by the architect Edward Durell Stone of Hartford's museum, the Gallery of Modern Art. The Courbets and Dalís that had graced its walls had long since been sold. The building itself had been taken over by the City of New York. The only artworks left in this house were a half-dozen paintings and sculptures by Marjorie Steele, second of the four very young, very beautiful women Hunt Hartford had married and divorced, partners in marriages that failed long before they ended.

On the bottom of a bookshelf in the living room were blueprints for Paradise Island, the $30 million Shangri-La he had built in the Bahamas. It had changed hands twice in the last five years; now, teetering on bankruptcy, it had become little more than a honky-tonk for midwestern honeymooners. Near the plans was a glassed-in model of a four-masted square-rigger; over fifty years before, the real boat had sailed through the Caribbean in search of lost pirate treasure. Not a single doubloon was ever found.

Thirty minutes passed, and the blonde returned. The old man, upstairs on the third floor, was ready to receive company.

Any preparations made for a visitor were impossible to discern. My host, a ringer for an aging, dissolute Jason Robards, was clad in a soiled blue cotton bathrobe. He was half sitting, half lying on his bed, a hospital cot adjacent to a large oak four-poster. The windows were closed and the curtains were drawn against the summer light; the air had the stench of a sickroom.

Compact discs, mostly opera recordings, were piled on one table. Bottles of Stolichnaya and Baileys Irish cream crowded the top of the television set. The bedstand was littered with pill bottles and candy-striped straws cut into thirds. Inside an open drawer were empty three-inch-square cellophane bags, each clouded by a film of white powder.

A thirtyish redhead in high heels entered and approached the old man. "Can I have seven dollars?" she asked. "I'm too tired to walk to Ginger's."

Slowly he raised himself up, climbed out of bed, and hobbled past a cedar chest that overflowed with scraps from his life: pictures of himself, his children, and assorted young women, whose names he had long since forgotten. He stopped before a massive cast-iron safe in the corner, and with his body blocking the dial from view, spun the combination, opened the door, and fished out some bills from a battered manila envelope leaning against a Maxwell House coffee can. Then, booty clutched in her fist, the redhead ran down the stairs to the ground floor, caroling to no one in particular, "I'm rich, I'm rich, I have seven dollars."

Meanwhile, the prince of this disarray—author, philanthropist, museum builder, developer of resorts, and heir to the great A&P grocery-store fortune—returned to his bed to talk of art. "I gave my Rembrandt, the best portrait I had, to Columbia University," he said in his New York bray. "They sold it. I want to see it one more time, but I don't know if it's going to be possible. Columbia hasn't answered my calls. . . . It's not asking so much."

George Huntington Hartford. The name could have been invented by Booth Tarkington for a nineteenth-century patrician rendered obsolete by the automobile age. This man, cleaned up and dressed up, with his shock of white hair and searing brown eyes, might still have played the part of Tarkington's antiquated aristocrat, George Amberson Minafer, in his golden years.

But Huntington Hartford aspired to more than the comforts of the leisure class. Piles of photographs and newspaper clippings in the chest at the foot of his bed attested to his celebrity; some hinted at his ambitions to be more than just another playboy. There was a laughing Huntington Hartford out on the town with Lana Turner; Huntington Hartford in a deep discussion with Errol Flynn on one of the zebra-striped banquettes at El Morocco; Huntington Hartford next to a smiling Richard Nixon on the golf course at his Paradise Island resort, playground for the rich and famous, and locus for a political intrigue whose cast of characters eventually included Nixon, Meyer Lansky, Howard Hughes, and Robert Vesco.

Huntington Hartford took the long fall; he ran through one of America's greatest fortunes. The Great Atlantic & Pacific Tea Company was built in the 1800s by his grandfather, George Huntington Hartford I. The grandson came into his portion of the legacy a full century later, inheriting some $100 million, worth more than four times that much in today's dollars.

One hundred million dollars gone. It wouldn't be hard to conjure images of Rabelaisian excess: women with weighty baubles, greenbacks piled high on a craps table. Those are some of the images of this tale, but they tell only a fraction of the story. Hartford was no Tommy Manville, frittering away tens of millions on gambling and women. He did not live a life of drunken dissolution as did Reginald Vanderbilt. Hartford believed that if he bought enough and built enough he could convert those boldface mentions in the society columns into lasting fame.

"I wanted to make an impact," Hartford said from his sickbed. "I knew I wasn't a genius, but I wanted to make a contribution."

"It was a great big spendorama," said his friend Herbert Smokler, a psychiatrist. "He loved to see his name on things."

If Hartford believed he could buy fame, he badly miscalculated. Buy and build he did, but there will be no Hearst Castle to immortalize the Hartford memory. His mansion on a 150-acre estate in the Hollywood Hills burned to the ground long ago; all that remain are an eroding tennis court; a graffiti-lined swimming pool awash with empty beer cans; and a gatekeeper's cottage, where a homeless teenager wearing a ragged Grateful Dead T-shirt has set up house.

Down the hill, just steps from the heart of Hollywood, stands the theater Hartford built in the fifties to bring culture to Babylon. "They took my name off," he said bitterly. "Go downstairs, see the commendation the city council gave me. I was the one who built it."

All of his life Huntington Hartford had been surrounded by girls and hangers-on, and that summer of 1985 was no different. "Anyone could live there," said one regular visitor to the Hartford household. "But I'm not sure why they would want to."

Huntington Hartford, a man whose name was once spoken in the same breath as those of Howard Hughes and J. Paul Getty, stayed in that wretched house for the same sorry reason everyone else did. He had no place left to go.

2

THE FOUNDING of Huntington Hartford's fortune had nothing to do with his family at all. The credit for launching what would eventually become The Great Atlantic & Pacific Tea Company belongs to George Gilman, a thirty-three-year-old leather trader from Maine, who in 1859 opened a tea-importing firm on Gold Street in New York City. Four years later, Gilman decided that he wanted to expand into the retail trade, and the Great American Tea Company opened its doors on Vesey Street, now the site of the World Trade Center towers. Gilman lured customers in with Barnumesque salesmanship. He turned the tea store into a Mandarin pageant, painting the exterior in vermilion imported from China and covering the interior with gilt-edged Chinese panels. The ceiling was a canopy of pressed tin; the cashier sat inside a gilded pagoda.

But thanks to a thirty-year-old clerk Gilman had hired some three years before, the tea company offered more than just glitz. George Huntington Hartford, son of a dry-goods salesman in Augusta, Maine, grandson of an English immigrant, came up with a unique sales strategy for his employer. What he called the club plan offered customers tea in bulk at a spectacularly low thirty cents a pound, when other retailers were charging a dollar. It was good for the consumer and even better for Gilman and Hartford. Bypassing the tea brokers meant they could charge less, attract more customers, and still turn a profit.

Gilman and Hartford aggressively trumpeted their prices, spending more money on advertising than any other tea merchant in the nation. In 1869, with the-bigger-the-better boosterism, they changed the name of their nascent enterprise to The Great Atlantic & Pacific Tea Company, a rather overblown monicker since the operation hardly spanned the eastern seaboard, let alone the entire continent. But the two-man team wanted to draw the blueprint for an empire. By the next year, the chain had a dozen stores, which had already started selling more than just tea: coffee, spices, soap, condensed milk, and baking powder were added to the shelves.

During the 1870s, Gilman and Hartford started moving west. They set down their first stakes in Chicago after the Great Fire in 1871, by sending a quickly exhausted consignment of goods and a small staff to aid the disaster-struck city. After the goodwill came the glitter—red-and-gilt wagons drawn by eight-horse teams. The A&P offered $500 in gold to the citizen who came closest to guessing the combined weight of the horse team.

The giveaways kept going once the customers passed through the A&P portals. Hartford originated the gift-with-purchase sales promotion. A&P tea customers received dishpans and lithographs of smiling babies with their purchases—all as a band played a ditty with the words: "Oh, this is the day they give babies away, with half a pound of tea."

Gilman retired in 1878, having signed a partnership agreement with Hartford that left the founder with a fifty-percent stake in the company and gave his onetime clerk managing control. Gilman died in 1901, and the next year Hartford bought out his estate. By then, along with two of his three sons, he was managing a two-hundred-store chain, headquartered not far from where most of the Hartford family had settled in Orange, New Jersey. There, Hartford became a pillar of local society and served a dozen years as the town's mayor.

The first ten years of the new century were good ones for the Hartfords. As of 1910, the A&P had 291 stores bringing in nearly $20 million in sales, and the company had even started paying its shareholders—the Hartford family—dividends. On July 24, 1911, when the entire clan gathered to mark the fiftieth wedding anniversary of George Huntington Hartford I and his wife, Josephine, the Hartfords were celebrating not just the occasion but their flourishing fortune as well.

A photograph taken at that anniversary shows a family awash in ornaments, the gregarious revelry of new money: Tiffany-style lamps illuminated the place settings, a carpet of rosebuds blossomed down the center of the table. Plaster fruit hung heavily off the mantelpiece molding. George Hartford's plump daughters—Marie Josephine, forty-eight, and Marie Louise, thirty-five—sat toward the end of the table with their husbands; the sons—George Ludlum, forty-five, Edward Vassallo, forty-one, and John Augustine, thirty-eight—stood closer to the photographer, stiff-necked in white-tie evening wear. Edward's daughter, a solemn-faced seven-year-old named Josephine, stood on one side of her father. The centerpiece of the portrait was the family matriarch, Josephine. She eyed the camera warily, her attention diverted by the infant in her arms. Edward's son, George Huntington Hartford II, born three months before, on April 18, was squalling for attention.

Looking away, as he always would be, was Edward Hartford, a difficult, reserved man who would die before his son turned twelve. Edward was the third of the five Hartford children, and the only son who refused to leave school to work for the family business: in his teens, having declared that ''one Hartford ought to be a gentleman,'' he matriculated at Stevens Institute in New Jersey. He dropped out before earning his degree, however, and took his dreams to France and India. When he returned to the United States in 1900, he brought back a motorcycle equipped with a Truffault spring fork that he had seen used by the winner of a motorcycle race at Versailles. The device absorbed the shock of bouncing and jittering so that steel parts of the motorcycle were not easily worn or broken.

Edward secured a patent for the device, and then adapted it to cushion the rough ride of the early automobile. The result was the Hartford shock absorber, which for a time was standard automotive equipment. According to Columbus O'Donnell, Edward's grandson, there were even a few years when his grandfather's automotive company made more money than the Hartfords' grocery empire.

Not only did Edward make more money than his brothers, he lived better. Unlike the other Hartfords, who lived quiet lives in suburban New Jersey, Edward and his wife, Henrietta, maintained their permanent residence on Fifth Avenue and spent occasional winters in Biarritz. The rest of the Hartfords were content to spend summers in a hotel in Spring Lake, New Jersey. Edward built a grand home of his own a few miles away in Deal, and it was there that his parents held that fiftieth-anniversary party.

When Edward married Henrietta Pollitzer in 1902, not long after meeting the dark-eyed South Carolina belle on a boat trip from Palm Beach to New York, he found a wife whose social ambitions exceeded his own. As her daughter put it: ''She believed, as Southerners do, that she was terribly grand.'' With her marriage to Edward Hartford, Henrietta finally had the money to match that grandeur.

Henrietta's mother, Mary Guerard, came from a prominent South Carolina family whose ancestors included one of the colonial governors.

That ancestry should have been a passport to high society, but Mary Guerard gave up those claims when she married Henry Pollitzer, an Austrian Jew whose family had emigrated to South Carolina in the 1860s. Even though the five Pollitzer children were raised in the Episcopal Church, they had lost their entrée into the Carolinian patriciate. Henrietta, the eldest, would spend a lifetime buying her way back in.

The French have an expression, *corriger la fortune*—to correct one's circumstances through denial of the past—that efficiently describes Henrietta's solution to her father's "problematic" heritage. She dropped her maiden name and used Guerard instead, and did everything else she could to hide her Jewish ancestry. So determined was she to turn the Hartford name into a pedigree that she had the three-chevron Hartford crest molded into the stucco house on the Deal estate as though it were the country manor of an English lord. Those chevrons were the imprimatur of a made-up aristocracy.

While Henrietta happily flaunted her shiny new fortune, her husband fretted over whether he could keep his business afloat. By the mid-teens, the profits from his automotive enterprise had started dropping; Edward needed new inventions, and he needed more money to finance them. But when he turned to his brothers for a loan, John and George refused to come to his aid. Their decision marked the beginning of a feud that festered for the balance of Edward's life.

In hindsight, it would appear that John and George rejected their brother's request not out of spite but simply because their grocery chain had no cash to spare. By the early teens, the premiums that the A&P had used to attract business started to take their toll on the balance sheet. Competing stores had started to underprice the A&P, and the only way for the grocery giant to keep prices down while keeping customers happy with free dishes and photographs was to sacrifice profits.

It was John, the younger and more creative of Edward's brothers, who came up with the remedy for the A&P's eroding balance sheet—and it was a solution that would revolutionize American grocery retailing. In 1912, John Hartford persuaded his father and oldest brother to open the first "cash-and-carry" store, in Jersey City. It was a bare-bones affair, plainly appointed, the storefront painted a dull red. There were no expensive Chinese pigments, no screens, no lanterns, no cashiers in pagodas—and no premiums. Customers fetched their own merchandise, so only one manager-clerk was needed for the entire operation. The point was low overhead, low prices, high volume.

The Jersey City store was profitable within six months. Because the chain stores were standardized, expansion came easily. Between 1913 and 1915, the A&P more than doubled its number of stores, to nearly 950. But all this growth meant that the grocer's slim profits had to be reinvested into the business. Funding Edward's highly speculative automotive-parts venture would have been next to impossible.

Edward, though, was incapable of acknowledging financial reality. "My father," explained Josephine, "had a fixation that the family betrayed him."

The only surviving evidence of the breach between the brothers is an undated typewritten letter from Edward Hartford to his mother. It is a self-indulgent and histrionic document, the musings of a man obsessed. Huntington Hartford kept the only copy of it locked away in his bedroom safe, harboring it as evidence that just as the family had conspired against the father, so too it would turn on his son.

In that letter, Edward Hartford contended that his brothers had refused him the loan because they envied his success; they wanted to obliterate his fame no matter what the cost. Edward had discovered that not only had his brothers refused him a loan, but their salaries at the A&P were double what he made as the company's secretary, a job that reflected his family ties rather than any real involvement in the business. Edward argued that it did not matter that he, unlike his brothers, did not work full-time for the A&P. He felt that the brothers' salaries were not actually wages, but rather a distribution of their father's wealth. Edward confronted his father with this disparity; George Hartford responded that he was merely acquiescing to John's demands, and he promised to readjust his sons' wages. But when the younger George and John learned what their brother had done, they were furious.

The confrontation came without warning. One evening, Edward traveled to Orange to see his mother. He entered the house unnoticed, but as he approached his mother's bedroom, he realized that he had walked in on a family conclave. Brother John was advising the rest of the family of Edward's exorbitant demands, decrying him as a lunatic.

While the brothers raged, the family patriarch stood by impassively. Only after the room had quieted did George Hartford take his second son aside. He told the young man not to worry, that he would resolve matters to everyone's satisfaction.

But the breach never mended. Edward claimed that he made overtures to his brothers, but they were rejected. Then, according to Edward, George and John forced their father to turn on his middle son. They threatened to leave the business unless he agreed to change his will. The threat would have been a potent one. By 1915, the elder George Hartford was eighty-two, and the two sons had taken full charge of his business. If they deserted the helm, the grocery empire might not survive. George gave his two sons what they wanted. Instead of splitting control of the A&P among the three brothers, he agreed to put the entire enterprise into a trust. Two classes of stock were created, common and preferred. The common shares could be bequeathed to relatives or simply sold on the open market (they were traded on the American Stock Exchange); the preferred provided holders with voting rights and the bulk of the dividends but could not be sold so long as any of George Hartford's children were alive; thus it was guaranteed that the business would be held by the family for at least one generation. The shares were divided equally, twenty percent to each of the five Hartford children.

George Hartford put the younger George and John in charge of the company and cut Edward out of any active role in management. Edward was livid. He ignored the fact that the trust specifically put him on equal financial footing with his two brothers and two sisters. He was convinced that he was the Hartford family martyr, and likened himself to that icon of miscarried justice, Alfred Dreyfus, the French army officer who was wrongly convicted of treason, stripped of his medals, and sent to Devil's Island.

Edward Hartford conjured his own purgatory. In the months after his father rewrote his will, Edward was plagued with a series of ailments. First he could no longer see clearly. His eyes ached and burned, and no treatments seemed to help. Then came the pains in his legs. When doctors told him that his symptoms might simply be the result of some serious nervous shock, Edward blamed his brothers; he was disconsolate that the family he loved could inflict such punishment on their kin. There would, he vowed, be a reckoning someday.

That reckoning never came. By the time George Huntington Hartford I died in 1917, the power had already shifted to George and John. Edward withdrew into melancholia, and his children almost never saw either their grandmother or their uncles during the rest of their father's lifetime.

It was Hartford's sister, Josephine, who mourned the loss of those visits. According to Josephine, her grandparents had always had a warm, affectionate household—altogether different from the cool climate at her own home in Deal. As for her brother, Josephine, who was seven years older, hardly knew him at all. "We had different nurses," she explained.

Josephine was a tall, awkward child endowed with a good deal of intelligence and scant beauty. At Miss Doddsworth's dancing classes she was never picked until the end, one of the unfortunates paired up with another girl to learn how to waltz. With her hard-set jaw, she looked a bit like a World War I commander, a schoolgirl version of General Pershing. Her features would soften into handsomeness with age, but she was an unpretty child whom her mother disdained.

Huntington, in contrast, was a Little Lord Fauntleroy, with an almost feminine, pretty face and long curls that weren't cut until he was five or six. In his velvet sailor suits, he was a caricature of the spoiled little rich boy, whom money and Mother cushioned from a rough-and-tumble childhood. Huntington was reared apart from other children, served by tutors, a chauffeur, and a beloved British governess named Rose.

Deal, New Jersey, was a halcyon, if isolated, place for a child. The boy's playtime was spent in the garden, where he climbed endlessly over an old bright-red Mercer racer, outfitted by his father with a Rolls-Royce radiator and German components on the dashboard. The estate had a croquet lawn and tennis courts and a miniature nine-hole golf course, designed especially for Edward. But by the time his son would have been old enough to join him on the greens, Edward rarely emerged from his study.

Henrietta, meanwhile, had turned her attentions from her unstable husband to her son. She cooed over how handsome her ebony-eyed boy was becoming, and told him over and over how his low-set ears were most certainly a sign of genius. Henrietta's ambitions for her cherished son had more to do with social stature than with actual achievement, however. In the daytime the two of them would play croquet; in the evening they would walk around the porch, mallets in the small of their backs, following her regimen for proper posture.

Henrietta was a hot-tempered woman, whose love, while potent, was less than consistent. "His mother didn't love him, she possessed him," said one of Hunt's former sisters-in-law. There were even suggestions that this possession included not just her son's life but his bed as well.

Henrietta managed her son as one might a small, overly pedigreed dog; a short lead confined his every move. One of his pinkies still has a crook in it, lasting evidence of one of Henrietta's attempts to bring the boy into line with her image of perfection. Annoyed because the boy was making a fuss when she wanted to go out for the evening, Henrietta locked young Huntington, aged seven or eight, into a closet. The boy kept screaming, but she ignored his cries. When she finally unlocked the door hours later, she discovered he had been screaming in pain: his little finger had been slammed in the closet door.

▲

When it came to Edward Hartford, his son would always say he just didn't recall much about him. One evening in 1985, Hunt spent hours leafing through a cache of childhood photographs with his nurse, the fifth or sixth of a string of attendants who cared for the heir during his seventy-fifth year. "Is that your father?" she asked as her patient turned up a photograph of a dashing mustachioed youth.

"No," he answered. "He was my mother's boyfriend when I was growing up. And when she dropped him he ditched me like hotcakes too."

"Is that your father?" the nurse repeated as the heir retrieved another fading snapshot, this one showing Hartford himself at age ten or eleven, leaning against a Rolls-Royce next to another young man in a boxy double-breasted suit. "No," he said, sighing, "I think it was the chauffeur.

"There are only two little details I remember about my father," he continued. "Whenever he had a cup of coffee he'd spill half of it because he was shaking so much. And once he bought me a shiny silver balloon. I blew it up too big and it exploded. I always felt bad about that."

In all, Hartford's father had as unsteady a presence in his only son's life as that fragile, evanescent balloon.

Edward Hartford died in the Devon Hotel in Manhattan on June 13, 1922. His son believed that his father, a Christian Scientist, had refused medical help after he cut his leg, and then died because blood poisoning set in. His daughter recalled it slightly differently. "There was that row, and he brooded and brooded. We were told that the ends of his nerves got tied up. I never really understood it," Josephine recalled. "In the end, I think he finally died of peritonitis." Regardless of what killed him, his death certified a loss that had taken place years before.

Edward's will was a curt ten-line document which left his entire estate to his "beloved wife." As it turned out, that estate didn't amount to much. There were the house in Deal and a few worthless patents. The bulk of the Hartford wealth was tied up in the controversial trust Edward's father had created, and the beneficiaries of that were Edward's children, not his wife.

Over the next year, Henrietta, always a strong force in her son's life, became the only influence. Josephine wanted no part of her mother's household. In 1923, she escaped into her first marriage, to Charles Oliver

O'Donnell, a member of the very social Iselin family, descendants of one of the signers of the Declaration of Independence.

George and John Hartford were both childless, but neither sought any say in how their nephew was raised. John spent what little spare time he had with his wife's sister's family. Taciturn George preferred tinkering with automobiles in his garage to the company of his nephew.

Thus Henrietta Hartford was left in full charge of her adolescent son. Hunt would have his millions, but no one who would teach the overly mothered boy the lesson he most needed to learn: how strong men used their wealth to wield power.

3

AFTER HER HUSBAND DIED, Henrietta Hartford began her social ascent in earnest. She set her sights on the queen of the seaside resorts: Newport, Rhode Island.

Social Newport began at the top of Bellevue Avenue, where cottage after multimillion-dollar cottage punctuated the winding road that represented the summit of American resort extravagance.

In Newport's turn-of-the-century heyday, hostesses shyly revealed that they could give dinners for a hundred without calling in extra help; ten-course meals were eaten off solid-gold service. At one dinner, a stream flowed tastefully down the middle of the table. At another, the center of the table was covered with sand; each guest was given his own small sterling-silver pail and shovel, and at the end of the evening, the guests dug for favors: emeralds, rubies, sapphires.

Hunt, then fourteen, and Henrietta spent their first season in Newport in 1925. Josephine Hartford O'Donnell, married with a family of her own, rarely visited her mother's Newport household, a series of rented summer cottages. First came Chastellux, the residence of Major Lorillard Spencer on Halion Hill, then King Cottage, the villa owned by Frederic Rhinelander King on Bellevue Avenue. By the late twenties Henrietta decided that she wanted to buy, and she needed more than her late husband's legacy provided.

She turned instead to her bashful son and that generation-skipping trust created by his grandfather. Although the A&P dividends added up to about $1 million a year, the New Jersey Surrogates' Court had approved an allowance of just $100,000. (The balance of the boy's income would be placed in a trust, which could not be tapped until he reached his majority.) And for Henrietta, that was simply not enough to support her son in the style to which he (and she) deserved to become accustomed. In 1926, Henrietta petitioned the court for an increase in her son's allowance. She contended that under current circumstances she was forced to draw on her own resources and that this resulted in "constant need for curtailment, which seems uncalled for." One hundred thousand dollars was not enough to afford her son such "necessities" as his own car and chauffeur, nor could she pay for the yacht (and two hands) that her son desperately desired. "As his guardian," Henrietta wrote to the court, "[I] consider it extremely unwise to curtail him in such reasonable demands as he may now make, and I do not believe that he should come into his inheritance with desires ungratified and wishes thwarted." The court cleared Henrietta's request, and the boy's allowance was raised by half, to $150,000 a year.

In 1927, after two years of Newport rentals, Henrietta took a piece of the magnificently plebeian Hartford fortune and acquired Seaverge, the estate built by one of Newport's greatest snobs, Commodore Elbridge Gerry, grandson of a signer of the Declaration of Independence. The mansion, bordering Bellevue Avenue, was perched on the end of a five-acre plot that ran all the way to the sea. Not only was Seaverge perfectly situated physically, it was socially strategic as well. Next door was Rough Point, where Doris Duke, heiress to the tobacco fortune, lived; just across the street was the Aspegrens' Aspen Hall.

But by the time the Hartfords moved into their Newport manse, the resort was already a Gilded Age artifact, a relic of an era when well-brought-up girls grew into ladies and boys aspired to be white-suited yachtsmen, so many Tom and Daisy Buchanans. When the government instituted a national income tax in 1916, many of Newport's oldest families were forced to sell. By 1924, the year before the Hartfords' first season, Newport was already being dismissed as "a little too garish, a little shopworn, a little past its prime, as is American society itself."

Still, Henrietta Hartford clung to her prelapsarian notions of luxury. She decorated the place with determined opulence. She converted an old barn on the property into a glassed-in tennis court, the better for her son to perfect his game. She spread tiger skins across the divans and the floors before a huge fireplace, decorated walls with murals of Cleopatra vamping Mark Antony on a barge. Seaverge had its own greenhouse, where carefully grown cantaloupes were cradled in little net hammocks so that they would not become soiled. Henrietta invented family colors, blue and gold, and used them on the grosgrain ribbons decorating the uniforms for the footmen, who stood in their breeches behind each chair at her dinner parties.

The right school was, of course, as important as the right residence. In 1924, Henrietta packed her thirteen-year-old into the family Rolls and sat next to him as they were chauffeured up to St. Paul's School in Concord, New Hampshire.

The boarding school, America's answer to Eton and Harrow, had been educating Biddles, Sedgwicks, and Astors since the Civil War. With its Dickensian dormitories and rules forbidding ostentatious shows of wealth—students were allowed neither bicycles nor cars—St. Paul's excelled at teaching the scions of America's industrialists the primary tenet of the reigning Anglo-Saxon aristocracy: The more money one had, the less one should be showing it.

St. Paul's had been founded in 1855, and by the turn of the century, the school was admitting new money along with the old, assimilating the sons of America's recently rich Protestant tycoons. Henrietta intended for it to do just that for herself and her son, but from the beginning Hunt's patrician classmates never really accepted him as one of their own.

For Hartford, St. Paul's turned a troubled childhood into an impossible adolescence. In his seventies, he winced when asked for his recollections of boarding school, the pain unblunted by the many years that had passed. "They were," he said, "the worst years of my life." At St. Paul's, where the understatement of wealth was all-important, the A&P heir became aware that he was wealthier than most of his classmates. That realization quickly turned to discomfort, and it drove a deep chasm between Hartford and his peers.

Henrietta, guiding a fortune not quite as old as the century, flagrantly flouted the subtleties of status, and her son bore the brunt of her indiscretion. "Old money comes in old cars and old clothes," sniffed one aging alumnus. "The Hartfords were not old money."

The petite overdressed martinet spent virtually every weekend in Concord, and she took little stock in Andrew Carnegie's dictum that jewel-wearing was a relic of barbarism. She flashed into the sleepy town wearing high-fashion silks and high-priced gems. Outfitted for a Newport ball, she would escort her son to the drab Eagle Tavern, a factory-style New England hotel that was the only place in town where visiting parents could take their children to dinner. "If only she'd stop getting dressed halfway through," Hunt Hartford used to say.

"Of course I remember her," said Beekman Cox Cannon, like Hartford a member of the form of 1930, when asked about Henrietta. "She looked like Anita Loos. She didn't know enough to dress in a country way, the way you'd expect to find in New England when a parent is visiting a child at boarding school. She was terribly socially pushy and tried to make a lineup for any men who were available, even my poor aging father. It must have been very hard for a boy not to be embarrassed by what his mother was about."

"He wasn't well liked," recalled Philadelphian William Foulke, another member of the form of 1930. "And he thought money entered into it. But the truth was, we were more interested in whether he could play sports or made good grades than in how much money he had. After all, Alfred Vanderbilt was in the class behind us. But the fact that he was uncomfortable with the money made everyone else uncomfortable with him."

No one was supposed to like the spare trappings at St. Paul's, but Hunt Hartford had been an exceptionally cosseted child, and he was ill equipped to handle the rigors of boarding school. The boy who grew up on Newport banquets loathed the meager Sunday suppers of fishballs and sausages. He disdained the stiff collars and old blue suits, the eight-A.M. bell chiming to wake the boys for the first trip to church. They marched single file into the English Gothic chapel and paraded to assigned seats in the high-backed pews. Latecomers, Hunt frequently among them, sat in a drafty anteroom on cane-backed chairs.

Most of all, Hunt resented the boys who carried around the collection plates. Every fourth Sunday, two boys came around with change so that students would have no excuse for not giving the amount they had pledged. "I think he felt people were trying to take advantage of him," said Foulke. "He tried to be canny and didn't want to give away anything." Teachers singled him out for unwelcome attention as well. The school's infirmary deemed him underweight and ordered him to go on a special diet: extra milk and jelly sandwiches served every morning between classes. In class, to his face, the instructors called him the "million-dollar milk-fed baby."

His ostracism wasn't simply the result of the newness of his money and the frailty of his physique. Although years later his classmates claimed not to recall that Hartford's maternal grandfather was Jewish, anti-Semitism apparently had a role in his rejection. The heir's broad, swarthy features clashed with those of his fine-boned Anglo-Saxon class-mates. "He wasn't very attractive," said one member of his class, whose father had also graduated from St. Paul's. "He looked," he added, grappling for an acceptable euphemism, "Eastern European."

Nor did his classmates talk about what Hartford's second wife referred to as shower-room ribbings, abuse she believed had lifelong repercussions. In the white-tiled steamy communal showers, the boys attacked Hunt's fragile adolescent ego. As she discreetly explained, "He got a lot of ridicule." She felt that the boys at St. Paul's destroyed his confidence about his masculinity and triggered his relentless, obsessive pursuit of young women.

After five long years at St. Paul's, the derision that had dogged him finally began to abate. He didn't play team sports; he excelled instead at one-on-one competition. During his senior year, sixth form, Hunt Hartford won the school championship in squash; he was the second-best tennis player, losing a final championship match to William Foulke in four sets.

During his last year, Hartford started writing as well. Each semester the editors of the school literary magazine, *Horae Scholasticae*, chose the top essay. In the winter of 1930, they picked "On Conventional Vacations" by George Huntington Hartford II, a revealing four-page piece that lauded the value of self-sufficiency in young men. According to Hartford, there were three types of youths who liked to spend summer holidays traveling—"the cut and dried aesthetes who see and study life but do not live it . . . the superficial idlers who live life and yet do not understand nor study it," and more admirable, boys who do not "have to keep begging Mother and Father to let them be free from family ties for a month or so: these boys' parents . . . have conceived the astonishing idea that children exist to more advantage on their own than in the bosom of the families."

Hartford tracked the adventures of such a youth, who one summer biked alone through the English countryside and the next traveled through Europe with nothing more than a hundred-dollar bill and a ticket home. "He is now a noted novelist," he concluded, "and I dare say that his early environment had as much to do with his success as any inborn writing ability."

The essay was Hunt Hartford's plea for autonomy, a plaint that Henrietta was determined not to hear.

▲

Hartford's six years at St. Paul's apparently ended as badly as they had begun. Hartford would never discuss just what happened when he finished his last year at St. Paul's; about all he said was that he "didn't remember being at graduation." That much is absolutely clear; his name is missing from the roster of boys who graduated from the school in June 1930. Just why his name is missing is less certain.

In addition to its standard diplomas, St. Paul's issues "certificates of completion," to students who have run afoul of the school's rules regarding grades or conduct but in the months after graduation have proven themselves worthy of a diploma, albeit a downgrade one. St. Paul's refuses to release information about which students have been given those deferred diplomas, but it seems probable that Hartford received one.

The problem, his classmates said later, came during senior exams. The boys collected their tests in the main building, then took them to study rooms; proctors patrolled the halls outside. According to his classmates, one proctor walked in and saw Hartford peeking over another boy's shoulder. "The odd thing," reflected one classmate, "was that George knew more than the fellow in front of him."

Whether or not Hartford used the answers he saw didn't matter; to be charged by a proctor with peering at another boy's paper would have been enough to keep a boy from graduating with his class. Initially, classmates said, it appeared an exception might be made for the young A&P heir. Then, as now, boarding schools ran on fairly tight budgets, and by 1930 the country was well into the Depression. Alumni who might otherwise have been relied on for generous gifts were still reeling from the previous October, when a seventy-point drop in the stock market sent the nation's economy tumbling. The story at St. Paul's was that Henrietta had offered to donate a new gymnasium in return for her son's being permitted to participate in the commencement ceremonies.

Then the St. Paul's student council became involved. "We decided in a furious session that we would refuse to accept our diplomas if Hartford were allowed to graduate with us," said one of the council's surviving members. "The rector thought we were nuts, but we were young and we still had our principles."

Ultimately, no gymnasium was built. Hartford stayed away from the celebrations, and with or without a proper diploma he started Harvard in the fall.

Hartford wasn't to have his final word on St. Paul's until the twenty-fifth anniversary of his Harvard graduation, in a commemorative yearbook published for the occasion:

My inferiority complex started around the time I went to fashionable
St. Paul's School. . . . Why should I, a young boy who in the eyes
of the world had everything have felt so inferior in boarding school
and, in fact, been quite miserable till long after I got out of college?
A combination, I believe, of a loving and determined mother . . .
(my father died when I was twelve [*sic*]); of being possessor of what
the rector of St. Paul's called "that most dreadful thing, a sensitive
disposition"; of being spoiled in some quarters and resented in
others because I [had] a lot of money and, finally, because of the
inordinate emphasis at St. Paul's on church and Christianity which
turned me into an embarrassingly shy and humble little mouse.

The ostracism from St. Paul's would echo for the rest of his life.
Huntington Hartford would forever bar men who were his social and
intellectual peers from his innermost circle of friends.

Henrietta was apparently less concerned with her son's troubles at St.
Paul's than she was with her own entry into Newport society. The Hearst
columnist Maury Henry Biddle Paul, who signed his pieces "Cholly
Knickerbocker" and served as arbiter and chronicler for high society,
took fairly derisive note of her first season on Newport's Halion Hill.
"Madame waited for social success to trail her there with its tail, if
necessary, between its legs," wrote Paul. "To say that it didn't is rather
a too harsh way of putting it; but to say that it did is equally beside the
point."

Still, she persisted, and by April 1928, Henrietta had moved to Seaverge and charmed Maury Paul into her camp. "Why, I ask, should not
this matron become part of the fashionable fabric of the famous city
wherein more history of its particular kind has been woven than in any
similar place in the new world?" Paul asked. "For Mrs. Hartford is
exceedingly rich . . . and she has influential friends who will see that
she is correctly advised and directed. . . . Sheltered by such a traditional
roof tree as Seaverge and possessing the friendship of certain very powerful Newport personages, she is destined to mount to the heights."

At the end of that summer season, those powerful personages threw
their support behind her first ball.

Newport was then host to the International Intercollegiate Tennis tournament, at the Casino on Bellevue Avenue. The event was the culmi-
nation of the social season, and Henrietta chose it to launch her full
entry into Newport society. At the start of Tennis Week, Henrietta invited five hundred Newporters to celebrate at Seaverge. She had a spe-

cial dance platform, eighty by fifty feet, constructed on the south side of the mansion facing the Atlantic. Its boards were stained blue, illumination was provided by large fern-draped and hand-painted yellow chandeliers. Gladiolas were made to blossom out of the walls, the illusion provided by vases camouflaged behind bunches of ferns. Rhinelanders and Astors and Vanderbilts were invited and, more to the point, they came.

The Seaverge extravaganza had the desired effect. In 1929, Henrietta and her son became the first Hartfords to make it into the Social Register.

They also were the only ones. Social striving meant little to the men who were running the business that financed Henrietta's balls. Instead, Hunt Hartford's uncles led aggressively quiet lives, so quiet that their entries in *Who's Who* were restricted to their names, titles, and addresses. If anything, Henrietta's extravagance served only to alienate them further from their brother's family.

For both George and John Hartford, the business of the A&P came first—and that business was booming. In 1923, just six years after George Hartford I died, the A&P had surpassed Sears, Roebuck in annual volume, becoming the largest chain store in the world. Two years later, in a move befitting the kings of American retailing, the Hartfords transferred their headquarters from a nine-story warehouse in Jersey City to the Graybar Building in Manhattan, adjacent to Grand Central Terminal.

The differences between the two brothers had become more exaggerated as they aged. John Hartford had begun to enjoy his status. In 1925, he bought 360 acres in Westchester County, a few miles north of White Plains, and began building an estate. Buena Vista Farm had a thirty-room Tudor house with a bathroom of imported marble and solid-gold fixtures, as well as stables, a riding ring, and its own nine-hole golf course. John's attire reflected his newfound corporate gentility. His silk shirts and ties were specially tailored at Sulka; his suits were from Savile Row. He became part of the corporate oligarchy, with invitations to join various boards of directors; Chrysler Motors' was among the ones he accepted.

George, ever staid, had his sole allegiance to the A&P. He did not move from his modest home in Orange, New Jersey. In his ill-fitting black suit and black shoes, he looked more like a small-town mortician than the chairman of the country's biggest grocery chain.

The brothers' differences in style proved profitable when it came to the substance of business. John was the gambler, willing to risk every-thing on a new idea, while George would carefully husband every last penny. With John's foot firmly on the gas pedal and George applying the brakes, they had the perfect team for building a colossus of American business. In 1929, a full year ahead of schedule, the A&P topped $1 billion in sales.

In large part, the A&P owed its growth to the good times buoying all of the United States. In the mid-twenties, the country was in the midst of an unprecedented economic boom, and it looked as if the stock mar-ket could go nowhere but up. But that overabundance of prosperity made stodgy old George Hartford edgy. As the stock market soared ever higher, George became increasingly conservative. Stores' leases were to be for no longer than one year, no exceptions. Surplus cash was divvied up among a variety of banks so no single collapse could destroy the corporation.

In October 1929, when the stock market crashed, George Hartford's sense of foreboding proved prescient. His overriding conservatism would ultimately enable the A&P to weather the Depression. His insistence on one-year leases meant individual stores that were seriously hurt by the effects of unemployment could close down without consequence to the corporation. Since the equipment investment per store was nominal and the fixtures portable, the company could easily shift operations to lo-cations where there was business.

With virtually no formal education beyond a few years of high school, these two men had built one of the most resilient retail empires in the nation. They had the righteousness of self-made men, and when they observed their nephew, they saw a young man who had all the advantages that they had never had, and they saw him putting them to no good end. When John Hartford, who had had to sacrifice his own schooling to help with the family business, learned that Hunt had failed to graduate prop-erly from St. Paul's, he told one of his nieces that he was appalled that such privilege had been squandered.

As for Henrietta, she tightened her grip on her son as he went from boarding school to college. For years, Hunt Hartford told the story of how his mother finally bought him his first car—then had a governor put on it.

Hunt did spend the summer after he left St. Paul's traveling through Europe, but Henrietta was always at his side. It was hardly the sort of salutary autonomy he had described in that essay he wrote at St. Paul's. "Due to the coolness that exists between Mrs. Hartford and her recently married daughter, her whole life is centered on Huntington," wrote Maury Paul. "She has consistently given up all her own personal pleasure to insure Huntington's future happiness."

In the fall of 1930, Henrietta followed her son to Harvard; she took an apartment in Boston. "Local society saw but little of Mrs. Hartford during the past season," reported Paul. "For months she has occupied an apartment at the Copley Plaza in Boston to be near Huntington, an undergraduate at Harvard. Having much spare time on her hands she took a course in economics, and friends who dropped in at the Hartford suite on various occasions tell me they frequently saw devoted mother and son studying side by side."

The Harvard that Huntington Hartford entered in 1930 was straight out of J. P. Marquand. As Marquand put it in *The Late George Apley,* it was a society peopled with students for whom "the clock struck twelve while they were undergraduates at Harvard, and in the interval remaining to them between youth and grave they underwent no further change." They were the ones who took their intellectual education from the classroom and their social education at the club, which, for boys from St. Paul's, generally meant either Porcellian or A.D., the top clubs at Harvard.

Henrietta wanted her son to become vested in that closed society, but he had no interest in reentering a world that had made his adolescence unbearable. And even if he had wanted to join that elite fraternity, it is unlikely that he would have been welcome. His untoward exodus from St. Paul's had made him a pariah among the boys who his mother hoped would become his peers.

"Frankly, I was surprised he was there," said a St. Paul's graduate who went on to Harvard with Hunt. "After the cheating incident I, well, just didn't think he was very nice."

The only St. Paul's boy who did associate with Hunt was his freshman roommate. Edward "Ned" Rollins was a mediocre student who had barely squeaked through St. Paul's, and he would leave after his first year of Harvard. "I didn't study," recalled Rollins, who eventually retreated to Maine to run the family dairy. By his own admission, he was more interested in having a good time, and during his first and only year in Cambridge he took Hunt along for the ride.

That year, young Hartford finally began to show some spunk. Never mind Prohibition; Hunt Hartford had enough money to keep the liquor flowing. He and Rollins had their own messenger on call to keep them well supplied with bootleg whiskey. And together they took in the pleasures of the local nightlife. "When I was nineteen, Ned Rollins took me out to this house near Cambridge," Hartford remembered. "I think I must have been drunk. I got one of these fishskins, they don't shrink or anything. I was absolutely terrified; I'd never done anything like that before. I went back to Harvard in a trolley—it was about seven A.M. and a gray, gray dawn. I was terrified that I was going to get syphilis. Then I was afraid she was going to get pregnant. That was my introduction to sex."

When Henrietta Hartford began to suspect that her son was making the rounds of Boston's seamier establishments, she was not happy. For months she had been angling for a matchup between her son and their Newport neighbor, the tobacco heiress Doris Duke. The society columnist in the New York *World-Telegram* crowed: "Richest boy courts richest girl."

But there was little chance that Henrietta's match would take. The youngsters were too rich to have much use for one another. Duke's secretary laughed at the report: "It must be a joke. Miss Duke saw him a few times, but there was never anything serious."

Fifty-odd years later, Hartford still pooh-poohed the idea. "Nobody would get paired up with Doris Duke. She was so ugly, she had a big chin." (Eventually she would have it reduced surgically.)

Even if her son had no future with the tobacco heiress, Henrietta apparently panicked at the thought that her ambitions for her son and herself might be derailed by a local harlot. Within months of Hunt's arrival at Harvard, Henrietta was consulting friends at the New England Conservatory of Music, looking for a young woman who could be surreptitiously introduced into Hunt's life, someone who would make sure that he met girls with the correct social patina. She ended up hiring a redhead named Mildred King, an eminently presentable piano student from the eminently respectable Back Bay.

At a Sunday-afternoon tea dance at the Savoy Hotel, King introduced Hunt to Mary Lee Epling, the eighteen-year-old daughter of a West Virginia dentist. Mary Lee was a pretty, wide-eyed brunette studying to be a kindergarten teacher at Lesley College, a finishing school for young ladies whose major draw was its proximity to Harvard. In the words of one man who knew her, Mary Lee was "the kind of girl who always became president of her class . . . a tremendous politician in a quiet way." The capture of Hunt Hartford was her first big campaign, and her southern charm served her well.

Six months later, spring break, 1931: Hartford drove his two-seater Daimler down to the Greenbrier resort in Hot Springs, West Virginia, with Ned Rollins. "Hunt left one morning and said, 'I'm going to be busy,' '' Rollins remembered. "I thought nothing of it. He came back and said, 'I've just gotten married.' That was the first I'd heard of it.''

The wedding was a perfunctory affair. Hunt met Mary Lee at the First Presbyterian Church in Covington, West Virginia. They recruited two strangers to serve as witnesses, and just before noon on April 18, 1931, Hunt Hartford's twentieth birthday, the young heir and the dentist's daughter pledged their troth.

More than a half-century later, Hartford scarcely recalled the day of his first marriage, but he did remember why they had wed so precipitately. "The only person that had control or had any effect on me was my mother," he explained. "I was a mama's boy, and instinctively I wanted to have a little more freedom."

Hunt and Mary Lee waited weeks before they told their respective families. Henrietta was hysterical—she lay down on the floor and screamed and cried her dismay. Mary Lee's parents were similarly—though less demonstratively—displeased. The parents agreed to keep the wedding a secret, and to do what they could to keep their children apart. Hartford went back to his dormitory room in Winthrop House and finished an otherwise unremarkable freshman year.

That summer, Henrietta Hartford took the newlyweds on a cruise to Hawaii, part vacation, mostly an attempt to browbeat them into having their marriage annulled. She wasn't successful, but she refused to give up. As long as news of the marriage was kept out of the papers, she believed that there was hope of ending it. But on September 8, ten days before the beginning of the fall semester at Harvard, Henrietta's hopes were dashed: Mildred King sued her for $100,000.

As King told her story at the time, Henrietta originally had hired her to save her son from an unnamed temptress, to introduce him to a series of socially acceptable young women in order to cure him of his interest in women of lesser repute. And King contended that she had done exactly that. "I was not a lure," she insisted. "My job was to see that he met only nice girls. . . . There was no sentiment of lovemaking involved. I interested him in music as well as the different girls I introduced."

But Henrietta, King said, failed to make good on her part of the deal, a promise to adopt the young redhead or pay her $100,000. "Newport Woman Sued over Son's Love Case" headlined *The New York Times*. "Girl Sues Rich Society Widow for $100,000" ran the New York *Journal-American*. When reporters asked Henrietta about Mildred King, she denied ever having met the woman who had introduced her son to his wife, a wife whose very existence she was still desperately trying to keep out of the papers. "It's one of those cases wealthy people have to put up with," she told the New York *Mirror*.

Within days of King's filing, word of the Hartford wedding was leaked to the papers. The *New York Post* headlined the news: "Apron Strings Guide Heir to Altar." The *World-Telegram* summed up Henrietta's aversion to her son's spouse with a single sentence at the bottom of its front-page story: "The former Miss Epling is not listed in the Social Register."

In September, after the marriage had been revealed, Maury Paul came to Henrietta's defense.

> If you happen to enjoy even a bowing acquaintance with the petite and attractive Mrs. Edward Hartford, it is not difficult to understand her present perturbed state of mind over the unpleasant publicity that has followed in the wake of Miss King's suit. Personally, I know and like Mrs. Hartford, and while I have no way of ascertaining definitely if there is any foundation for the claims made by the young lady who is asking for a mere $100,000 for (to put it politely) "services rendered" I am inclined to doubt that a woman as sagacious as Mrs. Hartford would find it necessary to enter into an agreement with anyone to "rescue" her son, Huntington, from the wiles of any woman.

Apparently, that very sagacity ensured that King's lawsuit never went to trial. In mid-December, just over three months after the suit was filed, Henrietta Hartford paid Mildred King the not inconsiderable settlement of $26,000. In return, King agreed to "desist from any publicity," according to a letter from Henrietta's attorney, Bronson Winthrop. As Winthrop noted in his letter to Henrietta: "We all realize that the amount paid is large, but it will relieve you from a great deal of unpleasantness."

Not only did Henrietta manage to control the King incident, for the first few years of their marriage she even managed to hold some sway over Hunt and Mary Lee. Hunt kept his dormitory room, although he usually stayed in his mother's hotel suite. Mary Lee stayed in an apartment with roommates; the couple spent an occasional weekend together under Henrietta's watchful eye at her suite at the Copley Plaza.

While Mary Lee studied to be a kindergarten teacher, her husband attended classes and played tennis and squash. After the uncomfortable intimacy of St. Paul's, Hartford reveled in the relative anonymity of Harvard's large student body; virtually none of his housemates remembered him. Hartford's only accomplishment listed in the Harvard yearbook was membership on the squash and tennis teams. Although his teammates were impressed with his skill, they were not with his character. The problems were much the same as those he had had at St. Paul's. "He was regarded with some distrust by most of us," recalled Jack Barnaby, who was number two to Hartford's number three on the squash team and number three to his number two in tennis. "One year he drove up to the courts in a twelve-cylinder Cadillac, the next year he had a Jaguar. I asked him what happened to the Cadillac and he said, 'I didn't like it.' That's the kind of money his mother gave him. He lived like the Shah of Persia instead of another student.

"We all felt it was unfortunate to have been brought up without the values that we rated pretty high—like not displaying your wealth and not throwing money around. Other wealthy parents made their kids scrape the bottom of the yacht if they wanted to go sailing in it—they were brought up right. Hartford was a silver-spoon kid—he was bright, he was a talented athlete, but he had no discipline, no restraint, no limits. None of us got too close."

The only relationship that lasted from his four years at Harvard was with Mary Lee. That marriage was Hunt Hartford's first attempt to break away from his mother, and he celebrated it. Years later, he still had a file drawer full of copies of the newspaper clippings reporting his marriage. They marked his first timid move toward adulthood—proof that he was something more than Henrietta Hartford's weak-willed son.

4

*B*Y JUNE 1934, Huntington Hartford had graduated from college
and celebrated his third wedding
anniversary, but he still made sure to sit at the far end of his mother's
dining room table so that she wouldn't try to cut his meat for him.
Henrietta's hold on her son wasn't simply psychological. She continued
to manage his income from the A&P trust, which made her the final
arbiter on virtually every decision he made. To no one's surprise (and
Mary Lee's consternation), when Henrietta insisted that her son and his
wife take a cottage next door to Seaverge, Hunt quickly complied.

By the mid-thirties, the Hartfords had arrived in Newport society.
Newporters, then as now, are imbued with Yankee pragmatism, the understanding that continuous infusions of new capital are necessary for
the community to survive. So it was that Hunt and Mary Lee Hartford,
sufficiently attractive and amply monied, were warmly received.

That summer was typically languid. Mary Lee golfed and lunched.
Hunt spoke vaguely of becoming a writer (he had, after all, listed that
as his intended career in the Harvard yearbook), but mostly he played
tennis and squash and circulated through Newport's endless stream of
social functions. The young Hartfords made a regular foursome with
Jack and Ellen "Tuckie" Astor, who married that summer in a lavish
wedding in New York City.

John Jacob Astor VI, brand-name society, seemed to be everything
George Huntington Hartford II was not. He was the second son of John
Jacob Astor IV, the chivalric legend who perished on the *Titanic* after
escorting his pregnant wife (with Jack VI in utero) onto a lifeboat. But
in the world, the son was less impressive, a prep school dropout whom

columnists sniggeringly called "Jackaster." Jack's older half brother, Vincent, was willed the bulk of the family fortune; but even if Vincent wore the mantle of familial responsibility, Jack was not wanting for funds. Thanks to a trust set up by his father, the younger Astor had sufficient income to lead a thoroughly aimless existence; he became a boorish patrician who excelled at misbehaving while never breaking with his set.

Luncheons were a favorite forum for his antics. At one meal, he started by juggling the finger bowls, then moved on to the dessert plates, which were painted with words from French folk songs. Astor launched into an impromptu performance, first singing the lyrics from his own plate, then grabbing Hunt's, then Mary Lee's, cadging every piece of china at the table to keep the act going. Mary Lee thought him crude, but Hunt enjoyed the commotion created in Jack Astor's wake.

Jack and Hunt and Tuckie and Mary Lee would spend evenings at parties, then lose the next morning recovering. The day barely began before lunch, and each afternoon was inaugurated with a game of back-gammon, followed by tennis on Seaverge's indoor courts.

One frequent partner on the courts was Frank Shields, the dashingly handsome tennis champion. Shields, grandfather of the actress-model Brooke Shields, was an Irish charmer whose place in Newport society was based on athletic talent rather than social standing. Like Astor, Shields was prone to high drama, although his behavior was born of alcohol rather than an overbred sensibility gone slightly awry.

"Hartford liked Frank because he was off the wall, and he liked the idea of Frank with these gorgeous women," remembered Jules Seligson, who was part of the Newport tennis set and later employed Shields as an insurance salesman. "Frank was the antithesis of an intellectual, so he was no threat [in that respect] to Hunt, who fancied himself an intellectual of sorts." Hartford had a hard time accepting Shields's superiority in the one arena where the athlete excelled—on the tennis court. According to Seligson, the easygoing Shields would often lose games deliberately in order to humor the grocery-chain heir.

Hartford had finished his education, and it should have been time for him to start thinking about what he was going to do for the rest of his life. He was too passive to take exception to his mother's judgment on his future. Henrietta had done her best to discourage her son from pursuing a business career, even one in the family business. In her ongoing attempt to ape Victorian social standards, she was convinced commerce was beneath her son's social status. Just like a latter-day Tarkington character, her boy would be a yachtsman.

Hunt was content to lounge in Newport, making sporadic stabs at being a novelist. It was an easy life, one in which achievements were fuzzily defined by status rather than worldly success. As one Newport dowager explained it, "There are people who have succeeded in Newport whose feet never touched reality."

Mary Lee wanted more from her young husband. While she enjoyed being a wealthy man's wife, she wanted his status to be based on his own accomplishments, and that was an impossibility as long as they lived in his mother's shadow. By midsummer Mary Lee persuaded him to ask his uncles for a job at the A&P. Before the season was over, Huntington Hartford had started his first job, as a statistics clerk at the nation's largest grocery chain.

An outsider might expect that the Hartford uncles would have been delighted to have the heir working for them. But George and John Hartford had no interest in grooming their feckless nephew for the company they had worked so hard to construct. They had developed a strong management team from within the working ranks of their company; not unreasonably, they believed that errant shows of nepotism would erode the loyalty of the men who helped build their empire.

And while under the best of circumstances Hunt Hartford would have been a difficult employee, these were hardly the best of circumstances. In 1934, the Hartford brothers were approaching the biggest crisis in the sixty-five-year history of the A&P. Even though overall revenues were burgeoning, volume on a per-store basis was decreasing. Only by constantly increasing the number of stores could the A&P continue to keep profits growing, and this perilous strategy could easily cause the entire operation to self-destruct.

Making matters worse was a former A&P employee named Michael Cullen. In 1930, Cullen transformed a huge, empty garage in Queens into a no-frills warehouse store, where prices were set only slightly above cost. Over the next few years, King Kullen changed the course of grocery retailing. Instead of small shops with relatively few items, these new stores, called supermarkets, were veritable warehouses. By stocking a larger number of items, Cullen could afford to cut his prices; volume made up for what he lost on margin. This was, after all, the Depression, and consumers were especially price-conscious. Cullen's King Kullen store was imitated by Big Bear, which occupied an abandoned automobile plant in New Jersey. Customers began leaving the A&P in droves.

By 1934, A&P sales had dropped a precipitous ten percent. John argued that the supermarket, in whatever form, must be the wave of the future. George, ever cautious, insisted that the higher fixture and inventory costs would be a stone around the A&P's neck, diminishing the liquidity that had saved the company during the Depression and putting it on the road to bankruptcy.

While the brothers Hartford argued and anguished, their nephew was assigned to keep track of the sales of bread and pound cake. Each day, Hunt Hartford would arrive at the cramped A&P offices on the eighth floor of the Graybar Building. He would unlock the cabinet in which the various record books were kept, then carry them over to his desk, one of the look-alike wooden tables lined up on the floor just beneath George and John's glass-enclosed offices, perches from which they could watch the work going on below.

For the first few weeks of his tenure, Hunt stuck to his tallies. But it wasn't long before he found himself doodling little poems on his notepads. With an heir's audacity, he asked the company typists to print up his verses. "I had an income of over a million dollars a year," said Hartford. "Can you imagine me sitting out with a bunch of clerks?"

Instead of working on the bakery statistics, he spent much of his time on the phone. There were art dealers wanting to sell Turners and Rembrandts, and debutantes' mothers inviting him to their daughters' balls. Finally the uncles left a note on his desk: The phones at the grocery headquarters were not for the personal use of employees.

Clerks were supposed to be at their desks by nine, but because of his all too active nightlife—Hartford was a regular at such Prohibition-era clubs as "21" and El Morocco—he generally showed up at least an hour later. One day he arrived at eleven, his eyelids heavy. He gathered his statistics books from the cabinet, piled them on his desk, pushed his chair in, and lay prostrate on the floor. The other clerks simply edged around the sleeping heir as they went about their business.

"Hunt Hartford was a disturbing influence in the office," said William Walsh, who spent more than forty years working at the A&P before retiring in 1981 to write a bitter history of the grocery chain, *The Rise and Decline of The Great Atlantic & Pacific Tea Company.* "He'd come in like the playboy of the Western world. . . . He would sit there talking about buying a yacht—meanwhile the $65-a-week clerks were busy tallying up bakery statistics."

Despite his wretched comportment, Hunt genuinely wanted to win the approval of his Uncle John. One day Hunt made his way into his uncles' great glassed offices. He told them he wanted to become more involved, do something more personal, get to know Uncle John, even work as his secretary. The answer was no. If Hunt Hartford was going to succeed in the family business, he would have to show some discipline.

Hunt survived that first rejection, then returned with a second idea: he would write a company history. Again he was rebuffed. If their nephew couldn't be relied on for the simple drudgery of statistics, he certainly couldn't be trusted to tell the public the story of the very private Hartford brothers.

Mary Lee saw it differently; she was convinced that the uncles should have put their nephew to work. "He could have done so many things there," she said, "advertising, writing." This was, after all, the era when 16 million American radio listeners made a musical variety show known as *The A&P Band Wagon,* which starred Kate Smith, the most popular program in America. But John and George said it was statistics or nothing.

For Hunt Hartford, the end of the A&P came in less than six months. "These were the days when workers put in a half-day on Saturdays," said Walsh. "Hunt asked for the day off to head back to Cambridge to watch the Harvard–Yale game. His uncles decided he would be given no special treatment. They told Hartford's boss, the head of the statistics department, Dan McCarthy, to tell their nephew that if he took the day off, he need not come back to work."

Yale stopped Harvard 14–0 on November 24, 1934, and Hunt and Mary Lee were there to see it. Thus ended his career at the A&P.

"It just didn't work out," John Hartford would say if anyone asked. "There he was, surrounded by people who really had to work for a living, and he was receiving callers who wanted to sell him paintings."

Hunt never recovered from that rejection. "I adored Uncle John like a god," he said. "If he had been willing to be friendly with me, none of this would have happened. . . . All I would have liked was to have my uncles invite me to lunch occasionally."

Had the Hartford uncles been inclined to indulge their nephew, he probably would have ended up like so many other dissipated heirs who had positions in the family business, but no real jobs, the sort of men who had one too many martinis at lunch and maintained the merest pretense of activity. But when John and George closed the doors to the A&P their nephew was forced to start casting about for an alternative career, one that might eventually earn his uncles' esteem. "He was the only one carrying the name, and he felt he had to live up to it," said a cousin, Michael McIntosh, a descendant of one of George Hartford I's daughters. "If Hunt had been able to work in the company, I'm not sure he would have had the need for all the publicity he generated. . . . It might have taken care of that desire for recognition.''

Hunt and Mary Lee Hartford's marriage was born of impetuousness and nurtured by tepid affection. It would not be enough to sustain them. Hunt Hartford was a niggler. Chief among his obsessions was physical appearance. He brooded over his own countenance, and decided that his nose was placed wrong, his ears were too low, his brow too thick. He was even more critical of his wife's features. Mary Lee had a round, feminine form that did not quite jibe with Hartford's androgynous ideal. He was constantly nagging his wife to lose weight, and once he even sent her to a plastic surgeon to see about correcting a slight crook in her nose. To his credit, the doctor told her the proposed operation was senseless.

Hartford, though, wanted more than aesthetic perfection. He wanted his wife to be an actress, a writer, or an artist—the realization of his own inchoate ambitions. But Mary Lee had little interest in charting her own career; most of her ambitions were social.

Hunt and Mary Lee stayed in New York after he lost his job at the A&P. At Tuckie Astor's side, Mary Lee became increasingly successful as one of the ladies who lunched. Her husband, meanwhile, was growing increasingly apathetic toward the social set. Hunt withdrew to his study, his writing, his books. He spent months laboring over a fictionalized version of his short-lived job at the A&P and of life in Newport. He submitted portions of it to a variety of magazines, including *Esquire* and *Writer's Digest.* His name inevitably merited a personal rejection slip, but it was a rejection just the same.

There are sparks of insight in that incomplete autobiographical work, and an occasionally elegant sketch. Discussing Jack Astor, Hartford went through a litany of his hypochrondriacal complaints; his description of the root of his friend's self-indulgence was dead-on. Astor's problems, according to Hartford, were the result of too much leisure and a syco-phant doctor who was paid to listen to Astor's imagined ills. In another too brief passage, Hartford saw the tables at one Newport ball as ''lined up like Fascist tanks on parade.'' In the end, though, what survived was a clutch of finely crafted fragments; there was no evidence that he ever wove those elegant details together into a coherent whole.

Not only was Hartford plagued by an overattention to detail; when it came to actually *working,* he lapsed into a paralytic indolence. He in-dulged himself, purposefully drinking Sanka instead of coffee in the morning so that he wouldn't be kept awake all day. He had, he noted a bit hyperbolically, little resemblance to Balzac, who worked eighteen or twenty hours a day.

Hartford believed that his problem went beyond shoddy work habits. He contended that there were two great subjects, character and drama. While he had little trouble getting at the character, he was always searching for a way to fathom the drama.

Hunt and Mary Lee spent their fourth anniversary with Henrietta at Wando Plantation, Henrietta's winter home near Charleston, South Carolina. The thirty-two-room mansion, designed by the New York architect William Delano and modeled after low-country plantation homes of the early 1800s, was yet another of Henrietta's attempts to reincarnate herself as a nineteenth-century aristocrat, and the effect was worthy of Margaret Mitchell. The two-and-a-half-story main house had beveled glass windows looking out onto a garden shaded by trees covered with Spanish moss; the pathway from the street was an avenue lined with oaks.

About a quarter-mile from the mansion, on the banks of the Wando River, was "Little Wando," a log cabin furnished in finely wrought bentwood. And it was there that Hunt and Mary Lee were permitted to stay, and retain a modicum of privacy. Early in the visit, Henrietta ventured over (she made sure Mary Lee was out) to tell her son, "If you married a Negress I would have accepted her." That sort of acceptance, he replied, was likely to give Mary Lee the impression that Henrietta didn't like her. "If you don't want me around," Henrietta snapped back, "I'll just go off to Europe and leave you two alone."

Hunt tried to calm his mother, extolling his wife's social graces, her performance on the New York and Newport social stages. That did nothing to allay Henrietta's displeasure. "All she did," retorted Henrietta, "was take over the friends I made for you."

The dinner to celebrate Hunt and Mary Lee's anniversary was a sorry, expensive affair. The table's centerpiece was a wooden model of St. Michael's Church in Charleston, complete with a toy bride and groom. Henrietta carried on about all the trouble and expense she had had arranging for it to be built for the occasion. Mary Lee kept quiet, but afterward she told her husband that on a previous visit to Charleston she had seen that very model collecting dust in a shop window.

By the time their stay was over, a battle had erupted between husband

and wife. The subject, predictably, was money. Hunt confided to Mary Lee that he wanted to buy a yacht. She insisted he tell his mother.

"Why should I?" he responded. "You always tell me I should wear the pants in the family. Why do you keep interfering with my affairs?"

Mary Lee reddened. "I have no interest in your affairs. Everything belongs to you two. I hate you and your whole damn family," she said, throwing a glass bowl full of cereal to the floor, where it shattered at her feet.

In the end, of course, Henrietta was consulted, and inevitably she approved the purchase. The acquisition was perfectly suited to her antique ambitions for her son.

The yacht was the *Joseph Conrad,* the smallest full-rigged ship in the world. Built in 1882, she was originally called the *Georg Stage,* after the son of the man who commissioned her. Alan Villiers, a gentleman author, had bought her in 1934, renamed her, and replaced the figurehead of Stage with a bust of the Polish novelist.

Villiers sailed the *Conrad* around the world, then wrote a book about his voyage. But on New Year's Day 1935, the ship's anchor chain parted in the teeth of a northwest gale; the boat was a wreck, her hull splintered on the rocks near the Brooklyn end of New York Harbor.

Hartford spotted the *Conrad* in 1936. His best recollection was that he was originally interested in the figurehead, and he contacted Villiers to find out if it was for sale. Villiers told him it wasn't. "Can I buy the ship, then?" Hartford asked.

Villiers, who lacked the funds to repair the *Conrad,* offered the wreck to Hartford for $15,000. That was just the beginning. Originally the *Conrad* had had rudimentary fittings, triple-decker bunks, and a couple of heads. But Hartford decided to re-create her as an opulently appointed yacht, appropriate for the Newport harbor, and by the time he finished, she had five bedrooms, each finished with white panels with gold molding and mahogany capping on the beams. The five bathrooms were fitted with porcelain, and the grand saloon was warmed by an open fireplace. Cost of the entire enterprise: $100,000.

In the spring of 1937, after a year of refurbishing, Hartford took off on his first expedition. The captain was A. E. Toonian, former senior lieutenant in the Imperial Russian Navy and, more recently, master of the *Vamarie,* a yacht owned by Hartford's sister's second husband, Vadim Makaroff, an Imperial Russian Navy commander turned caviar importer.

The passenger list included Mary Lee, Virginia French, who was Jack Astor's sister-in-law, and two scientists—Dr. Waldo Schmidt, curator of marine invertebrates at the Smithsonian Institution, and his assistant, G. Robert Lunz, curator of crustacea at the Charleston Museum—brought along to give the trip the veneer of a scientific expedition.

Hartford was less interested in the oceanographic aspects of the journey than in some romantic notion of finding pirate riches. He brought along the Charleston writer DuBose Heyward, author of *Porgy* (later immortalized by George Gershwin), to share his fantasies.

Henrietta did everything short of coming along for the ride. She insisted that, along with the captain and a dozen-odd hands, her son take Carlson, the family butler; then she saw the ship off in Charleston. As Hartford later described the scene in an article for *Esquire*:

> She was looking slightly younger than myself, and the only claim she had to her eyelashes was the fact that she had paid for them. She did not bother much with me, but went and confided to the captain (as he later reported) that I was to have Walker-Gordon milk shipped by plane and that I was to have it every morning for breakfast instead of coffee, which might keep me awake all day. Then she gave me a big kiss, gave nine sailors a glance which incapacitated them for eighteen hours, and left.

Hartford's pursuit of high drama turned into something out of Gilbert and Sullivan. Every morning the scientists dutifully put out their nets, the women took out their backgammon boards, and Hartford and Heyward puzzled over yellowing maps of lost schooners. Each evening there was a cocktail hour, complete with champagne and canapés; dinner was served by white-jacketed waiters. The scientists managed to come back with a couple of new species of crustacea, but the heir never found any sign of wrecks, pirates, or treasures.

Still, the trip was not without its rewards. The heir in search of adventure was not unaware of the comic elements of his three-month voyage. He kept a diary, and part of it became that article in *Esquire,* his first piece of writing accepted for publication. "Gone Without the Wind," published in October 1938, was a not unamusing tale of the foibles of a rich kid who yearns for a seafaring romance and ends up with a high-priced cocktail party.

> For years I had the hazily romantic notion that I wanted to sail in a square-rigger. . . . How grand it would be, I dreamed, to bowl over the seas in the wake of such swaggering adventurers as Morgan and Red Legs, Blackbeard and Dampier; to ride my horse on deck and

drink a health in gunpowder and salt water; to line up all my ene-
mies and make them walk the plank; to maroon whichever of my
crew I found obnoxious to me; to capture many an iron-studded
casket full of doubloons and moidores and pieces of eight, and having melted them down for safety's sake, to fill the hollow masts of
my ship with ever-flowing molten gold. Little did I know that my
dream was soon to be realized; that I was to own such a ship and
more gold was to be poured into her than I had ever imagined—my
own gold however.

Indeed, "Gone Without the Wind" was probably one of the most
expensive investments a young writer ever made in starting his career.
Ralph Burger, a bespectacled functionary who served as John Hartford's
secretary, made sure to pass on to the Hartford brothers the less than
flattering description of their flirtatious sister-in-law. It undoubtedly was,
in their estimation, the sort of publicity the family could do without.

As for Henrietta, she probably didn't even notice the slight. For the
first time in the sixteen years since her husband had died, she was too
preoccupied with her own troubles to pay much mind to her son's affairs.

II

❖

STEPPING OUT
Café Society and
the Hollywood Years

*Inherited wealth is a real handicap to happiness. It is as
certain death to ambition as cocaine is to morality.*
WILLIAM K. VANDERBILT

Hunt and Mary Lee Hartford in Newport (1937). Theirs was a
union bound by pragmatism rather than passion.
(Courtesy of The Hartford Family Foundation)

5

*I*N 1937, Henrietta Hartford made another pass at establishing social legitimacy. She tried to catch up with the parade of American heiresses who wed European noblemen with titles far grander than their fortunes. The September issue of *Le Carnet Mondain,* a European chronicle of high society, featured "Donna Henriette Pignatelli, nata Hartford [*sic*], la gentile consorte di don Guido Pignatelli dei duchi di montecalvo" on its cover. Although the fifty-six-year-old bride was on her second marriage, the photograph depicts a woman looking aggressively virginal in diaphanous white tulle embroidered in silver. Maury Paul described the groom as "small, dark and not bad looking and he must have considerable fascination for susceptible women." In the words of another man who knew him, Henrietta Hartford's second husband was a "pathological charmer."

Prince Guido Pignatelli, son of General Pompeo dei Duchi di Montecalvo and Princess Helene Narisehkin Pignatelli of Naples, got his title from an ancestor who had been pope. He had a brief and desultory career as a "customers man" on Wall Street; it turned most profitable when he made a call to sell corporate bonds to a rich widow named Henrietta Hartford.

As with her other efforts at attaining social credibility, this effort was also somewhat passé. The golden era for European title acquisition had begun more than fifty years before, in the 1870s, when a couple of girls whose families had been rejected by New York society married English aristocrats: Jennie Jerome, daughter of the upstart stock speculator Leonard Jerome, became Lady Randolph Churchill in 1874; Consuelo Yznaga, Cuban-born daughter of a Louisiana plantation owner, married the Duke of Manchester in 1876. By the turn of the century, when titular marriages were practically de rigueur for monied young women, Consuelo Vanderbilt's mother forced her to marry the Duke of Marlborough.

It wasn't long, though, before it emerged that all too often these matches didn't work. Consuelo Yznaga was virtually abandoned by her husband; Lady Churchill had to contend with a disastrously syphilitic spouse. Consuelo Vanderbilt divorced her duke, leaving her family out some $10 million. There was more finishing the trend than simply a slew of bad marriages. As the United States moved into the twentieth century, the nation's power was sufficient that the monied class was no longer obliged to look abroad for legitimacy.

Henrietta's shopworn quest for aristocratic success foundered as well. For although her relationship with Pignatelli was sufficiently amicable, she failed to achieve clear title to the pedigree that should have gone with the marriage.

Henrietta had always told Hunt that if she ever remarried, she would ask him—"her favorite boyfriend"—first. But her second wedding, on April 25, 1937, came as a surprise not only to her son, off with Mary Lee on a *Conrad* expedition, and her daughter, then in Hawaii on her own third honeymoon. When Henrietta married Guido Pignatelli at St. Vincent's Church in Los Angeles, his Reno divorce decree was less than twenty-four hours old, and he had never bothered to tell his first wife, Constance Wilcox Pignatelli, that he was leaving her. She didn't learn about the marriage until weeks afterward, when someone mistakenly sent *her* a congratulatory telegram.

Constance Pignatelli, a Connecticut heiress who had supported her prince throughout their ten-year marriage, refused to give up her title without a tussle. In September 1937, while the newlyweds were on their honeymoon boar-hunting in Czechoslovakia, Constance filed suit in New York, contending that Guido's divorce was invalid.

During the weeklong trial, held in January 1938, the papers carried stories of the various Pignatellis trooping in and out of court—along with delicious bits of trial testimony. It was bad enough that Henrietta had stolen her husband and her title, Constance testified, but Henrietta's age made matters even worse. "All my friends called my attention to the fact that she was a grandmother," said Constance at trial. "It annoyed me terribly."

Guido and Henrietta both declined to take the stand, and the judge eventually ruled that Constance still reigned in New York. (New York State, he noted, did not recognize a Reno divorce unless both spouses had attorneys present at the hearing, and Constance had not been represented.)

Guido's divorce lawyer declared that the ruling would not affect the prince's marriage to Henrietta, "since he is a legal resident of Nevada and does not intend to return to New York," the only place the ruling applied. But Nevada residency wasn't quite good enough for Guido. First he obtained an annulment from the archbishop of Los Angeles, and then he had his marriage to Henrietta declared legal in California. Annulment document in hand, he went to court in Florence, Italy; the court ruled against him. In July 1939, he appealed to the Italian Court of Cassation, which declared his divorce from Constance in effect; that verdict was sustained by a court in Perugia.

References to the prince in Hartford's journals never mention Pignatelli by name; it is always "the foreigner married to my mother." According to Hartford's sister, there was a certain amount of rivalry between them, but the stepson was reticent and the stepfather courtly; civility reigned. Still, the underlying tension between Henrietta's son and her husband, coupled with the court ruling invalidating her marriage in New York State, where Hunt and Mary Lee spent most of their time, slackened the bond between mother and son.

Without his mother there to manage his life, Hartford started to spin out of control. It was then that his compulsive womanizing began. His obsession had twin, contradictory drives: the chase appeared to be Hartford's attempt in part to replace Henrietta, in part to flout her. Either way, Mary Lee made it easy; she was already spending more and more time apart from her husband, traveling alone to California and Hot Springs, West Virginia. Hunt, meanwhile, became a fixture on the banquettes at El Morocco, legendary for ordering milk when everyone else was downing post-Prohibition highballs. Thirties café society was going full swing, and the clubs were cluttered with beautiful young women in search of bright futures, just the sort to whom Hartford was drawn. For him, a man already constitutionally self-occupied and buffered even more by his wealth, those girls were his passport to the outside world.

He spent days mooning over one girl or another: Jane Bradley, an heiress from Milwaukee who had a role in the Broadway production of *Stage Door,* the starlet Arline Judge, Gene Tierney, Betty Hutton, Carole Landis, Peggy Cummins, Carol Marcus (who later married William Saroyan and then Walter Matthau), Marta Toren, and Lana Turner—all made gossip-column appearances with the A&P heir.

But before these evanescent beauties there was Mary Chastain Grund-hoefer, a high-strung chorine who used the stage name Mary Barton. Born in New York in 1915, the doe-eyed brunette spent her childhood in the Bronx; her parents died when she was thirteen, and she was adopted by family friends, William and Florence "Florrie" Grundhoefer, an auto company employee and his wife.

Mary struck out on her own at sixteen; she took a small apartment in Manhattan and within the year landed a job in the chorus line at the Roxy, where Hartford first spotted her. He sent her flowers after each performance until she agreed to go out with him. He made little effort to keep his infatuation with Mary clandestine, leaving a messy trail Mary Lee couldn't help but discover.

Hartford never could resist the late-night telephone call, and he would creep down the hall from the bedroom to the library, then tiptoe back to bed. "It's bad enough that you have to call her, but does she have to keep me awake too?" Mary Lee would complain when he returned. One night he even brought along Tuckie Astor, Jack's wife and Mary Lee's best friend, to see Mary Barton perform. When Mary Lee learned of the excursion, she was of course outraged.

Then, in early 1938, Mary discovered she was expecting a child. "When she wired me that she was pregnant, instead of being terribly shocked, I said okay, I'd go along with it," recalled Hartford. "I asked if she wanted to get married, and she said no. But she wanted to go ahead and have the baby. I told my sister, she said she would be glad to adopt it. It was extraordinary that my sister, who was very socially conscious, was willing to do it."

But Josephine never had to make good on her offer. "The stepmother [sic] wouldn't allow it," Hartford said. "She wanted to hold onto the trust." Florrie, Mary's adoptive mother, was by then living in Florida, divorced from William Grundhoefer and remarried to an ex-convict named John Colt. She demanded custody of Hartford's firstborn.

Florrie wanted Mary to go to Florida for the birth, but, she later told a reporter, Hartford insisted that the child be born at LeRoy Sanitarium in New York, a plush private hospital popular with society women because its food came from the fashionable Colony restaurant next door.

George Huntington Hartford II's first child, a son, was born on August 18, 1938. At his insistence, the Hartford name was kept off the birth certificate. Instead, Florence Grundhoefer Colt and her new husband were listed as the child's parents. Within the month, the boy, named Edward for his grandfather, was taken to Florida to be raised by Florence Colt.

Mary Barton rejected Hartford's initial attempts to make some sort of financial settlement. She had reconsidered his offer of marriage and decided to hold out for his divorce from Mary Lee. But although Hunt and Mary Lee split up less than six months later, he would never make good on his promise to Mary Barton.

Had she not borne his child, the Roxy chorine probably would have passed quietly out of Hartford's life. For even as he was fretting over Mary's pregnancy, Hunt was distracted by yet another young woman. In the spring of 1938, he spotted Jane Bradley, a fine-boned blonde, watching him play tennis in Hot Springs. He asked her to dinner. The infatuation continued through the year, and in December she even took him to Milwaukee to meet her parents.

By that time, Hunt and Mary Lee's union was mostly a matter of appearances. She wintered in Palm Beach; he shuttled between New York and Milwaukee. By day, he wrote in his journal; by night, he caroused with Frank Shields, his beard when he met Jane. But even though Hartford would occasionally ask Mary Lee for his freedom, he had never made any serious moves toward divorce. In January 1939, however, she had a suitor of her own. There was no reason left to keep up the slim pretense sustaining their marriage.

Mary Lee had met Douglas Fairbanks, Jr., on New Year's Day 1939 at the estate of Herbert Bayard Swope, the bombastic editor of the New York *World*. As Mary Lee told the story, she spent New Year's Eve at the Swopes' and received a call in the morning from her husband saying he wanted to end their marriage. She left the phone and went downstairs, where Swope introduced her to the young actor, who had arrived for the day. Swope, Fairbanks, and Mary Lee strolled about the Long Island estate. When they returned to the house, Swope excused himself, and the young couple retired to the library, deep in conversation. After an hour, Mary Lee suggested that it was time to rejoin the party. But when Fairbanks went to open the door, which he had surreptitiously closed, it wouldn't budge. The two started shouting for help. Finally, thanks to a good shove by the butler, the door gave way. The couple emerged to much teasing from the other guests. Fairbanks asked Mary Lee to lunch the following week, then to dinner—and the next week she was off to the lawyers to discuss a divorce.

Hartford remembered the circumstances leading to his first divorce slightly differently. He too heard about the stuck library door, and he also knew about Mary Lee's interest in the debonair young actor. Hartford conceded that he had asked to be given his freedom, but he insisted that he wasn't really serious. It was Mary Lee, he said, who turned his idle conversation into action.

Hartford's version of events seems the more credible of the two. With Henrietta remarried and his uncles unwilling to have any part of him, Mary Lee was the only anchor in his drifting life. For him, the arrangement, however tenuous, was more desirable than none at all.

When Mary Lee began to press Hunt for a divorce, he asked her to think about a temporary separation. But Mary Lee insisted on a permanent break. And although her attorneys told her it could imperil her divorce settlement, she continued to see Fairbanks on the sly.

Still, the Hartfords' breakup started out amicably, with Hunt going so far as to suggest that Henrietta adopt Mary Lee and make her his sister instead of his wife. Little emotion inflamed the dissolution; even so, there was the problem of a financial settlement. Mary Lee demanded more than $1 million. When Hunt told his mother how much she wanted, Henrietta, who still controlled his finances, pressed him for the details of his adulterous affairs.

Hunt told her about Mary Barton and the baby. Henrietta calmly informed her son that she had suspected something of the sort and suggested that, along with his divorce, he straighten out that problem as well. As for Mary Lee, Henrietta added, she was willing to agree to some sort of settlement, but the demands were excessive.

Hunt Hartford, the weak-willed son and manipulated husband, became little more than a courier between his wife and mother, a passive man drawn taut between two strong-willed women. The last days of his marriage not only drew finely the faults of that first union but were a blueprint for the rest of his life.

Hunt sided with his wife against his mother; he felt that Mary Lee should get whatever settlement she asked for. Hunt told Mary Lee what his mother had said, and she conceded that there was little to do but wait. Her attorneys had told her that her only alternative was to sue in open court, and even with the scandal, there was little chance that she would be awarded a judgment as big as the out-of-court settlement she was seeking.

But Mary Lee was not going to give up without a fight. She proceeded to badger her soon-to-be ex-husband subtly, suggesting that he put more pressure on his relatives, asking him to point out that she could expose his bastard son. She wouldn't threaten his mother directly, she said, nor would she ever really go public with what she knew. But if his mother thought she might, it could force Henrietta's hand.

Hunt told Mary Lee he was unwilling to do anything that might have the appearance of blackmail. For one thing, he didn't want his family to think he would submit to that kind of pressure. For another, he did not want the Hartfords to part with Mary Lee on unfriendly terms.

Several days passed, and Hunt went back to his mother to see if she would acquiesce to Mary Lee's demands. Henrietta said she might, but only if her son agreed not to remarry for a minimum of one year. Hunt said that would be impossible. Henrietta then said she was tired of fighting and that she, after all, had problems of her own. She asked him to take the matter up with his Uncle John.

Hunt called his uncle and, scruples about blackmail notwithstanding, warned him that if he didn't settle with Mary Lee the matter of his illegitimate son would likely become public. From a selfish viewpoint, John told him, he would have liked to see the matter cleaned up quickly and quietly. But ultimately, the publicity would not affect the company a great deal.

The A&P had already weathered a far more critical storm. In 1935, profits had slid to $16.6 million, their lowest point in nearly ten years. Finally, in 1936, John convinced George that he needed to convert to King Kullen–style supermarkets, and George agreed to remodel a hundred stores. The number doubled the next year, and by 1938, the A&P operated more than 1,100 supermarkets. By 1939, the downward spiral was reversed, and profits started increasing again, up to nearly $20 million in six years. In the face of that accomplishment, their heir's affairs appeared inconsequential.

But while John wasn't particularly concerned about the potential for scandal, he was worried that if Mary Lee sued she might end up with voting stock in the A&P. And he was adamant that those shares not slip out of family hands. As long as Mary Lee didn't get the stock, he reasoned, the settlement was none of the uncles' affair. Henrietta could resolve the matter herself. And after some haggling, the mother struck a deal with her son: He would not marry for a year after the divorce; in return, she would give Mary Lee the settlement (no A&P stock included) she wanted.

Mary Lee and Hunt spent one winter morning signing separation papers in his attorney's office. Then Mary Lee went to pack up her belongings at their Fifth Avenue apartment, which Hunt would be keeping. The next day, dressed to the nines, he went from the hotel room where he had been staying to the apartment. It would be the last time he would see Mary Lee as her husband, and he wanted to make a good last impression. He spent the morning dickering over the last of their possessions, dividing golf clubs into male and female sets. Hunt wandered into the bathroom and noticed the blue toilet seat was gone. "You shouldn't have any use for it," she replied when he asked what had happened to it.

Finally he took Mary Lee to her train, the Orange Blossom. When he returned to the apartment, the reality of the divorce hit him; Mary Lee was gone, off to a new life in Florida, where he could not even telephone her without a struggle. He looked around the newly emptied rooms and suddenly realized that for the first time he would be facing life on his own. He thought that maybe their split came too soon, that perhaps somehow they could reconcile. But there would be no going back. In mid-January, Mary Lee went to an out-of-the-way courthouse in Okeechobee, Florida, and filed for divorce on the grounds of "extreme cruelty." Hartford's first marriage thus ended as furtively as it had begun.

The divorce became final three months later, and on April 22, 1939, Mary Lee married Douglas Fairbanks, Jr., at the Westwood Methodist–Episcopal Church on Wilshire Boulevard, just beyond Beverly Hills. Douglas Fairbanks, Sr., served as his son's best man.

"Hunt wanted to be a Pygmalion," explained Mary Lee. "I wasn't the type [to play along]."

After Mary Lee had announced her remarriage, Mary Barton finally understood that Hartford had no intention of marrying *her*. She began to press for a financial settlement for her child; Henrietta's attorneys handled the arrangements. Barton received a modest $5,000, with the agreement that she would receive $100,000 more upon the liquidation of George Hartford I's trust. Young Edward Colt, nicknamed "Buzzy," was set for life: Hunt Hartford put $300,000 in trust for the infant and made Florence Colt trustee, the income to be used to support the boy. Barton agreed never again to press Hunt for funds to support their child.

By May 1939, Hunt Hartford had discharged all of his obligations, and had virtually no idea what he was going to do with the rest of his life.

Into that breach slipped Ralph Ingersoll, the founding editor of *Fortune* magazine, who had been working since 1937 to raise money for a new publication that, as he planned it, would incorporate the finer aspects of magazine journalism into an afternoon newspaper. *PM* would have fine photographs (the dummy contained work by Margaret Bourke-White) and stories that were as well written as they were reported. Lillian Hellman, Dashiell Hammett, Dorothy Parker, and Heywood

Broun worked with Ingersoll to prepare the dummy. By the middle of 1939, a stable of investors, including the Sears heirs Marian Stern and Lessing Rosenwald, and Marshall Field, heir to the Chicago department store fortune, had purchased shares in the fledgling paper. But Ingersoll remained short of the $1.5 million he needed to start it.

According to Ingersoll's biographer, Roy Hoopes, a photographer Ingersoll had known when he was editor of *Fortune* approached him on behalf of Hartford and told him the A&P heir might be interested in investing in his project. The photographer explained that the Hartford family was worried about Hunt, since he was recently divorced and didn't quite know where to direct himself. Hunt had once remarked that he would like to be a reporter, and an adviser had suggested that instead of starting up a newspaper himself, it would be easier to let someone like Ingersoll do it, using Hartford money, of course.

A few days after the photographer's visit, Hartford dropped by the office, "a slim good-looking boy, immaculately dressed, shy and somewhat ill at ease," the publisher later told Hoopes. Ingersoll assumed Hartford was barely out of college, rather than nearing thirty. Hunt stammered and stammered, clearly trying to muster the nerve to ask for a job. Finally, Ingersoll said he was a long way from hiring anybody and was still trying to raise money. "I'd be interested in that too," Hartford responded.

"Some other time," replied Ingersoll, who assumed that there was no way Hartford handled his own money. And that, he figured, was the end of it.

But several months later, Ingersoll was approached by H. C. North, who was employed by A&P and acted as an agent for the Hartford family. North informed Ingersoll that the heir was still interested in the project, and that "any problem of a Hartford is a problem of ours. . . . We don't give a damn how much money you lose, as long as it's respectable. And if you can keep him in a job for a year, we'll bless the hell out of you.

"But," he added, "you've got one more job. The princess wants to see you. She's going to ask you to dinner."

For Ingersoll, the Hartford money would mean he could afford to publish his paper. He agreed to have dinner with the princess and her son. The three dined in Hartford's Fifth Avenue apartment. Conversation was slow; in the presence of his mother, Ingersoll noted, Hunt had nothing much to say, and the princess herself seemed interested only in seeing how much she could read of Ingersoll's character with her intense and continuous stare. After the last course was removed from the table,

Henrietta dismissed her son with a gesture that seemed to be sending him to his room.

"As soon as Hunt was gone," Ingersoll recalled, "the princess's attitude changed. With a nod and a smile, she suddenly assumed everything was settled between us and launched into an embarrassingly intimate analysis of what she considered her son's character and how I was to look after him when he became my ward."

The agreement was that Hunt would purchase one of *PM*'s remaining $100,000 units and would be guaranteed a position as a cub reporter at minimum wage for at least one year when the paper was launched. And so Huntington Hartford got himself his first paying job outside the family business, even if he did have to pay for it.

Unlike most of his old Newport cronies, Hartford was uncomfortable with straight-out indolence. Jack Astor was the worst of the lot. He had managed a brief stint in 1934 at a Wall Street brokerage house controlled by his older half brother, Vincent, but he had little interest in working for a living. "I didn't finish until five o'clock," he said, "and by the time I got uptown it was six. And then I had to get up the next morning."

For the most part, those other heirs were at least two generations removed from the source of their wealth. But Hartford's legacy was more immediate, and he still felt obligated to try to match his uncles' accomplishments with achievements of his own.

To that end, Hartford came up with a plan to match his spending with his $120-a-month salary. He envisioned a system in which he would give himself a dollar from his trust for every dollar he made in salary. If he didn't receive a salary, he couldn't use the money from his trust. By the time he actually started working, his discipline had slackened. He upped the ante to four-to-one, but even that didn't hold up for very long. Earned money just didn't have much meaning for a man who had been receiving an income of more than $1 million a year for virtually all of his adult life.

During his tenure at *PM* he rarely even collected his salary. "The business manager once asked me if we had anyone on the staff named Huntington Hartford," recalled *PM*'s managing editor, Rae Weimer. "I asked why. She said, 'He never comes to get his paychecks.'"

Still, Hartford continued to maintain the fantasy that he would someday live without his income. In the early days at *PM* he told Jules Seligson that he wanted to live like a "real" reporter.

"I've taken an apartment down in the Village, and I'm going to live down there alone," he announced. "I'm going to try to be in the same mold, the same environment as a reporter would be. I want to inject the element of struggle in my life.''

''Huntington, that's marvelous,'' Seligson responded. ''But if you're serious, get John [Hartford's butler] to go on sabbatical for six months. Close up your apartment . . . and let your secretary go for six months. And then you're a reporter. If you find yourself at three A.M. at the Stork Club, you can't call your chauffeur and have him pick you up and take you home. You can get on the subway or, if you can afford a taxi, take a taxi.''

Hartford paused and considered the implications of Seligson's suggestions. ''I can't do that,'' he said. ''That would be going too far.''

Seligson was a spectator to the constant stream of women parading in and out of Hartford's life; he figured this obsession was another attempt by Hartford to escape the A&P wealth. ''One day he said to me, 'Barbara Hutton is after me, and I'm tired of it,' '' recalled Seligson. ''He had a stable of some of the most beautiful women in America, but he wanted to get down to the lower levels. One night he said, 'Let's go out and see if we can pick up some girls at Childs [a chain of New York City coffee shops]. I'd like to talk to a young girl if she's pretty and has brains, and maybe make a date with her.'

''He wasn't arrogant,'' said Seligson, shaking his head at the memory, ''he wasn't outlandish, but he was weird.''

For his first few months at *PM*, Hartford kept after the city editor for assignments, but even with his pestering he rarely received any. Mostly he just sat around the office, writing in his journal, talking on the phone. He never sent in an expense account; instead, he took his expenses out on the telephone.

PM's city editor quickly learned the danger of sending Hartford out on assignments alone. On one occasion, he dispatched Hartford to cover some forgettable incident on Long Island. Instead of taking the train, Hartford used his own forty-foot boat. He arrived back in Manhattan on a floating dock in the East River that, unfortunately, was a long way offshore; he needed a rowboat to land. For nearly an hour he waited in the same spot, surrounded by the waters of the East River, flagging all boats in an attempt to hitch a ride to shore. By the time he returned to the office, his story was hours overdue.

Hartford said that he covered the Murder, Inc., trial in Monticello, New York. But Hunt Hartford, cub reporter, appears to have been more observer than reporter; the stories carried in *PM* bore the byline of John Kobler, a more seasoned staffer.

Not surprisingly, Hartford didn't mix particularly well with the other *PM* reporters. Despite all his talk of modest living, he generally used his limousine as transportation to and from assignments, and his colleagues found the affectation amusing but not particularly endearing. Nor was Hartford comfortable writing in the communal bustle of the newsroom. Instead, he asked Shields, who shared a suite with Seligson in the Sardi's building, if he could use their offices. There he spent his days toiling away on his own idiosyncratic stories that never quite made it to print. He spent weeks tailing a blind beggar around the city, returning to tell Shields and Seligson of his adventures each afternoon.

While Hartford had fewer than a dozen bylines during his six-month stint at *PM*, he had no trouble grabbing headlines on his own. In 1940, he started going out with one of the more flamboyant starlets around, Arline Judge. By the time Hartford met Judge, she had starred in a handful of films, but her real fame lay in her many marriages. Her first husband was the film director Wesley Ruggles. They divorced in 1937, and within two weeks she married the tin-fortune heir Daniel Reid Topping. She had two sons, one from each marriage.

Hartford chased her down to the Kentucky Derby in April, then back to New York, where she was still seeing another man on the sly, Hartford's friend James McKinley Bryant, who served as chief greeter at the Sherry-Netherland Hotel. Where *PM* failed to bring out Hartford's reportorial instincts, Arline Judge succeeded. Her hotel room at the Derby adjoined Bryant's, and Hartford regularly left a slip of paper in the door separating the two suites so he could see later if it had been opened— more times than not it had. When he confronted her with his telltale evidence of infidelity, she just laughed and called him her "Junior G-Man."

Still, Hartford wooed on. In August, he bought Judge a $65,000 orchid-pink diamond. The nation was still reeling from the Depression; it wasn't hard for the public to be outraged by his extravagance.

The New York *World-Telegram* headlined its story: "Consumers' Nickels and Dimes Pay for the $65,000 Diamond A&P Heir Gave Hollywood Cutie Pie." Hartford's coworkers at *PM* were similarly disdainful. In the newsroom, his political callousness became legend. In the summer of 1940, El Morocco held a benefit auction for Vichy France. Outside, *PM* reporters picketed, protesting the fascist regime. Inside, *PM* reporters covered the story for the paper. Hartford was there as well, "bidding on baubles for Arline Judge, a cutie-pie starlet," recalled a *PM* reporter named Penn Kimball. "I didn't have the impression he was a person of electric social conscience."

▲

As with so many glittering editorial enterprises, *PM* had grave problems on the business side; its circulation was less than half what it needed to break even. By September 1940, it had become clear to Ingersoll that additional financing was needed. Hartford, along with several other of the original backers, was willing to put up the money, but it never came to that. On October 15, *PM*'s shareholders convened, and Marshall Field offered to buy them all out for twenty cents on the dollar. Hartford and the others agreed to the buyout, and within the month he had resigned from the paper. (Field kept pumping cash into the ailing paper for the next few years. In 1946, the department store heir finally insisted that the paper include advertising, and Ingersoll quit. New editors changed the name to *The Star,* and that paper folded in 1949.)

By the beginning of 1941, Hartford was without a job. And despite the diamond, his relationship with Judge had evaporated as well. Once again, the heir went looking for moorings.

This time, history intervened. Germany had invaded Holland, Belgium, and Luxembourg; Italy had declared war on Britain and France. Franklin Roosevelt announced the buildup of a peacetime army, and Huntington Hartford prepared to go off to war.

6

IN 1944, the United States government did what no one had ever done before: put Huntington Hartford in a position of authority. That April, after eighteen months' service in Los Angeles Harbor, a three-month stint in the Canadian Arctic on the Greenland Patrol, and five months of officers' training school in Florida, Hartford was named commander of a supply boat docked in Los Angeles. The boat, with a cargo of three hundred tons of canned pineapple (not to mention mosquito netting and quinine provided by Henrietta to ward off malaria), headed first to Hawaii, then the Philippines.

Hartford's commission was a tradeoff, pure and simple. "I got into the Coast Guard because I gave my boat to them," he later explained. (Initially, the Coast Guard refitted the *Joseph Conrad* as a training vessel, but it quickly decided there wasn't much need to train ensigns on a square-rigger. In 1947, by special government act, the *Conrad* was given to Mystic Seaport in Connecticut, where she is still docked.) Apparently, the Coast Guard assumed that if Hartford could manage the *Conrad,* he would have no trouble as captain of the *FT-179,* a supply ship only slightly larger than the yacht. The Coast Guard assumed wrong.

"Serving under Hunt was like being under the command of a combination of Mr. Roberts and Lieutenant Pulver—the guy played by Jack Lemmon in the movie, who inadvertently blew up the ship's laundry," recalled one of the men who served under Hartford.

Fortunately for the Allies, the closest Hartford's ship came to combat was at Tacloban harbor in the Philippines when three inebriated Marines charged aboard and demanded the crew shuttle them to their own boat in the outer harbor. One of Hartford's crewmen pulled out his pistol and fired a few warning shots in the air, and the drunken sailors headed off down the dock.

Still, Hartford and crew did better in port than on the open sea. He managed to run the ship aground twice, both times coming out of a channel. The first time, he said, a mismarked map was to blame. He had no such excuse for the second mishap; he had simply misread the map. "I mistook feet for fathoms. We finally had to get a tug to pull us out."

Hartford kept in loose contact with Mary Barton for the first months he was stationed in Calfornia. Three years and two failed marriages after her baby was born, Barton was trying to reestablish herself as a dancer in New York. But the fresh-faced chorine Hartford had fallen in love with was no more. At twenty-six, Mary looked a good bit older, her face finely mapped with age lines, her brown eyes empty.

In May 1941, while on leave from the Coast Guard, Hartford went to New York and met with Mary for what would be the last time. When he arrived at her apartment on West Sixtieth Street, she told him that she wanted her son back. She implored him to intercede with Florrie Colt.

But Hartford did nothing. And over the next months, Mary grew increasingly disconsolate. She pleaded with Florrie to return her child, but Florrie refused.

On the afternoon of September 8, 1941, Mary's landlord, Thelma Erickson, received a phone call from someone who identified himself only as a friend of Barton's. He informed Erickson that her tenant had sent him a letter saying she was leaving for California, and that while passing by her apartment he had noticed that the windows were open. Would the landlady be so good as to close them?

The building's janitor, Lewis Larsen, was dispatched. When he went up to the apartment, he saw Mary lying on her bed, assumed she was sleeping, and left.

Three days later, Mary's gentleman friend called once more. This time, Erickson told him that her tenants were well able to take care of their own windows. A few hours later, though, he phoned yet again, pleading with the landlady to go and check on his friend. This time, the landlady complied. She went upstairs and opened the door on an operatic tableau of death. Mary was half sitting on the bed, her henna-dyed hair spread on the pillow. The sheet, which covered her body to the chest, and the blanket, which lay folded at her feet, were completely unwrinkled. The room was banked with four dozen American Beauty roses.

The next time Mary's friend called, Erickson told him what she found—and asked him to come over. "No sir, not me," he responded. After a week, and repeated pleas to the public from the police, the man finally came forward on his own and identified himself. He turned out to be Benjamin Van Raalte, a Park Avenue stockbroker. "My client hardly knew Miss Barton," said his attorney at the time. "He was slightly interested in her professional career." (Van Raalte's second wife didn't quite see it that way. "It pretty much ruined his first marriage," she said, chortling, some forty years later. "I always did tell him he was a damn fool for getting involved.")

The medical examiner, Dr. Robert Fisher, determined that Mary Barton had died of an overdose of sleeping tablets on the afternoon of September 8. The coroner dismissed any suspicion of foul play, but just why the windows were open and how the roses got into the room would remain a mystery forever.

Mary Barton would be remembered more for her death—and the son she left behind—than for anything she did in life. Her body would languish at the morgue before it was finally released to her adoptive father, William Grundhoefer, who hadn't seen her for five years.

Grundhoefer took charge of the funeral and, on September 15, was appointed administrator of her estate. When he began sorting through Mary's effects, he discovered documents relating to her son's trust fund. And for the first time since the boy's birth, he began taking very serious interest in his affairs.

On December 30, 1942, Grundhoefer filed suit in New York State Supreme Court, asking for custody of the boy—and control of his trust account. Grundhoefer argued that his ex-wife and her new husband were unfit guardians; as proof he offered John Colt's conviction for having destroyed a car in order to collect insurance.

The next month, Grundhoefer filed a petition demanding that Hartford testify about the trust fund. Hartford didn't respond to the petition, but on January 20, 1943, Mary Barton's closest friend, Virginia Caserta, a self-described exotic dancer who used the stage name Tangia (she was pictured in the tabloids wearing a spangled décolletage that would have done Gypsy Rose Lee proud), did. In a sworn affidavit, Caserta linked Hartford to the dead dancer—and to her illegitimate son:

> Mary told me that a trust fund had been established which she stated
> at various times to be between a quarter and a half million dollars

by Huntington Hartford for the benefit of the child. . . . She told me that this fund was paying an income which varied between $900 and $1,200 a month to her foster [*sic*] mother, Florence [Grundhoefer] Colt.

Colt was supposed to use the money to support Mary's child, but Mary told me that Florence was using this money for her own private purposes and wasting the money on automobiles, private homes, servants and other useless expenditures. Shortly before Mary died, she told me she had consulted an attorney for the purpose of obtaining custody of her child.

Although Hartford stayed away from court, he couldn't keep the story out of the headlines. "Playboy Pledged Fund to Dancer's Boy" ran the New York *Journal-American*. "A&P Heir Named as Love Child's $500,000 Friend" trumpeted the *Daily News*. Grundhoefer pressed the court to compel Hartford to testify about the nature of the trust fund, but the judge refused to order him back to New York. Without Hartford's testimony, there was no way Grundhoefer could prove that the boy's trust fund was being mishandled—or even that it was Hartford who had established it in the first place. Ultimately, the suit was dropped.

Although Hartford kept his distance from the trial, he maintained close ties with Florence Colt, who had been sending him pictures of the boy from the moment they moved to Florida.

Florrie Colt was not a glamorous woman. With her buxom, maternal figure and gray hair in tight curls, she bore a distinct resemblance to Bess Truman. Still, the men who knew her say she was charming, and by the mid-forties, Florence Colt had moved on to her fourth husband. Roy Brangenberg was a widower, a onetime dance instructor with two daughters, Nelda and Janet, both older than Buzzy Colt. After Florrie and Buzzy moved into the Brangenberg household, they shared the front bedroom.

That house became Florrie's fortress, and she practically refused to leave. "She was afraid someone was going to kidnap Buzzy," explained Janet. "She didn't want want strange sitters in the house. She lived for the day he would turn twenty-one, and get access to that trust."

From the time Florrie and Buzzy moved in with the Brangenbergs, Hunt Hartford was a regular visitor. He swept into the patchwork household at odd hours of the night, generally with some young actress on his arm, his purpose to show his son off like some sort of trophy. One time, said Nelda, he brought Lana Turner, who came carrying her pet cheetah.

"Hartford would come in, wake Buzzy up, and bring him downstairs," recalled Nelda. "Hartford would just sit there and grin, eating his cookies and milk. It was as though he were saying, 'Here is evidence of my masculinity. This is the one thing in life I really produced, the one thing I'm really responsible for.' "

For Hartford, the relationship with his son was so important that he decided to move the entire Brangenberg family from Florida to Los Angeles, his base during his stint with the Coast Guard. He bought them a stucco Spanish spread at the corner of Flores and Fountain in Hollywood, not far from where he was living. The relationship with Hartford quickly became the focus of the family's existence. Florrie spent a lifetime leeching, first off her adopted daughter's legacy and then off that of the boy she left behind. The boy was Florrie's link to real money, and she exploited it for all it was worth. She kept aging photographs of Mary Barton in silver frames in the living room, telling Buzzy the woman was his older sister. She coached the child for his visits to his so-called uncle, visits made in the company of his "stepsisters," who were expected to chauffeur him to and from Hartford's home.

Buzzy never asked, but it wasn't hard for him to figure out just what his relationship to Hartford really was; the physical resemblance between the two was unmistakable. "People would see Buzz and ask if he was Hunt's son," remembered Nelda. "And Buzz would say no. Then they'd say, 'But you look so much like him.' "

What Buzzy could not believe, though, was that Florrie was his mother, which is what she had told him. According to the Brangenberg sisters, when Buzzy was about ten or eleven, he sat down, looked at Florrie, and said, "I don't understand something. I know Hunt is my father, but how can you be my mother? You're so much older."

Florrie brought out pictures and sat down and told him the story of Mary Barton. She told Buzzy that Hunt and Mary had been very much in love, that when Mary found out she was pregnant Hunt promised to get a divorce and marry her. Mary, Florrie told him, was so unhappy when Hartford broke that promise that she committed suicide.

Buzzy listened quietly to the tale. What hit him hardest was not his father's betrayal of his mother but rather that this man was his only blood relative, his only real family. Ed Colt would spend his life trying to forge a bond to the father who would never publicly claim him as his own.

The identification photograph on Hartford's discharge papers from the Coast Guard depicts a soft-featured man who looks more twenty-five than thirty-five. His chin is weak and his dark eyes have an uncertain focus. Under the section labeled "Job Field Preference" he entered: "Writing fiction."

Although he still spent some time in New York, Hartford lived most of the year in California, on an estate nestled in the Hollywood Hills, the biggest piece of private property in Hollywood. The estate was built by Carmen Randolph Runyon (it still bears the name Runyon Canyon) and was sold to the Irish tenor John McCormack in the twenties. Hartford bought it in 1942, just a year after he made his first move west. A winding road traversed the estate, coursing up a hill past tennis courts and a swimming pool with a commanding view of the city. An English Gothic mansion was perched just inside the wrought-iron gates leading to the grounds—the ideal habitat for the ersatz Edwardian heir.

Moving into the aeries of Hollywood came easily for Hartford. Hollywood in the 1940s was an impossible, imaginary paradise, populated by moguls and gangsters and an overabundance of starlets and molls. Hollywood was divvied up into studio city-states, with Louis B. Mayer, Carl Laemmle, Jr., Adolph Zukor, and Harry Cohn making up the oligarchy. It was a place where a handful of mostly lowborn Jews created their own vision of America, ruling a nation's fantasies and choosing its gods.

In this El Dorado where old money was a fortune made on last year's movie, Hartford passed as a blue-blood aristocrat, something he could never be back at St. Paul's. In 1940, the Securities and Exchange Commission declared the Hartfords one of the five richest families in America, just behind the Du Ponts, Rockefellers, and Mellons, and for Hollywood, that was pedigree enough.

"I remember Hunt would always send the car and chauffeur to pick up girls. That procedure didn't work with me," recalled Robert Neal, heir to the Maxwell House coffee fortune and a regular on the Hollywood circuit. "Not that I didn't have a chauffeur, but with Hunt they accepted it. For the girls, being with Hunt Hartford was like being projected into royalty."

As the token East Coast patrician, Hartford was given a certain leeway when it came to his sometimes erratic behavior: his ill manners were construed as amusing quirks. "One night I was with some girl—I called them the 'faceless wonders'—and Hunt said that Gene Tierney was giving a party and that we should all go over," remembered Neal. "He wanted to go hunting—that's what we called it.

"We arrived and we went to the pool, and Gene came over and said,

'Hunt, I didn't know you were in town. I would have invited you. Oh, Huntington, you're so bohemian.' ''

In the thirties, Hollywood entertained at home, but by the time Hartford arrived, café society had finally gone west. In January 1940, Billy Wilkerson opened Ciro's, and the stars started venturing out on the town, congregating at Hollywood's newest hotspot. What they found was a club with a streamlined façade and a baroque interior, walls draped in heavy ribbed silk dyed a pale green, and a ceiling painted American Beauty red. Bronze columns and urns served as lighting fixtures, flanking the bandstand. "Everybody that's anybody will be at Ciro's," announced *The Hollywood Reporter.*

"Hollywood was like a private club in those years," recalled Joseph Perrin, a real estate broker who handled much of the celebrities' business. "There were the golden boys, Howard Hughes, Howard Hawks, Errol Flynn." Hartford wired into the social circuit, joining the pantheon of playboys who controlled tables at Mocambo and Ciro's, fetching girls with the desultory flick of a finger.

Of that lot, Hartford and Hughes perhaps had the most in common. Hughes, six years older than Hartford, was also an heir trying to prove himself worthy of his legacy. His father had created the Hughes Tool Company, whose patent for a newfangled drill bit revolutionized the oil industry. But unlike Hartford, who was still struggling to shape his identity, Hughes had already met and surpassed his father's accomplishments.

By the forties, Hughes had already established himself as a producer with *Hell's Angels,* which featured Jean Harlow and which Hughes also directed, and *Scarface,* a thinly fictionalized biography of Al Capone. And Hughes was more than a moviemaker. *Hell's Angels* was essentially a celebration of World War I pilots and Hughes's fascination with aviation (he leased or acquired eighty-seven vintage planes to make the film), and in 1932 he decided to make another movie with special flight sequences. He began focusing his attention on developing a new, streamlined airplane, and formed Hughes Aircraft to fund development. The film never was made, but the H-1, a single-seat, open-cockpit plane with a series of innovations (retractable landing gear among them) was. With the H-1, Hughes set virtually every transcontinental speed record of consequence.

Hughes, with his successes, and Hartford, notably without any of his own, had an antipathy for each other. "They looked at each other like bulls looking at bastard calves,'' remembered Gregson Bautzer, Hughes's attorney. ''They didn't know each other, and they didn't want to.''

Still, according to Bautzer, who knew both men well, they showed some distinct similarities—especially in their attitudes toward women. They were consumed by their pursuit of young women, but both were essentially shy men, inept at the chase. Hughes would have women summoned for assignations—then leave them waiting for hours or not show up at all. ''Hartford,'' Bautzer recalled, ''was capable of extraordinary spurts of generosity, then, like Howard, he would be penurious about rather simple things. He had a series of ladies that lived with him, but they always complained that he didn't take proper care of them. He didn't know how to keep his women in style.''

Nonetheless, Bautzer willingly introduced women of his acquaintance to Hartford, most notably Lana Turner, who at seventeen had lost her virginity to the lawyer. Bautzer also claimed credit for arranging Turner's introduction to Howard Hughes, whom she nearly married.

''I had a big crush on Lana Turner when I was out in California,'' Hartford recalled. ''And Bautzer was very friendly with her.'' Bautzer agreed to arrange for them to meet, but he told the heir that he had to give her ''a beautiful present.''

The actress, said Hartford, looked better from afar. ''I was very disappointed,'' he recalled. ''She had shaved her hairline, she had put on weight. She really didn't look very good. I gave her a cigarette lighter that my mother had given me, but she felt it wasn't elaborate enough. I guess we were both disappointed.''

The link between Turner and the two heirs inspired a widely circulated—and apparently apocryphal—tale regarding the actress's linens. Turner, the story went, was so sure of her betrothal to Hughes that she had her sheets and towels initialed HH. When Hughes refused to marry her, she said, ''But I've already had the monograms made.'' To which Hughes supposedly retorted, ''Well, you can always marry Huntington Hartford.''

In the first years after the war, Hartford's professional life, if one could call it that, was as scattered as his personal affairs.

He tried to turn his Coast Guard adventures into a novella. The result was a rambling 134 pages that tracked a young lieutenant through the South Seas. Peppered with allusions to Joseph Conrad and Sir Walter Scott, the work was not badly written, but there had been nothing much in the voyage worth recounting. And although he flogged it for the next thirty-odd years, he never sold the story. In 1985, some forty years after the misbegotten voyage to the Philippines, his agent was still shopping the manuscript to various publishing houses.

As for business ventures, he simply wasn't interested. "You couldn't bring Hartford a project," recalled Perrin, who attempted to get him in on his real estate deals. "Hartford would send you to his advisers, they would say they'd discuss it with Hartford, then the whole thing would stall." Some of the ones that got away were beauties. "He had a chance to get Orange County at $600, $1,000 an acre," marveled Perrin. "Those orange groves are now Irvine—with high-rise buildings going for $100 a [square] foot."

By the end of the forties, having failed as a novelist and approaching middle age, Hartford resolved to prove himself more than just another playboy. He determined to elevate the Hartford name into that pantheon of American patrons—Rockefeller, Morgan, Mellon, Vanderbilt. Huntington Hartford decided to build not just one project, or two or three—he would try to blaze the Hartford name across a half-dozen buildings in New York and Los Angeles.

First came an aborted attempt to turn the grounds of his Hollywood Hills estate into the Huntington Hartford Play Resort and Sports Club and Cottage Group Center, a members-only resort for two thousand. Hartford commissioned Frank Lloyd Wright, then past seventy and in his last, fallow days in Los Angeles, to draw up plans for the canyon retreat. Wright planned a hotel for the base of the canyon, accommodating some three to four hundred guests. It was to be a cottage-group hotel, not one big building, made to follow the topography of the canyon.

For the sports club, Wright proposed a monumental concrete pyramid atop the canyon. Jutting out just below the peak of the pyramid would be three large disks, one a room for dancing, another a casino, the third a cabaret. In a curious update of the tennis courts his mother had built for him in Newport, Hartford planned four courts at the base of the pyramid for tournament tennis. There was to be a swimming pool as well; its water would cascade into the canyon below. Hartford was to have his own private apartment in the club, and his own residence and stables elsewhere on the property.

It was a Disneyland construct, "Frisbees impaled on a ship's prow," in the words of Wright's biographer Ron McCrea. And it was structurally improbable from the start. Although Hartford allotted some $500,000 for the development, the setting alone made that price tag seem low. Runyon Canyon was largely steep, steep hillside that, because of the difficulty of building on the rocky slope, has remained undeveloped to this day.

But Hartford never had to cope with the topographic obstacles. In order to build, he needed to obtain a zoning change—and local residents objected to the plan. In August 1947, some six hundred Hollywood residents called a protest meeting to inform Hartford and Wright that they didn't want a "monstrosity like that" in their neighborhood. The retreat, they complained, would create a traffic nuisance. "So I won't use the highway," Hartford replied. "I'll have the guests come up a side road and ride an elevator to the top of the cliff." But the community board held firm, refusing Hartford a zoning variance.

"It went on for two or three years," said Bruce Pfeiffer, director of the Frank Lloyd Wright Archives. "Finally Mr. Wright said, '[Hartford] is the sort of man who will come up with an idea, pinch it in the fanny and run.' And that was it."

And so, for a time, Hartford preserved his fortune in spite of himself.

Since being somebody in Hollywood meant being somebody in the movie business, Hartford made a pass at moguldom. There were rumors that he was going to buy Republic Pictures, the studio with the bald-eagle trademark and a reputation for B-grade cowboy pictures that later rode to fame on a score of John Wayne films. Hartford talked to the Nassour brothers about buying their production studios and lot on Sunset Boulevard, where he maintained his office. Then he pursued Howard Hughes's RKO studio.

According to Greg Bautzer, Hartford and Hughes met at midnight in one of the bungalows at the Beverly Hills Hotel. "Howard told Hartford that before there could be any serious discussions he had to know where Hartford was going to get the money," Bautzer said. "It had to be all cash, no mortgages, no paper. We never heard another word from [Hartford]."

After that failed attempt to buy RKO, Hartford finally turned up a project that did come to fruition—and for a time actually thrived. He turned his avocation for pretty girls into a vocation and launched a modeling agency that briefly was number one in the business.

Stephen Elliot, then a fashion photographer and the husband of one of the top models, Georgia Hamilton, recalled that Hartford first started talking of forming an agency at a Christmas party at his studio in 1947: "He had said to me, 'Boy, I really envy you, doing something that you really love to do, having all these beautiful girls around—it's terrific.' He asked if he could come and watch while I worked; I said anytime. He would come and watch. What was he trying to do? He just wanted to be somebody, a [top agency owner, like] John Powers, Harry Conover. As though that were something.''

But there was more to it than that. Like those aspiring actresses Hartford had courted at the Stork Club, the models became vessels for his own stunted dreams. ''He had this hopeful quality,'' recalled Elliot, ''as if in guiding those young girls he could find his own direction.''

Despite the constant chase, Hartford's reputation among the models remained surprisingly benign. ''For all that activity, almost no consummation,'' mused Jerry Ford, president of Ford Models, founded in 1948 and now the nation's largest. ''This is a small business, and everyone is very anxious to talk about what so-and-so does. Hunt used all this money and [built] his agency and not much ever happened. Any model who was established and good wasn't bothered by him. . . . The [good models] weren't really approachable and he wasn't stupid enough to try.''

''It was a religious thing with him, just to be near them,'' said Elliot. ''Those girls were goddesses to him. They had fame. He'd walk past the newsstand and see their photographs. They were masterpieces, natural wonders. He couldn't quite believe they could walk and talk and that they actually had natural functions like the rest of us. For him they were a miraculous thing.''

It wasn't hard for Hartford to work his way to the pinnacle of the modeling business. In the 1940s, the agencies were scarcely businesses at all: the girls would come up, do a job, sign a release, then take that release back to the agency. Every two or three months they would receive a check; it was typical for them to lose roughly twenty percent of their income through dishonesty or bad bookkeeping.

Into this came Hunt Hartford, who, by trying to create a lure for girls, suddenly turned the modeling game into a profession. In order to attract models from other agencies, Hartford instituted a voucher system. Instead of waiting months to be reimbursed for a job, the girls were paid as soon as the work was completed. ''A lot of very good models went there simply because they got paid every day,'' explained Ford. ''He was a terrific threat to the rest of us, because none of us had the money. He had the rest of us running back to our bankers for more money.'' Ford and the other agencies were eventually forced to adopt the voucher system.

Hartford's operation had another draw: unlike the other agencies, Hartford's had offices in Los Angeles as well as New York. He wasn't interested just in the images on the printed page. As a Svengali, he needed a larger stage than *Vogue*. The girls lined up to join Hartford's models, and eventually a few did go on to some measure of success: the actress Ellen Burstyn, for one, got her start with Hartford's agency.

One reason Hartford was able to contemplate the California resort and launch the modeling agency was that, for the first time in his life, he could get his hands on his money without his mother's permission. In 1946, Henrietta Hartford was diagnosed with leukemia, and after more than thirty years of control, she was finally forced to loosen her grip on the trust's purse strings.

After the verdict that invalidated her marriage to Pignatelli in New York, Henrietta had spent much of the forties living in Washington, D.C., where her prince was attached to the diplomatic corps. When she took ill, however, she moved full-time to Melody Farm, an estate she had purchased in rural New Jersey. As Henrietta Hartford's health deteriorated, Hunt's trips to New York became increasingly frequent. But he was not with her when she died on June 3, 1948. The obituaries likely would have pleased her almost as much as those mentions in Maury Paul's society columns. The New York papers memorialized the half-Jewish girl spurned by Charleston society as a princess.

Hartford and his sister, who spent most of her time in Newport and New York while her brother was in California, reunited for their mother's funeral in Charleston. But any harmony was brief. In life, Henrietta had never hidden her preference for her son, and her will was a lasting legacy of her disparate devotions. To her daughter Henrietta bequeathed 2,215 shares of A&P common stock, worth just over $300,000, and a single pearl necklace. Virtually everything else, some $4 million worth of stock, gems, and antiques, she left to her son.

To add further insult, Henrietta's will prescribed that should Huntington die before her, her legacy would go to his children. Should he have no children, it would go to Josephine's offspring, bypassing her daughter altogether.

Although Hunt Hartford was aware of the inequity, he made no effort to rectify it. "My mother definitely preferred me to my sister," he later reflected, "and if I'd had more maturity, I'd have tried to straighten that out." But of course he never did.

The jewels—Henrietta's emeralds, diamonds, sapphires, and rubies— remained with her son. They would be used by his wives and, in later years, lost to pawnshops and thieves.

Guido Pignatelli saw little from his wife's estate. She bequeathed him

$50,000 outright, along with a living trust that would provide him with $10,000 a year, the principal to revert to Huntington upon Pignatelli's death. As a memorandum of one of Henrietta's attorneys noted: "Her husband had virtually no property or income." Henrietta's paltry trust was hardly enough to keep him in style.

But for Pignatelli that problem proved transient. Four months after Henrietta died, her Italian prince remarried in Reno. His bride, Barbara Eastman, was a Manhattan-bred debutante with old money and her own old name; she was a descendant of Roger Eastman, one of the earliest settlers of Massachusetts.

Death may have taken his mother, but Hartford kept her retainers. One of her attorneys and her longtime secretary were charged with maintaining fiscal order in his life. Hartford abdicated his financial responsibilities to them just as he had to his mother before them.

The secretary, Agnes Hardecker, was a small woman with a tremulous voice that often sounded as if she were choking. She lived with her deaf sister in an apartment adorned with crosses and was the sort of servant who had little life outside the family for whom she worked. Her hair, steel gray, was worn in a rigid permanent. "She looked as if she were born at the age of fifty," recalled Phyllis Sher, the widow of the lawyer who tried to hold the reins on Hartford's spending.

David Sher, a soft-spoken partner with Stroock and Stroock and Lavan, did not have many years on Hartford, but bald and wizened even in his forties, he appeared far older. He assumed a paternal role in Hartford's life almost from the start. "Before his mother died, she asked my husband to watch over Huntington and do everything he could to keep him from going into gambling or drink," remembered Sher's widow. It was a quaint request: those vices would turn out to be among the precious few Hartford resisted.

Three months after Henrietta Hartford died, her son met the woman who would become his second and most beloved wife. The story of their meeting was the kind of dream-stuff Hollywood was made of.

In September 1948, Hartford and Dick Cowell, an oil heir crowned by the gossip columns as glamour boy of that year, were at Ciro's. Cowell was with Ava Gardner, Hartford with Yvonne De Carlo. The foursome encamped at the center table in front of the stage, occupied that night by Sophie Tucker.

Hartford had little interest in Tucker and less in De Carlo. His attention was fixed on a cinnamon-haired, gap-toothed beauty in stiletto heels who was peddling cigarettes from table to table. When she passed by their table, Hartford, a nonsmoker, shot up after her and disappeared from view. "When he came back he dumped her entire load on the table," recalled Cowell. "Sophie Tucker came out, took one look at our table, and said, 'My God, you must smoke a lot.' "

The cigarette girl was eighteen-year-old Marjorie Steele, an aspiring actress who had arrived in Los Angeles from a small town in northern California months before and had won a scholarship to the Actors' Lab, Charlie Chaplin's acting school. At first Hartford's attentions left her cold. But he pressed on for weeks, leaving messages, sending flowers. Finally Marjorie agreed to a date. The relationship progressed slowly until it nearly derailed when Hartford was away on a trip to New York.

The evening before Hartford left, he dined with Marjorie at Romanoff's. Marjorie spotted Charlie Chaplin at a corner table and demanded that Hartford introduce her to him (Chaplin was an occasional tennis partner of his). The next day, Marjorie was at the Actors' Lab cafeteria, and Chaplin's son Sydney approached her.

"Do you know a girl called Marjorie Steele?" he asked.

"I'm Marjorie Steele," she replied.

At which point he introduced himself and said, "My father told me I should take you to dinner."

"We went out that night and every night after that," Marjorie recalled.

Hartford got word that Marjorie was seeing the young Chaplin. He summoned her to New York and had her read for a play he was "thinking of producing." The reading went poorly, but he managed to keep her in New York, ensconced at the Ritz-Carlton.

"It seemed like Hunt barely knew I was there," Marjorie remembered. "He was always accompanied by some beautiful model, and I just felt worse and worse." After two weeks, Hartford finally called on her at her hotel. But even then he was out the door before ten at night.

"Just after Hunt left, the telephone rang," said Marjorie. "It was Sydney. 'I just talked it over with my father,' he said, 'and I think we should get married. Will you marry me?' I said, 'Yes, definitely yes.' "

Then came a knock on the door. It was Hartford. His second date for the evening had stood him up, and he asked Marjorie to go for a drive. Marjorie told him about the proposal.

"You're not going to marry Sydney," he said.

"I am," said Marjorie.

"No, you're not," he announced. "You're going to marry me."

"If I say yes to you and no to Sydney, you'll eventually see one of your pretty models and say yes to her and then I won't have anybody."

They backed and forthed until finally he convinced her that this time he would be faithful. Several days after she agreed to marry him, Hartford presented Marjorie with a twenty-two-carat blue-white diamond ring.

Marjorie returned to Los Angeles and headed straight for the Chaplins'. "[Charlie] Chaplin took the ring off my finger, gave it to his wife, Oona, and told her to take it to the jeweler and find out if [it was] real." If the diamond was genuine, Chaplin told her, it would be proof of Hartford's intentions. The elder Chaplin advised his son's fiancée that if she gave up her chance to marry the heir, forfeited the opportunity to be a rich man's wife, she would always regret it.

Sydney was furious. "Money doesn't matter," he told his father. "I'm going to marry Marjorie. It's as simple as that."

"If you marry Marjorie, I'm going to send you to England," Chaplin responded. "You're not going to ruin this girl's life."

Shortly Oona Chaplin returned with the ring and pronounced the stone genuine. "A few days later Sydney and I talked it over," recalled Marjorie. "He said, 'It is true what my father says. I could ruin your whole life and you'd never forgive me.' "

Still, Marjorie wavered. And still Hartford lobbied on, arranging for Marjorie's first break in the movie business, a role in *Tough Assignment,* an hourlong B melodrama.

"Hartford was infatuated with this girl, and he had competition," recalled Murray Lerner, executive producer of Lippert Productions, the studio that made the movie. "He had to make his position stronger in a hurry." Hartford, who shared rented offices with Lippert at Nassour Studios, approached Lerner about putting Marjorie into a movie. "I made him a proposition; he loaned us $25,000—no interest, I think. He came up with the cash, wrote a check like it was nothing. It was a favor for a favor," Lerner said.

The reviews were predictably so-so: "Okay for secondary billing in nabes and subsequent runs," sniffed *Variety.* Marjorie did get a nod from *The Hollywood Reporter*: "[She] is attractive and portrays the courageous young wife extremely well." But the point of the picture had less to do with reviews than with the Hartford–Steele romance. And on that score, it went exceedingly well.

"Everybody got what they wanted," said Lippert. "Marjorie got a movie, I got the money, and Hartford got the girl."

"We lived very happily for a couple of years," Marjorie remembered. It would be those years—fewer than could be tallied on the fingers of a single hand—that Hartford would later count as the best of his life.

7

H UNTINGTON HARTFORD and Marjorie Steele, then just nineteen, were married on September 10, 1949, by a justice of the peace in an efficient ceremony in Gardnerville, Nevada, a tiny town along U.S. 395 whose chief distinction was that Clark Gable and Carole Lombard had honeymooned there. Hartford had planned to go to Reno, but Marjorie had a bad cold and, after the eight-hour trek from Los Angeles to Gardnerville, she couldn't face the additional hour to Reno.

The marriage did not begin well.

What Marjorie remembered of her wedding day was not the ceremony but the quick stop made at a restaurant just after they took their vows. "Hunt said, 'I'm going to make a telephone call.' I knew what that meant, even on my first day of marriage. . . . He was going to cruise around the place and see if there were any pretty girls. Right after our wedding.

"He finally came to our table. He started circling and giving me what I call green eyes. He then went like this"—she put the heel of her hand to her forehead, miming surprise—"and said, 'You're my wife.' In other words, he hadn't realized who I was and just thought he found a pretty girl that was his type."

Still, Hartford was less satyr than lepidopterist. Like a butterfly collector, he seemed to feel he could catch hold of beauty by taking possession of a corporeal presence. And while his sort of philandering became almost a reflex, Hartford would remain devoted to his second wife. For unlike Mary Lee, Marjorie had aspirations of her own. She had the creative drive Hartford sought in himself, and for a time Marjorie became both his Galatea and his muse.

Before the Hartfords eloped to Nevada, Herman Hover, owner of Ciro's and Marjorie's ex-boss, had promised Hartford he would host a reception for the couple on their return.

He threw the bash at his home on Bedford Drive in Beverly Hills. Clark Gable showed up with Virginia Grey, a blonde who lived near him in the San Fernando Valley; Shirley Temple came, as did Carmen Miranda. The guests of honor, however, did not. At one point, the "Brazilian Bombshell" cornered Hover and asked, "Who is this goddamn party for?"

As dusk rolled into evening, Hover heard someone shout his name. He elbowed through the crowd to his fitness trainer, who served as the bouncer for the party.

"There's a couple at the door I can't get rid of," he told Hover.

"Crashers?" asked Hover.

"Looks that way," he replied. "They're improperly dressed."

Hover pushed through to the door, where he found Hunt and Marjorie, both clad in tennis whites.

"Herman," Hartford began apologetically, "we were just passing by and saw the cars and thought there must be a party. Mind if we crash?"

"Not at all," Hover responded. "After all, it's your party, remember?"

That sort of incident was hardly an anomaly with Hartford, a man never quite in sync with circumstance, aggressively inattentive to the details of life.

Over the next fifteen years Hartford would be frenzied with projects: a theater, a museum, an artists' retreat, an island resort, two movies, and a play among them. Each was inspired by the sprite who got her start selling cigarettes at Ciro's, and each was intended to impress the uncles who had cast him out of the family business.

"Hunt had to have projects," said Marjorie. "He had to do things. If you've made your own money, you know you can make it again if you lose it. Those born rich aren't sure emotionally. Hunt spent his money the way he did to try to show that he could do serious things."

In the beginning, Marjorie was the happy beneficiary of her husband's ambitions. "I think probably the happiest time in my life was the first

few years in my marriage to Hunt,'' she reflected. ''I learned so much
from him. He had such confidence in me, and I had none. I felt like a
big zero wherever I was. He took a real interest in my education. We'd
have games, slides we'd set up, trying to guess who a painter was, who
he was influenced by.''

They spent much of their first year of marriage traveling through Europe, where Hartford guided Marjorie, her sketchbook in hand, through
a series of Continental collections. When they returned to Hollywood,
Hartford started buying up potential film properties, including ''Dusk
Before the Fireworks,'' a Dorothy Parker short story about a philan-
derer, and ''Hello Out There,'' based on a slight William Saroyan jail-
house drama about a convict and the sweet young cook who befriends
him. He ended up producing the Saroyan piece, and hired James Whale,
who did *Frankenstein* and *The Invisible Man,* to direct; Harry Morgan,
who went on to fame in *Dragnet* and then *M*A*S*H,* played the convict, and Marjorie was the plain-faced cook.

The filming was largely uneventful, although Morgan did recall a
minor skirmish during the shooting of one particularly difficult scene.
''I said to Marjorie, 'Well, you wanted to be an actress.' She said, 'I
am an actress' . . . about which there may have been a little bit of
doubt. She did get a little petulant.'' Morgan never saw the finished
movie, which was never released. ''I was supposed to get a print,'' he
said, ''but I never did. But I did get paid.''

The Hartfords divided their time among New York, Palm Beach, and
Los Angeles—with an occasional sojourn at their house at Cap d'An-
tibes, purchased because Marjorie loved to go skin-diving. It seemed an
aristocratic idyll. Springs were spent in Manhattan in a penthouse in
River House, a high-rise overlooking the East River that was also home
to Cornelius Vanderbilt Whitney and Henry Luce. (Hartford and Marjorie threw a number of parties at River House; Marlon Brando made
an appearance at one. At a certain point that evening, Hartford recalled,
''we suddenly realized we hadn't seen him for a long time. We found
him at the top of the water tower.'')

They wintered in Palm Beach in a seventeen-room house Hartford
had had built during his marriage to Mary Lee. Bougainvillea festooned
every archway of the rambling two-acre property on El Vedado Road.
But the Hartfords' real home was the Runyon Canyon estate in the Hollywood Hills. Days started with breakfast, followed by a constitutional
around the gardens. Then Hartford would work on his writing or have

meetings on the project of the moment. Marjorie would paint or, if she was working on a play, put in a few hours rehearsing her lines. Evenings were spent on the nightclub circuit—Ciro's, Conga, dinner and dancing.

In the nineteenth century, doers of deeds became heroic. In the twentieth century, they became celebrities: creatures of gossip and public opinion, the ephemeral images in magazines and newspapers. The modern public man no longer needed a private secretary as much as he needed a public-relations representative.

That was the world of Huntington Hartford. He hired a press agent, Dorothi Pierre, to help push him and Marjorie out from the society columns and into feature stories. The Hartfords' tale bought easy fame. Hunt, with his dark good looks, and Marjorie, with her open-faced beauty, were an ideal focus for the public's ongoing fascination with wealth. They were young, they were handsome, and they gave the impression of purpose. The heir and his rags-to-riches bride were the perfect icons for America in the anything-is-possible postwar years.

In January 1950, Hartford's efforts started to pay off. In an article headlined "Huntington Hartford Is Pouring Millions into the Arts," Maury Paul extolled the virtues of the heir's efforts:

> Huntingford Hartford is throwing his A&P millions into various ventures. The biggest amount of cash will go into the Hartford Fund, which the artistically-inclined Hunt is founding to sponsor all the Arts. Frankly, I think it is gratifying to see a young man of Hartford's wealth, who has always been labeled a playboy, using his money for such a civilized venture. Evidently marriage is doing Hunt good, and he's turning over a new leaf. From playboy to . . . patron of the arts.

The New York *Daily News* ran a spread headlined "The Handicap of Wealth—The Huntington Hartfords Hope to Prove Something to Themselves in Spite of Money." "He can go through life buying whatever he wants," the *Journal-American* wrote, "but to him money is not the most important thing. People are. That's why Huntington Hartford is another of THE MOST MAGNETIC MEN."

The New York *Sunday Mirror* did a three-page piece bannered "Where the Versatile Cigaret Cinderella Led the Millionaire Grocer Boy." In *Look,* "Millionaire's Wife at Work" ran to five pages. Marjorie Steele, the young Mrs. Huntington Hartford, who "would rather juggle two careers than have a life of leisure," is pictured next to her husband at River House. Marjorie is painting the skyline out their window; Hunt is reading by her side. The caption: "She's a modern Cinderella whose pet luxury is working."

Edward R. Murrow came to call at the Hartford penthouse and interviewed Hunt and Marjorie for *Person to Person*. The man who may well have been television's finest journalist asked the grocery-store heir which of his myriad projects was the most important, expecting, no doubt, an answer that involved the arts. Murrow then listened patiently as Hartford expounded on the subject of handwriting analysis. Since graduating from college, Hartford had styled himself a handwriting expert; he believed that a man's penmanship was the key to his character. "It's not just a hobby, it's a serious scientific study," Hartford explained, and went on about the powerful microscope he was using to determine whether a man's script could predict not just his abilities but also his susceptibility to various illnesses.

"I'm sure all subjects are interesting if one gives them enough study," Murrow diplomatically replied, before nudging Hartford onto a subject of somewhat broader interest: art collecting. Hartford displayed two recent purchases, a Degas and a Courbet, then brought out several works by his "favorite" artist, Marjorie Steele, while she stood behind him and blushed.

"He wanted to be well known for what he could do—and for what I could do," Marjorie said later. "He was always talking about us becoming the most famous couple in America."

Huntington Hartford started building in earnest within months of his marriage to Marjorie. He wanted to reshape the city he shared with her, to turn Hollywood, then not much more than a cinematic wasteland where composers scored only movies and the only writing was dialogue for the screen, into the cultural mecca he had left in Manhattan.

For Hartford, the climate in Los Angeles seemed far more salubrious than that of liberal New York. Where the latter reveled in the eclectic, Los Angeles was rather xenophobic. There, the art establishment demanded neutral, objective, apolitical work. Not for Angelenos were the messy passions of a Jackson Pollock or a Mark Rothko. When the abstract expressionists were first shown in Los Angeles in the mid-fifties they were greeted by a line of picketers protesting the "Red propaganda."

As Hartford's own sensibility veered sharply to the right, he expected that Los Angeles would prove hospitable to his patronage. The planning that started with the resort designed by Frank Lloyd Wright evolved into an artists' retreat, an effort to make the world a little safer for struggling artists, writers, and musicians. Hartford purchased 145 acres in the Santa Monica Mountains and christened the compound the Huntington Hartford Foundation. Hartford took his inspiration for the Foundation from the MacDowell Colony, started by Mrs. Edward MacDowell in 1907 in Peterborough, New Hampshire, as a place for artists to leave behind quotidian cares and attend to their work. But where MacDowell offered only the most rustic of accommodations—four residences and simple stone-sided studios—Hartford was intent on providing his artists with an aristocrat's amenities. The grounds had a swimming pool and stables, and the resident artists—each of whom occupied a studio apartment designed by Lloyd Wright, Frank's son—could explore the surrounding mountains. A chauffeur-driven station wagon brought the Foundation fellows to and from the city below.

"The directors have created the ideal climate for the creative worker," said one fellow, a minor novelist named Martin Dibner. "Every necessity is provided—every lure, snare, distraction is removed."

But for many of the artists, those very amenities, coupled with the languor endemic to southern California, proved to be an obstacle to productivity. "For the younger guys transplanted from New York, the colony was a strange, Nathanael West–ish experience. We were penned in," reported writer Seymour Krim, a New Yorker and a charter member of the Beat Generation, and author of *Shake It for the World, Smartass*. "We had to wait for the house station wagon to take us to town. Too much was done for us. We felt like children. It was so opposite to what we thought of as an artists' colony. There was wine at dinner, courtesy of the house. . . . It was more of a holiday."

Little surprise, then, that much of the work done at the colony was unfinished or uneven. Nonetheless, at least initially the place had a veneer of seriousness. Christopher Isherwood and Robert Penn Warren were on one of the first selection committees. Edward Hopper painted watercolors at the colony, and Ernest Toch composed a Pulitzer Prize–winning symphony during his stay.

Hartford was happy to support the artists as a sort of southern California Medici, but he was never quite comfortable mixing with them. He would attend only the occasional dinner, quietly sitting off to one corner and disappearing long before the evening's end.

Indeed, Hartford's choice for the head of the Foundation showed just how far his sensibilities were from those of the artists he was supporting. The director was Michael Gasynski, a self-described Polish count who had been attached to his country's embassy in Washington until the communists took over in his homeland in 1947. More recently, Gasynski had been selling cheesecakes in a bakery shop at the Farmer's Market in Los Angeles, which is where Hartford found him.

Gasynski's imperious manner offended many of the colony's artists, and by 1952, Hartford was deluged with mail accusing the count of everything from snooty behavior (he was apparently more concerned with artists' social connections than with their artistic abilities) to examining fellows' mail and eavesdropping on their outgoing telephone conversations. In 1953, Hartford replaced Gasynski with a more credible director, John Vincent, a composer on the faculty of UCLA.

The artists' foundation was to be just the beginning. In the early fifties Hartford bought up two square blocks on Wilshire Boulevard, just across from the La Brea tar pits. He envisioned a "Theater Square," a vast new center for the dramatic arts. Lloyd Wright drew up elaborate plans with three theaters—a main production hall, a smaller one for circle-style workshops, and a third for showing art films. Surrounding the theaters would be an office complex, in which Hartford hoped to centralize the headquarters of the various movie studios, then, as now, scattered widely about the sprawling city.

But the center was never to be realized. Hartford left California in 1955, before ground was broken, and the property was eventually sold. He turned an accidental profit of about $500,000—one of the few times he made any money on one of his ventures.

There is no record of what the elder Hartfords thought of their nephew's philanthropic endeavors, but they probably paid little mind. While Hunt was spending his dividends on various artistic ventures, the Hartford brothers were scrambling to ensure that the source of that income, the A&P, remained intact.

For nearly twenty years, the United States government had been battling to dismember the A&P empire. The problems started in 1938, when Representative Wright Patman, a sponsor of the 1936 Robinson–Patman Act, advocated that chain stores be required to pay surplus taxes to compensate for their lock grip on the market. His new bill called for a per-store tax up to an annual maximum of $1,000 multiplied by the number of states in which the chain operated. At the A&P, the tax would have added up to more than $300 million, approximately thirty percent of total sales.

Thanks to the brothers' aggressive lobbying efforts, Patman's bill died in Congress. But that defeat ended just the first battle in the war between the government and the A&P. In November 1942, the Department of Justice charged the A&P with conspiring to monopolize American trade in food, a violation of the Sherman Antitrust Act. The Hartford brothers protested; in January 1945, even their nephew tried to get into the fray and sent a letter to President Roosevelt. Rather than address the merits of the case, Hunt Hartford ingenuously argued that his uncles' monopoly on the grocery trade was, in fact, an act of patriotism, their way of supplying the war effort.

Hartford's naiveté regarding commerce and government was perhaps predictable, but his revelation of strained relations with his uncles must have taken the reader—a complete stranger—by surprise. Hartford confided that he had never had much in the way of financial acumen; he had never paid much mind to the money he had or to how the fortune might be maintained. Indeed, he noted, his impracticality about money matters may have been precisely why his uncles had never wanted him to be part of the A&P. Hartford contended that his disfranchisement from the family business made him an even better advocate for his uncles. It wasn't that he had a personal interest in maintaining the A&P, he said; he was simply proud of his uncles' accomplishments and he wanted them to be rewarded, not chastised, for the building of a great American institution.

An assistant attorney general named Wendell Berge wrote back. He ignored Hartford's personal comments and simply pointed out that the government's charges had nothing to do with the war effort; rather, they concerned "the preservation of one of our most traditional of American precepts—free competitive enterprise."

Although his own letter had no effect on the government's suit, Hunt had a copy sent to his uncles. They were apparently unimpressed. Within a week of its arrival, their secretary returned the document—with no accompanying word of gratitude from either George or John.

The Hartford brothers' trial began in April 1945 and dragged on for more than a year—5,000 exhibits, 30,000 pages of testimony. In September 1946, Judge Walter Lindley found the defendants guilty. The A&P, he said, had conspired to monopolize a substantial part of the American grocery business. The corporation was fined over $175,000, and each Hartford brother faced a fine of $10,000 and a two-year prison term.

The Hartfords appealed the decision, but in February 1949, the conviction was upheld. Having already spent more than a million dollars in legal fees, the Hartfords decided it was more expedient simply to pay the fine than to continue the fight.

When the Hartfords declined to take their appeal to the Supreme Court, the Department of Justice set about trying to dismantle their empire, and filed a civil suit in New York that asked for the company's divisions to be torn asunder.

This time, the Hartfords went on the offensive. They launched a campaign in two thousand newspapers across the United States. The promotion went straight to the American consumer. "Do you want your A&P put out of business? Do you want higher prices?" the ads asked. The A&P was big, the ads said, because the American public had made it big.

The Hartfords' attorneys warned them that they might be sent to jail for contempt of court if they ran the ads, but the brothers were unfazed. They asked how long they would have to spend in prison, anticipating that it might be a year or two. The attorneys said thirty days would be more likely. "I'm not busy these days," said John Hartford. "I guess I can spare thirty days. What about you, George?" George said that he would not mind going to jail if he was allowed to fix radios there.

The brothers fought on. Not only were they taking out ads, but the usually press-shy men agreed to open their corporation to reporters. On November 13, 1950, Henry Luce put the brothers Hartford on the cover of *Time*. John was matinee-idol handsome; George looked like a slightly less foppish Alexander Woollcott. The eight-page feature lambasted those trying to bring down America's biggest grocery chain. *Time* cited a host of public champions for the giant corporation and concluded with a bigger-is-better quotation from John Hartford: "I don't know any grocer or anybody else who wants to stay small. They all dream about building something bigger. The whole country's growing—our cities, schools, labor unions, everything. I don't see how any businessman can limit his growth and stay healthy."

The Hartfords took out their ads and greeted the press, but ultimately the A&P overcame the government's threats less through its own efforts than because of a change in the White House. In 1952, when the Democrats finally lost to the Republicans, the Department of Justice slackened its approach to enforcing antitrust laws, and in 1954, George Hartford quietly signed a consent decree that left the A&P triumphant, intact save for a single supplier.

John Hartford did not live to see his victory. On September 21, 1951, after spending the morning at the A&P offices, he went to the Chrysler Building for a meeting of the auto company's board of directors. There was a discussion about the company's need for younger blood. Presently

John Hartford rose from his chair and announced, "Then you won't be needing me anymore"; he left the room and walked to the elevator, where he suffered a heart attack. He died before anyone could get him to a hospital.

John Hartford's will set aside $25,000 for Hunt Hartford and the same for his sister. He left the bulk of his estate to the John A. Hartford Foundation, established to aid various medical causes. It would be headed by Ralph Burger, his secretary, and would eventually hold not only John's stock but George's as well. With forty percent of the A&P voting shares, the Foundation would allow the brothers to maintain control of the A&P from beyond the grave. Ultimately it would nearly strangle the business they spent their lifetimes creating.

After John Hartford died, his nephew began a battle to gain the respect of his Uncle George. Not long after the funeral, Hunt went to see George. He implored the old man to give him another chance at the A&P. "We were ushered into a big office in the Graybar Building," recalled Marjorie. "He had a glass wall between [himself] and a score of secretaries. Hunt said he'd like to work in the business. He said he didn't mind starting out as a counterman in one of the supermarkets."

But George Hartford told his nephew there was no job for him at the A&P.

"I'll go to Safeway, then," Hartford angrily replied.

"You can do what you please," said George, "but no one in the family will work in this business."

"There was," said Marjorie, "no arguing with him."

Not long after that rejection, Hartford entered his first venture with a patina of fiscal credibility. He took $500,000 from his A&P dividend income and breathed life into a start-up business, later incorporated as The Oil Shale Corporation (Tosco). The company's raison d'être was the patented Swedish Aspegren process, which made possible a sort of petrochemical alchemy for extracting oil from oil shale deposits.

It was the sort of technology that appealed to Hartford's loose humanistic vision. If the Aspegren process were to prove economical, it could reshape the economy of South America, parts of which were rich in oil shale but crippled by debt. With Tosco, Hartford could lead the way to the liberation of an entire continent.

"I think Hartford stayed with Tosco because it fed back a lot," said Morton Winston, the company's onetime chief executive. "Tosco was

perceived by others as a quirky and difficult but potentially very interesting adventure. For Hartford, it reflected a certain amount of seriousness of purpose.''

Hartford was lured into Tosco by Rulon Neilson, a California oilman
who had been one of the witnesses at his Gardnerville wedding, and
Herbert Linden, a Swedish-born stock promoter. Linden ''was a cat-
skinner of the first order,'' according to Winston. ''Herbie could sell ice
cubes to Eskimos.''

Linden may have been ignorant of the oil industry, but he was imbued
with the fifties idealism that technology would do splendid things. He
truly believed that all of those innovations would make everybody a lot
of money, that all he would have to do was sit back, collect coupons,
and get rich. For Neilson, the investment was more calculated, a means
to enhance his own considerable real estate holdings, which were rich
in oil shale. If the technology worked, it would explode the value of his
assets, and if it didn't, his real estate could likely find another use.

Hartford wanted to bask in the glory of the venture (his $500,000
investment gave him the title of chairman), but he would never have the
sort of discipline needed to influence the company's direction effectively.
''He had no understanding of how power is manipulated inside corporate
structures,'' said Winston. Hartford rarely attended Tosco's board meetings, and he never really focused on the company's progress. ''He was
anything but a detail man,'' explained Neilson. ''He was interested in
endeavors but not in trying to address daily operations. Ultimately,
though, you can't handle things with your left hand and expect them to
thrive.''

Unlike his Uncle George, who as maker of the family fortune was
necessarily tethered to the base world of commerce, Huntington Hartford had been raised to be a member in good standing of the leisure
class. As the sociologist Thorstein Veblen explained it, members of that
patriciate have four acceptable avenues of endeavor: war, sports, government, and religion. Having failed at the first two, and having no
interest in government (despite his mother's urging that he follow Pignatelli into the diplomatic corps), Huntington Hartford got religion. He
became, in the words of the social critic Tom Wolfe, a new Martin
Luther, crusading for a reformation in the fine arts. Son of a woman
who had tried to become a nineteenth-century aristocrat decades too
late, Hartford likewise reached into the past for his values. He became
a reactionary aesthete, a sort of critical vector for the McCarthy era,
and just perhaps the kind of man his stodgy uncle could respect.

The 1950s saw the sanctification of abstract expressionism. In 1951, the Museum of Modern Art in New York ushered in Jackson Pollock, Mark Rothko, Arshile Gorky, and the rest with a full-scale exhibition. As the United States headed into an era of atomic anxiety, it seemed natural that "an age of disintegration must produce an art of disintegration," according to those artists' foremost promoter, the critic Clement Greenberg. It was an angry, difficult aesthetic, hardly suitable for a Newport parlor.

Huntington Hartford was determined to stave off abstract expressionism—and all the moral disorder it implied. At the end of 1951, he wrote a twenty-one-page pamphlet warning of the perils of contemporary art, literature, and music, then paid to have it printed and sent out to some four thousand opinion-makers across the country.

The cover of his booklet has a line drawing of eroding classical statuary along with a line from Balzac: "Has God Been Insulted Here?" On the title page, Hartford inscribed the full passage: "What fire from heaven has passed this way? What tribunal has ordered salt to be strewn upon this dwelling? Has God been insulted here? Has France been betrayed?" Balzac decried the bloody toll exacted by Robespierre's wayward idealism; Hartford was convinced that the permissiveness inherent in the current artistic state would deliver his nation to a similar fate.

The essay began with an unidentified passage:

> "You better win," Prew said, "goddam you. I ain't had a piece of ass in almost a month."
>
> "No wonder you're pissed off," Angelo grinned. "I ain't had one since last payday . . . Gimme a butt before I go."
>
> "Jesus Christ!" Prew said pained but he reached in his pocket and brought out one, a single tube, from the unseen pack. "Since when did I take you to raise!"
>
> "Whats a matter? You scared I'll steal your lousy tailor mades? After I win I'll buy you a whole carton. Now match me and I'm gone."
>
> "Is your mouth dry?" Prew said. "You want me to spit for you?"
>
> "Not on the floor," Angelo said, raising his eyebrows in mock horror. "Not on the floor. Wheres your manners?"
>
> "Ain't there something else I can do for you? Use my mouth as an ashtray? Cut off my balls and have a game of marbles? You oughta be able to think of something."

Then Hartford asked if the reader had determined the source of this colorful language. Pornography, perhaps?

Not at all, Hartford revealed. The dialogue was taken from James

Jones's *From Here to Eternity,* which was considered a masterpiece of the day. Hartford went on to decry the vulgarity in art that had reduced life to its basest elements. He railed against Pablo Picasso for his figures of despondence and lambasted Salvador Dalí for his nihilist oeuvre. He argued that the modern artist aspiring to attack the established order was motivated by envy, plain and simple.

Huntington Hartford was a voice in the wilderness, and there he was heard most keenly. Small-town editors—men who, like Hartford's staid Uncle George, were offended by the profligacy of the modern—offered their praise. This wildly unfashionable aristocrat gave credence to their condemnation of Willem de Kooning's mean-edged women and Pollock's bewildering paint-splattered canvases. Jones's raw view of military life could be dismissed with impunity.

George Hartford never bothered to tell his nephew what he thought of his essay—or even if he had read the pamphlet—but Hunt Hartford was delighted all the same. He basked in his newly achieved recognition and pasted clippings from scores of papers from the heartland—the *Daily Tribune,* in Pratt, Kansas; the *Evening Journal,* in Washington, Iowa; the *City Trail,* in Grass Valley, Nevada—into a leatherbound volume, its cover embossed "Has God Been Insulted Here?" in gilt letters.

Just after sending out the pamphlet, Hartford put his philosophy into action. He announced that the Huntington Hartford Foundation had rejected two painters' applications because their work was too abstract.

But what played well in small-town America did not go over in urban circles of influence. All seven members of the Foundation's advisory committee resigned in protest, and *Life* ran a four-page spread entitled "Art Trouble in Paradise." On one side there was "bad art": Joan Miró, Picasso, Georges Rouault, and Arthur Dove. On the facing page, "good art": Winslow Homer, John Singer Sargent, Paul Gauguin—and a portrait of Hartford himself, executed by Marjorie of course. Hartford was dismissed as a hopeless muddlehead, trying to save the world from something it had no reason to fear.

The New Yorker even ran a cartoon: A down-and-out artist is hunched over a bar, his face lined with despair. "He's an artist," the bartender explains, "and Huntington Hartford likes his paintings."

But Hartford kept tilting at his abstract expressionist windmill; critics made his attacks only more fervent. He appointed a new advisory committee to replace the seven members who had left, and the Foundation—and his battle—went on.

8

Since Huntington Hartford was in Hollywood, it was inevitable that his quixotic sensibility would find its way to the screen. In 1951, he moved into film production in earnest—no more B movies like *Tough Assignment.*

He took the title of his film, *Face to Face,* from the Kipling line "When two strong men stand face to face." The movie paired two short stories with a common theme: a strong-willed protagonist confronting enormous personal crisis. One tale was by Joseph Conrad, the other by Stephen Crane—both, naturally, creations of another century. Hartford intended to shape a new film form, novellas on the screen. "That something new . . . It's DUO-DRAMA," read the placards for *Face to Face.* "An exciting new step in screen entertainment . . . blending the talents of two top authors and two great stars." James Mason was cast in the episode adapted from Conrad's "The Secret Sharer"; Robert Preston took top billing in that adapted from Crane's "The Bride Comes to Yellow Sky."

Conrad's story is about an escaped murderer who swims to the side of a ship and is taken aboard and hidden by her captain. The fugitive, Leggatt, is the captain's own black side, his dark double; in an act of lunatic heroism, he nearly wrecks his ship on a jagged reef while trying to save his doppelgänger.

The story had familiar Conrad themes—the judge and the judged; reason versus emotion; the way in which actions verge on the heroic in one's innermost dreams, before reality, an unforeseen mishap, intervenes and plays havoc with those actions. "I wondered how far I should turn out faithful to that ideal conception of one's own personality every man has set up for himself secretly,'' reflected Conrad's captain. But unlike Kurtz in Conrad's *Heart of Darkness,* lost forever on his dark African river, the captain and his ship make it out to the light.

For Hartford, Conrad's captain must have embodied the drama missing from his own life. It was likely no coincidence that on the poster for *The Secret Sharer,* James Mason, resplendent in captain's whites, was a ringer for Hartford in his Coast Guard uniform.

The chief distinction of the second episode of *Face to Face* was its screenwriter, James Agee. Hartford's relationship with the writer, who was already acclaimed for *Let Us Now Praise Famous Men,* dated to 1949, when Hartford had commissioned Agee to do a screenplay adaptation of another Crane short story, "The Blue Hotel," about a dim-witted Swede who taunts an innocent man into killing him. Hartford made Agee write a sample sentence before he would hire him. Agee passed the test, despite his tight, tremulous scrawl; then he rushed through his adaptation, accumulating over a hundred pages of manuscript in just ten days. But instead of developing character, he crafted exquisite descriptions of the town, the landscape, and the stars above. It was impossible to translate Agee's literary descriptions to the screen; the movie was never produced.

Despite that initial disaster, Hartford turned to Agee two years later when he decided to try the second Crane story. In the interim, Agee had established his credibility in Hollywood, most notably with his script for *The African Queen.* He had also developed a disastrous drinking problem. Even so, Agee created an economical, witty, and filmable adaptation of Crane's whimsical sketch of a newlywed couple. The groom, Jack Potter (Robert Preston's role), is the marshal of Yellow Sky, Texas; his wife, played by a bright-eyed Marjorie Steele, is from San Antonio. The day they arrive in town, the local villain, Scratchy Wilson, goes on a drunken shooting rampage. When Scratchy confronts the unarmed marshal, his new wife by his side, he realizes he has been defeated by decorum and leaves town.

Agee took one liberty with the script and invented a new character, Frank Gudger, the town drunk, a likable man who let himself in and out of jail at will. The character was an acute observer of events taking place around him, an inebriated Greek chorus of one. Agee identified closely with the character—and persuaded Hartford to let him play the small role when the script was filmed.

Agee was fond of Marjorie, but he had nothing but flagrant contempt for her husband. After *The Bride Comes to Yellow Sky* was produced, Agee began work on a screenplay about Paul Gauguin. When Hartford heard of the project, he expressed interest. Agee then wrote to the proposed director of the film: "If Hartford wants to put his dough in fine; but if he wants to mess around in it to hell with him: he is an exceptionally stupid guy, it seems to me." Hartford was alerted to Agee's antipathy and withdrew from the project.

Surprisingly, *Face to Face* received extremely favorable reviews. "In advance, this film sounded like the preposterous undertaking of an amateur," noted *The New York Times*. "Whether it was beginner's luck or imaginative intuition, the film has turned out very well."

Even John McCarten, then the movie reviewer at the usually critical *New Yorker,* was laudatory. "Huntington Hartford, a young man I've always associated with mass-produced groceries . . . has emerged as a movie producer who deserves the congratulations of all of us. . . . Hartford might be the very one to convert *Lord Jim* into a movie. It's crying to be done."

Although *Lord Jim* eventually was made into a film in 1964 (James Mason, coincidentally, had one of the starring roles), Hartford had no part in the project. Despite his initial success at moviemaking, Hartford's career as producer ended with *Face to Face.* He felt it was the director, not the producer, who shaped the movie, and he wasn't interested in participating in a project if he couldn't have some creative control—and creative credit. Huntington Hartford had scant interest in being the anonymous benefactor; he demanded recognition.

In 1954, Hartford made yet another bid for immortality; he opened the first legitimate theater in Los Angeles in twenty-seven years.

In the early fifties, the only large playhouse left in the city was part of the Biltmore Hotel in downtown Los Angeles. Hartford set his sights on the heart of Hollywood and purchased a property a block south of Hollywood and Vine for $200,000. What he acquired was a ramshackle movie theater, then owned by the Columbia Broadcasting System. Originally it had been a legitimate playhouse, which had opened in 1927 with an adaptation of Theodore Dreiser's *An American Tragedy.* During the Depression it had been converted to a moviehouse and rechristened the Lux Radio Playhouse.

Hartford's theater had a dual purpose: he would continue his aesthetic crusade ("I'll shove culture down their throats," he said of his attempt to bring legitimate theater to Babylon), and he would create the perfect stage for his actress wife. One of the first productions would be a play he had written himself, an adaptation of *Jane Eyre* entitled *The Master of Thornfield.*

Reconstruction of the theater turned into another hands-off Hartford project. Within months of the purchase, Marjorie was cast in a London play, and Hartford, although he wasn't financing the production, went off to England to be with her.

Before he left for London he selected Helen Conway to redesign the Los Angeles playhouse. Conway was the sort of decorator used as much for her imprimatur of social respectability as for the quality of her work. Not only was she hired regularly by the Hollywood set, she was also the designer for what passed for old money in Los Angeles. She had done homes for the oil heir Edward Doheny III, the George Murphys, the William Holdens, Burns and Allen, the Jack Bennys, and the James Stewarts. At Hartford's urging, Conway designed a bar on the mezzanine that served both snacks and liquor. Although similar service had been offered in London for years, Hartford was the first to provide those amenities to the American theatergoer. Conway had the interior painted green, highlighted by stark black and gold. The carpet had a specially designed pattern of black and silver stars; the doors leading to the auditorium were black teak with gold fittings. The auditorium itself had gray-green walls with black pilasters rising from either side of the stage, extending from floor to ceiling and topped by large gold stars. "Any woman will look good in this theater because the background will not clash with her clothes or complexion," Conway said at the time. The price tag for perfection: $750,000, or $3 million in today's money.

To Hartford, the cost was of little consequence; what was most important were the words emblazoned across the façade of white Vermont marble: HUNTINGTON HARTFORD THEATRE.

KTLA, a local television station, broadcast the opening-night ceremonies live. Searchlights scraped the skies; a crowd of two thousand filled the bleachers lining Vine Street as celebrities paraded into the theater to see Helen Hayes in James Barrie's *What Every Woman Knows.*

Dina Merrill turned up, along with Joan Crawford; Norma Shearer brought her son, Irving Thalberg, Jr. The venerable Edward Everett Horton, a character actor who had played Fred Astaire's bumbling sidekick in *Top Hat,* and had appeared on the stage when it was still the Vine Street Theatre, was accompanied by his mother, "who used to be with me on all the opening nights." Cesar Romero said he hoped "it was the beginning of real theater for Hollywood."

Minutes before curtain time, Los Angeles councilwoman Rosalind Wyman presented Hartford with a resolution applauding his contribution to Hollywood. As for the production, the critical reception was at best lukewarm. The half-century-old play, the story of a Scottish spinster who is married off by her brothers to a younger man, then fights to regain his affections from a young rival, was already a period piece. It was a role Hayes had first played nearly thirty years before, and although her performance was well received, the four-act play was quietly dismissed. Even the usually flattering *Los Angeles Herald and Express* chided the work's "lagging scenes and antiquated situations" and added that "it would have been wonderful if [Helen Hayes] had arrived at the new theater in a new play." Hartford originally had planned to take the play to Broadway, but it never went beyond the West Coast.

Hartford always insisted that he chose the play because he was desperate for Hayes to open his theater, and it was the part she wanted. Indeed, she intended to give a speech thanking Hartford for his contribution after the final curtain.

But Hayes's attempt at expressing her gratitude misfired. After the curtain went down, no one could find the button to make it rise again. Finally, days later, a society columnist, Cobina Wright, published Hayes's tribute in the *Herald and Express.*

> I wanted to tell the audience . . . how every person connected with the play . . . will for the rest of our lives be grateful to Huntington Hartford, who has given the loveliest of theaters to this city and to the profession.

Hartford reveled in the recognition; still, the achievement remained incomplete: he received the honor alone. The woman for whom he had built his theater was on another continent, appearing on the London stage in *Sabrina Fair,* about an ingenue who opts for wealth over morality in her choice of mates.

Hartford had tried to play William Randolph Hearst to Marjorie's Marion Davies, but her pointed professionalism made it nearly impossible. Marjorie was determined to have her talents as both an actress and a painter stand on their own merits. By the mid-fifties, she had starred in plays in both London and New York, all without Hartford funding, and had had a one-woman show of her paintings at Wildenstein, an established Manhattan gallery. The reviews of her fifteen oils and ten drawings were respectful, though hardly raves. "There are signs of her struggle to find herself as a painter," wrote the reviewer for *Art Digest.* "She has a clear eye, a vigorous hand, and a talent for illustration. What is lacking is a poetic sense. Looking at a decanter of shiny glass, she paints only an expensive object. To paint a decanter in 1953 one must also look at Cézanne and into one's self."

By the end of that year, Marjorie had announced that she was severing all ties to her husband's ventures. "I didn't want to jeopardize my career," she explained later.

In 1955, Huntington Hartford reiterated his diatribe against modernism with "The Public Be Damned," a page-long tract that he paid to have published in a half-dozen newspapers around the country. If his critique four years before had been controversial, by the mid-fifties, an attack that equated abstract art with communism was so unfashionable as to be practically blasphemous. While New York intellectuals cooed over Jackson Pollock and Willem de Kooning, Hartford argued that their work was just so much balderdash, offensive pseudo-art whose only raison d'être was to pander to the cabal of museum directors, gallery owners, and critics who had willfully taken leave of their senses.

Hartford had some respectable company on the edge of his reactionary cliff. In the spring of 1953, a group of artists—Edward Hopper, Moses and Raphael Soyer, and Reginald Marsh among them—had written a "Reality Manifesto," addressed to the Museum of Modern Art, protesting what the artists perceived to be the museum's belief that "nonobjectivism has achieved some sort of aesthetic finality that precludes all other forms of expression." The artists argued not so much for what they called "humanism" as for pluralism. In the blindered pursuit of the abstract, they said, classicism was being unjustly ignored. What they wanted was equal time.

It was one thing for artists themselves to argue that they were being treated inequitably, but another entirely for an aristocrat who paid for the right to publish with income earned from a trust fund. Once again, the press took issue with Hartford's high-mindedness. Even in Los Angeles, it was too much. The art critic of the *Los Angeles Times,* Arthur Millier (one of the advisers of Hartford's foundation who resigned in protest after the publication of *Has God Been Insulted Here?*), wrote off the heir as little more than a crank. He suggested an alternative title for Hartford's essay: "Backward, Turn Backward, O Time, in Your Flight, Make Me a Child Again Just for Tonight!"

Even Eleanor Roosevelt stepped out to condemn Hartford's attempt to "buy public opinion," writing in the New York *World-Telegram:*

> Only a man with great wealth could have published this editorial and reached thousands of people with his opinions in an effort to put across his point of view with the hope of preventing such art as

he disliked. . . . We may not like or understand some of the experiments made by modern artists, but they have a right to experiment.

Time dismissed Hartford's views as "a three-lane, 40-mile-an-hour
parkway between photographic realism and emotional expressionism—
too pat to be persuasive." Even the marketplace judged him the fool.
His essay appeared just as a de Kooning show was opening at the Sidney
Janis Gallery; the paintings were sold almost instantly. "I never had it
so good," commented de Kooning, who was delighted with the free
publicity.

Still, from a distance of thirty-five years, Hartford's condemnation of
the abstract expressionists doesn't look quite as foolish as it did at the
time. Perhaps curiously, for a man so studiously behind the times, Hartford's call for a return to realism was less a case of getting it wrong than
of getting it early. "If today he launched something that would give
realism a chance, it would work," contended Thomas Hoving, a former
director of the Metropolitan Museum of Art. "His timing was just always absolutely bad. He was the brown sun, the lead touch.

"On balance, raw abstract work hasn't held up that well. . . . He
thought the abstract dangerous, morally turpitudinous. The fact is, styles
exist—the point is the subject. If the subject says hammer and sickle,
chances are it's propaganda, whether hammer and sickle are done in an
abstract manner or a cubist manner doesn't mean anything. Hartford
thought styles had political and moral overtones. Hartford's problem was
that he looked on artistic styles as philosophies, which is not so smart."

For the most part, Hartford's own collection would have been best
suited for the drawing rooms of his childhood. He was given to
nineteenth-century English painters, and collected the Pre-Raphaelites
when they were considered a quaint anachronism. The one deviation in
his otherwise antique sensibility was Salvador Dalí. While Hartford had
condemned him in *Has God Been Insulted Here?* Dalí was notably ab-
sent from the roster of transgressors in his later essay. The surrealist's
images were not actually that far removed from Hartford's credo, but
the heir's changed perspective on Dalí had less to do with ideological
considerations than with the artist's charm. "Dalí was the one person
that really hoodwinked Hunt, the only person that really pulled it off in
anything other than business matters," said Marjorie. "Dalí told Hunt
that he was the only one who had artistic understanding. It sounds ridiculous, but Hunt was an aspiring mogul, and you can't flatter a mogul
too much."

Dalí had enough of a sense of his patron to understand that showmanship was crucial to making the sale, and Dalí was a master show-man. He targeted Hartford for the purchase of *The Battle of Tetuan,* and virtually scripted a drama for the sales presentation.

Dalí arrived at his New York dealer, M. Knoedler & Co., a day before Hartford's appointment and had the painting cloaked by a curtain (he even sent a gallery assistant to Bloomingdale's for just the right fabric); then he and the head of the gallery, Roland Balaÿ, rehearsed the show. Two chairs sat across from the painting, one for Dalí, the other for Hartford. Balaÿ would stand. Dealer and painter would face the curtained canvas in silence, waiting for the collector to react. When Hartford spoke, Dalí would say grandly, "Roland, go and stand next to the picture," then, "Roland, pull the curtain."

"It sold the picture," said Balaÿ.

As with so many men with too many projects, Hartford's ardor for his aesthetic life was not replicated in his personal life. Marjorie gave birth to a daughter, Catherine, in 1950, and in 1953 the first legitimate Hartford namesake, John, was born. But as his children grew into tod-dlers, Hartford spent less and less time with them and their mother. Marjorie and the children divided their time between the house in Palm Beach and the triplex at One Beekman Place in Manhattan that the Hart-fords bought not long after John was born. Hartford, meanwhile, was spending most of his time in Hollywood.

Catherine and John were bruised by their father's inattention, but they were too young to voice protest. Hartford's illegitimate son, Edward, who in his teens had dropped the name Colt and begun using his moth-er's name, Barton, was not. In August 1955, Ed Barton went to court to resolve his relationship with his father, demanding that Hartford ac-knowledge his paternity and give him the family name.

The prospect of a subpoena sent Hartford into a panic. He was on a train out of California less than twenty-four hours after the lawsuit was filed.

III

❖

THE BUILDING BEGINS
New York to Nassau

There is no burden so great as a great opportunity.
BILLBOARD ON THE ROAD
BETWEEN LOS ANGELES AND PALM SPRINGS

Marjorie and Hunt Hartford with Errol Flynn (1957).
A drunken, dissolute Flynn made a shambles of Hartford's
theatrical aspirations.
(Queens Library/The New York Herald Tribune Morgue)

9

THE TROUBLE with Buzzy had begun the previous summer, when Florence Brangenberg, who was raising Hartford's illegitimate son, went on a vacation with the boy and her husband. When they returned, they discovered that the house where they had been living, the home Hunt Hartford bought to entice them to stay in California, had been sold.

In the years since he had moved the Brangenberg family to California, Hartford had remarried and distanced himself from his first son. Now, the ignominy of Buzz's illegitimacy and the furious pace of Hartford's spending (the Foundation, the theater, the movies) came together in the sale of the Hollywood house.

It wasn't the first time he had tried to move them out of the stucco house on Flores and Fountain. Not long before, he had suggested that Florrie sell the house and move in with Marjorie's widowed mother. "It was a crazy idea," said Florrie, who assumed that after scuttling that notion, Hartford would leave her in peace. When she returned from that brief vacation, she realized she had been wrong.

Hartford needed the money from the sale of the house, a relatively paltry $80,000, to help defray the cost of his quest to elevate himself into America's pantheon of patrons. The price of fame was proving to be more than even Huntington Hartford, with his ample A&P income, could afford. His A&P shares were worth close to $100 million, but Hartford couldn't get his hands on that principal. The generation-skipping trust established by his grandfather provided that the shares couldn't be sold until his last child died. As long as George Hartford was alive, the real A&P money was beyond his nephew's grasp.

But Hartford would not allow his finances to circumscribe his ambitions. When his projects began to demand more money than he had available, he began liquidating assets. He started outside the family, with a peculiar transaction with Harvard University. According to one of Hartford's financial advisers, Benjamin Buttenweiser, "Hartford needed some money in a hurry, so he sold a $5 million interest in his trust to Harvard University for $4.5 million." Harvard held onto its interest, and when George Hartford died a few years later, the university received $5 million.

With the sale of the Brangenbergs' house, Hartford's money-raising efforts became much more personal than that minor-league trust-fund bust. Initially, Hartford promised to give the Brangenbergs a portion of the proceeds from the sale of the house, whose title had been held in the name of his secretary, Agnes Hardecker. (Florrie had been told that there would be "tax problems" if the deed were put in her name.) But as he would do so often when it came to family financial commitments, Hartford reneged on that pledge. Finally, after months of haggling, he agreed to lend Florrie the money for a down payment on a two-bedroom house in suburban Westchester, not far from the Los Angeles airport. It was a comedown in both size and locale. Unlike the old Hollywood neighborhood, Westchester was a middle-class tract development, a Los Angeles Levittown.

The offense was made worse by the terms of the loan. Hartford secured the debt with Ed Barton's trust fund. (Under the terms of the trust, Barton would begin to gain access to the principal when he was twenty-one, five years later.) If Florrie failed to keep up with the mortgage payments, Hartford could attach his son's legacy, which was what Florrie saw as her financial ballast. Not only was Hartford taking her house away, he was mortgaging what little security she had left.

When Hartford first cajoled the Brangenbergs into moving west, he had promised a bright future. Hartford had told Roy Brangenberg that he would find him a job. "First he told my father he could run the Foundation," recalled Roy's daughter Nelda, "then it was the theater. It never happened. When my father called Hunt to find out what was going on, Hunt would say, 'We'll have lunch.' My father would ask when, and Hunt would say, 'Next week, next week.' That went on for months. My father became very depressed. He ended up working for the Pinkerton guard service. He got fired after he was caught in the president's office with his feet on the desk."

Not long after he was ousted from that last job, Roy was incapacitated by a cerebral hemorrhage, and eventually Florrie had him moved into a

Veterans Administration hospital. "First he didn't give Roy a job, and now Roy was sick," recalled Rico Zermeno, Janet Brangenberg's ex-husband and a close family friend. "Then he took the house away. Florrie was alone with Buzz, and she was afraid she would find herself without any money." For years, Florence Brangenberg had lived for the boy and his money, and she had long since made certain he knew where it came from. When Hartford said he needed money from the house, the only way Florrie felt she could save herself was to sue him.

Florence Brangenberg filed suit for Ed Barton on August 31, 1955 (she had to make the claim since he was still a minor); all he wanted was his right to the Hartford name. As Barton put it to a reporter who came to interview him after the suit was filed, he was desperate for an identity. "I wanted to go somewhere where no one would know me," he said. "And then I got to thinking about it and came to the realization that this situation was not of my own creation. Why should I be ashamed? I didn't ask to be born. All I want now is to have an identity and to belong to something legally." And although he demanded no additional money for support, Barton did ask for the right to it should it be needed in the future. The request seemed almost an afterthought. Florrie felt that if Hartford were forced to acknowledge paternity, he would be afraid to deny the family financial support.

The story hit the front pages of the Los Angeles papers the day the suit was filed. "Name Huntington Hartford in Boy's Paternity Suit," headlined the *Herald and Express*. The story featured a picture of a sad-eyed Mary Barton and side-by-side photographs of Hunt and his bastard son, a matched set with their dark curly hair, coal-colored eyes, and weak chins.

Superior court judge Elmer Doyle ordered Hartford to appear before him four weeks later to meet demands that he pay Barton's legal costs. By the time the process servers appeared at Hartford's house, he was gone, on a train to New York.

Barton and Brangenberg fought to bring Hartford back to California, but he successfully avoided the subpoena. Finally, at her attorney's suggestion, Florrie tried to win public support for her case by talking to the press. "The lawyer called and said she should talk to reporters. They came all the way to Westchester," recalled Zermeno. "They seemed so sympathetic. . . . Then they wrote the opposite. Florrie thought Hartford paid them off."

But Hartford didn't have to pay for good press. He had already given the boy a trust fund that, by 1955, was valued in excess of $500,000, more than enough to guarantee sympathy for his position. The New York *Daily News* titled its story "The Love Child Who May Win a Fortune" and made Florrie and Ed out to be greedy pretenders to the Hartford throne.

Society columnist Cobina Wright weighed in with another Hartford testimonial:

> In spite of the recent unpleasant headlines pertaining to Huntington Hartford, it seems to me that people should inquire carefully into the facts. When Mary Barton took an overdose of sleeping pills in 1941, Huntington was in the Navy [*sic*], fighting for his country. When he was accused of fathering her son, he set up a trust fund for the boy of $295,000, certainly more than an adequate amount for his support. Huntington believed he had done the humane thing, though it was never proven he was the father.
>
> The public here in Los Angeles should not forget that Hartford has given us the most beautiful theater in the world and also the Huntington Hartford Foundation where needy artists and writers have the opportunity to work. . . . There are so many millionaires who live only for their own pleasures and selfish interest, but Huntington Hartford believes in sharing his good fortune with others. He is happily married and has two adorable children and I think it is sad that after such a situation has been settled it has to be brought up again 17 years later.

As it turned out, it was not only sad but, for Ed Barton, ultimately futile. Hartford was never extradited, and the case was eventually dismissed.

Marjorie sided with her husband in the paternity suit, regarding it as an effort by Florrie to wring more money out of Hartford—as well as an attempt to displace her own son, born two years before the suit was filed, in the family hierarchy. "Buzzy and his grandmother were very, very greedy," said Marjorie. "That grandmother wanted him to be called Hartford—that was right after I had Jackie [John]. She wanted Jackie to be the second son."

But even as Marjorie defended her husband from outside attacks, the family was coming apart from within. By the sixth year of their marriage, there was a wide chasm between Hartford and his second wife. The problem, in large part, was his inability to sustain any sort of intimacy. His dealings with women had a percussive sameness: beauty was best perceived at a distance; his sexual relationships were rarely more than one-night stands.

"Let's put it this way. I could tell you when Jackie and Cathy were conceived," recalled Marjorie. "Sex with me never really got off the ground. He used to say at the dinner table, in front of everybody, 'Marjorie doesn't like sex, Marjorie isn't interested in sex.' I remember the first time he said it, out of the blue, when I had been plaguing him about it for six months. 'What's wrong with me? Why can't we have a decent sexual life?' I'd ask. 'You're not really interested in it,' he'd say. Then, after I would make such a fuss about it, he would say, 'You don't realize that having sex with you is like having incest.' "

The Hartfords' difficulties went beyond the bedroom. As their marriage evolved, they developed different sets of friends. Marjorie was drawn to New York and Hollywood intelligentsia, a crowd that left her husband decidedly ill at ease. The insecurities of his prep school days had only intensified with age. "The minute he got an intelligent person around, he felt inferior," Marjorie explained. His discomfort drew him apart, making him appear either shy or monstrously self-absorbed.

"I used to bring people to meet him," she said. "One night Budd Schulberg [author of *What Makes Sammy Run?* and screenwriter for *On the Waterfront*] came over. He started to read from the script from *A Face in the Crowd*. Then Hunt said, 'I have a script I'd like to read,' and started to read from *The Master of Thornfield*. When he was finished, he went around turning the lights out, and then, as he left, said, 'I'm sorry, Mr. Schulberg. I'm very tired and I'm going to go to bed.' "

Schulberg recalled another occasion, not long after, when he was sharing conversation and wine with Marjorie and several other guests in the Hartford living room. The master of the house was off in his study.

"He suddenly appeared in the living room; he had just finished an attack on modern art and he started reading it aloud," Schulberg related. "He was oblivious of other people's works, of other people's feelings. It was an eccentric, egocentric performance.

"Hartford carried with him the fervor of one of the born-agains. He had the unquestioning sense that he was right and everyone else was wrong and he was the one who would show the way. I thought he had rather a good mind, intelligent, but he was fixated. He put himself in creative blinders; he wouldn't listen to any other point of view.

"He was very much within himself—locked within himself. I always got the feeling that he felt he was in competition with me. It seemed people who had accomplished something in the field of the arts gave him a sense of inferiority."

For Hartford, graphology was a device that helped him cope with that lack of self-confidence, a seemingly scientific method for determining whom he could trust. "I'm not sure he was confident in his ability to judge character," reflected Paul DeGives, an acquaintance from Harvard whose mother was a palm reader and who shared Hartford's fascination with parapsychology. "Hartford felt that this was a good way to figure out a person's character without going into a lot of analysis."

In 1955, Hartford founded the Handwriting Institute in Manhattan, with a full complement of experts: six psychologists, a medical doctor, and three graphologists. "I don't feel that current intelligence tests accurately measure the capacity of a person," Hartford said at the time. "The trouble is they don't test the whole personality. We feel handwriting tests more. We feel the need of tests through handwriting to show drive, sensitivity, maturity, humor, and aggressiveness. If handwriting tests could be simplified, you could actually predict human behavior. You'd be able to predict a boy who was doing well in school was going out to kill his mother. Or take the guy who graduates summa cum laude and never does anything because of his beginning strokes and his unbalanced f's."

Hartford dismissed the various editors of psychology journals who considered graphology little more than a carnival sideshow: "They are naive. It stands to reason that the more you write as you were taught in school, the more immature you are. Your personality is imprinted on your school copy."

His was an extreme enthusiasm, and even Dr. Larry Epstein, the Institute psychologist and a fellow traveler in graphology circles (he coauthored a scholarly article with Hartford on graphology), was skeptical about his patron's views. "Mr. Hartford has a tendency to look at someone's handwriting," he said, "and indict him or her for being immature if the handwriting reveals primary [school] strokes. His wife has them. Lots of people have them. I have to settle Hunt down on this."

Hartford was particularly passionate about a phenomenon he called the "figure-eight *g.*" Hartford claimed to have discovered the figure-eight *g,* and he believed that people whose writing had it, as his own did, were especially sensitive and creative.

"I tried to convince Hunt that [just] because Albert Einstein didn't make a figure-eight *g,* he didn't necessarily lack sensitivity and creativeness," said Epstein.

The letter *f* was another Hartford fixation. Evenly balanced, it was taken as a sign of character. He also paid inordinate attention to how a person crossed a *t.* Those who crossed only halfway, he contended, were procrastinators; a bar slanting down was a sign of stubbornness. "I've thought about one thing and only one thing for the past five years,'' Hartford told a reporter. "And that is that slant is terribly important. My own handwriting, especially the final *d,* shows I'm a perfectionist. Never completely satisfied with things. My script is small. That's my indication of my caution, a certain modesty. . . . The basic fault with my writing is the rhythm. I'm very insecure, really. Emotionally unstable.''

He spent years collecting samples from eminent men and women he met, becoming sort of a graphological Vasari. "Take Admiral Nimitz and Admiral Halsey,'' Hartford said. "Nimitz' handwriting was straight up and down, and what was he? A desk man. Bull Halsey's handwriting slanted out. He was active in the field. That interests me. I firmly believe that people who have forward-leaning slants are more intelligent than those with up-and-down strokes.''

Hartford did not restrict his handwriting analysis to the laboratory. Virtually everyone hired onto a Hartford project had to be tested. Each had to write out the same sample sentence—"I'm walking the street to get the horse and buggy out of the old garage''—before being allowed into the Hartford sanctum, and most of those who supped at Hartford's table were briefed as to the proper shape for their *g*s and *t*s. "We knew how to rig the test,'' said Richard Schickel, a film critic for *Time* and a onetime Hartford employee.

"You can sell Hunt on an idea,'' a friend once said, "if he knows who recommended you and [if he] likes your handwriting.''

Unlike many of the very wealthy, who carefully insulate themselves from hangers-on, Hartford welcomed the flatterers. A secretary barely buffered him from his ever-ringing phone (the number then, as now, was listed in the Manhattan directory). Dick Cowell, the friend who was there when Hartford first met Marjorie, contrasted Hartford's accessibility to that of Howard Hughes. "When you tried to find Howard, you would call, leave your name and number, and if he felt like it he'd call back. You could never reach him directly. Hunt would answer the phone before his butler did.''

Hartford used his money to manipulate the men around him, to hoist himself up slightly higher than the surrounding crowd. "Hunt liked people to grovel,'' said Robin Moore, the coauthor of *The Happy Hooker* and a Hartford acquaintance since the late forties. "He could understand that.''

Marjorie would try to push her husband beyond his coterie of sycophants, but she met with little success. "He needed to be around people who gave him a sense of superiority,'' she said. "I used to plead with him. I said, 'You must meet some intelligent people so you can talk, you have no one to talk to but me.' ''

Just as Howard Hughes had Johnny Meyer, the onetime Warner Bros. public-relations man who would go out and tell whichever young woman caught the aviator's fancy that "Mr. Hughes would like to meet you," so Hartford had his entourage of men whose friendship was based as much on their ability to introduce him to women as on their camaraderie.

Marvin Finch, a Los Angeles bartender-boulevardier, was Hartford's sidekick in the late forties and early fifties. Finch, totally bald, with high cheekbones and sunken jowls, used to explain that he had "a skin toupee, there's hair underneath." He owned one bar in Acapulco, the Sí Como No, and a jazz club just across from the old Ambassador Hotel on Wilshire Boulevard. But Finch was less restaurateur than profiteer. "His commodity was pretty girls," said Robert Neal, who was part of Hartford's crowd in the forties. "Marvin scammed around"; having a pretty girl on his arm made it easier to belly up to the buffet table at a party, and with a svelte young thing no one cared if he was on the guest list or not.

Finch slipped from the Hartford set after the paternity suit forced Hartford to transfer his base back east. He was replaced by two Brooklyn-born operators—Seymour "Sy" Alter, a former store detective who, according to Marjorie, "looked like Humphrey Bogart after a car accident," and Larry Horn, another ersatz detective who was cued to follow Alter's lead.

Alter's first arranged encounter with Hartford set the tone for their relationship. "I ran into him a few times at parties," Alter recalled. Then John Talbot, a boulevardier turned real estate developer, invited him to come along for a Sunday at Melody Farm, the New Jersey estate Hartford had inherited from his mother. "I remember being very nervous about it. I said, 'He doesn't really know me.' Talbot told me not to worry."

Out at Melody Farm, "they were playing croquet," Alter remembered, his tongue clicking the *t* in "croquet." "I didn't know how to play well, and he kept hitting my ball all over the court. When he wasn't looking I moved it back to where it started. I kept cheating—but we had a lot of laughs."

Within months, Hartford installed Alter in an office in his modeling agency. His duties were ill defined at best. Although the hulking Alter described himself as Hartford's bodyguard, he was there more to introduce Hartford to the world than to protect him from it.

As Alter and his ilk drew closer to Hartford, Marjorie withdrew. She didn't like the men, and she didn't like the women they brought with them. Finally, said Marjorie, "I stopped going out with him altogether."

Marjorie's career helped her build that wall between herself and her family. In 1956, she replaced Barbara Bel Geddes as Maggie in *Cat on a Hot Tin Roof,* first on Broadway, then on tour. According to Eddie Dodds, the dresser who traveled with her during the show, "Marjorie was a sweet, naive girl who didn't seem to have any care about money. I remember Hartford bought her a mink coat while we were on tour— she was too embarrassed to wear it."

Hartford would show up occasionally, but for Marjorie, even those rare appearances could be harrowing. "I remember we went to see a university revue in Chicago," Dodds said. "Hartford kept getting up and cruising the girls in the show. It was obvious. Marjorie never said anything, but she grew increasingly tense."

Her husband's relentless philandering wore at her own esteem, and she drank to salve the wound. "I didn't want to go to nightclubs anymore, because of this thing about the girls. I understood it, but it was a humiliation that I couldn't take." With alcohol, Marjorie's unhappiness devolved into deep despair. As her daughter, Cathy, put it, "My mother was in the habit of trying to commit suicide."

One evening in New York, Sy Alter got a panicky phone call from Hartford. "Come over immediately," he said, with no explanation.

When Alter appeared, he found Marjorie naked, leaning off the balcony. One hand held a liquor bottle, the other grasped the railing. Hartford, desperate, asked Alter, "What are we going to do?"

Alter responded, "We're walking out of this room, because if she falls, I don't want anybody to say that we pushed."

Marjorie finally walked off the balcony and back into the apartment, and Alter took charge. "Something about the girls set her off," Alter recalled. "When she came in, I got her up to the bedroom and said, 'You're going to be calm, I'm your friend.' She gave me a whack. Hunt started to laugh. I said, 'Marjorie, if it feels so good, hit me again.' Son of a bitch, she hit me again. Finally she went to sleep, and the next day she was fine."

Roger Donoghue, an ex-prizefighter and a beau of one of Marjorie's younger sisters, Emily "Duffy" Steele, recalled a similar incident. In the summer of 1956, he and Duffy lived in a West End Avenue apartment and spent weekends at the Hartfords' triplex at One Beekman Place. "One night," he recounted, "Hartford came into our bedroom hollering. I followed him out, and there was Marjorie, drunk, sitting on the edge of a window overlooking the East River, her legs hanging over the side. Hunt said he was afraid that if he got near her she would jump. Duffy and I raced for her, grabbed her, and pulled her back. No one ever mentioned it again.''

Hunt Hartford was somehow thrilled by his wife's crises. Like those waitresses at Childs coffee shop years before, Marjorie became his way of touching reality. In her pain he began to find the drama he had been seeking for so long.

The Hartford children were brought up in opulent isolation. Both Hunt and Marjorie were too preoccupied with their own worlds to take much time out to be parents, and Cathy and Jackie, like so many children of affluence, ended up with an abundance of material goods and a paucity of parental care.

''Daddy was always on the phone,'' recalled Cathy. There were no family dinners in the Hartford household; the children were always served their meals separately from their parents. Said Marjorie: ''I tried to have lunch with them on weekends.''

As their father pursued his myriad projects and their mother went about her acting career, Cathy and Jackie were left to a German nanny named Amelia Kircher. The youngsters even spent their vacations traveling around West Germany, *sans* parents, with ''Kirchie,'' a nineteenth-century disciplinarian whom Marjorie found through the classified ads. ''She made me write a thousand times, 'I must not do this, I must not do that.' She used to slap me all the time, gave me a bloody nose. I was terrified of her,'' remembered Cathy.

The Hartford children grew up with too many houses and no real home. They were shipped willy-nilly from Palm Beach to New York to Los Angeles to London and back again, with the house in London providing the most precise measure of the breach between the Hartford parents and their offspring. The house—bought so Hartford could be near Marjorie when she was performing—was fairly small, just three stories and two bedrooms on Red Lion Yard in Mayfair. When they visited, the children were put up with their nanny at the Dorchester Hotel three blocks away.

''I had the most beautiful mother and father,'' said Cathy. ''I'd see them kissing in the living room, and they were a vision of the perfect mommy and daddy. But my real parent was the nurse. I never felt my parents were a part of my life.''

10

*B*Y THE MID-FIFTIES, Huntington Hartford was getting more press than the grocery giant that had spawned his fortune, and that sat just fine with the old men who ran the A&P.

After the battles with the government ended, the curtain dropped on the grocery chain. There were no press conferences, no quarterly reports; the company refused to join trade associations or even to supply data to A. C. Nielsen, the ratings service that tracks grocery sales.

Although George Hartford still showed up at the office at eleven each morning, he generally stayed only three hours before returning home to New Jersey. By then in his nineties, he had long since grown silent and senile; virtually all business affairs were handled by the company's president, Ralph Burger, who had originally been John Hartford's secretary.

Burger was an accidental dauphin. The son of an A&P employee, he joined the company as a $7-a-week clerk when he was still in his teens. He became a bookkeeper when the chain was still based in Jersey City, and by 1925 he had become secretary of several A&P corporations; he moved to the Graybar Building when the company transferred its headquarters there. Burger had never held a position with executive authority; he succeeded by insinuating himself into the brothers' lives. After John's wife died in 1948, Burger became his closest friend. His timing, as it turned out, was excellent.

By the late forties, the Hartford brothers had begun to think about passing the corporate mantle. In March 1949, they appointed David Boffinger, who had been head of the company's purchasing network, president; John became chairman; and George retained the treasurer's title. Boffinger held the job just nine months before dying of a heart attack. In June 1950, the brothers named Burger president of both the A&P and the John Hartford Foundation. He was to have been merely an interim chief executive, filling the slot until George and John came up with a better alternative. Then John died, and their temporary choice became permanent.

Burger's first act as chief executive was to visit each of the six divisions and thirty-seven operating units of the A&P, in an effort to reassure employees that the company was in good hands. He told them what John Hartford had told him when he was anointed as president: "During these last years you have been closer to me than anyone else; more than anyone else you know how I feel about this company, and as new problems arise I believe you more than anyone else would know how I might react and are most likely to react in the same way."

He spoke of his close friendship with John Hartford, of how he had turned down a salary as president of his foundation. Pointing out the red carnation boutonniere in his lapel, he told the assembled masses that he had instead agreed to accept one fresh flower each day from John's greenhouse in Valhalla. "This is Mr. John's suit I'm wearing," he added, as though that would somehow make the employees more comfortable with his assumption of the stewardship. "We were both the same size, and John Hartford would not have wanted his suits to go to waste."

Not surprisingly, Burger's appointment was not popular with A&P employees; they considered him little more than an obsequious office boy who had been promoted over his head. Most of the Hartford heirs (ten descendants of George and John's two sisters, along with Hunt and his sister, held sixty percent of the A&P voting shares) were equally unhappy with the Burger regime. And they were especially troubled by his appointment as president of the John Hartford Foundation, a position that gave him the power to vote the Foundation's stock after both John and George Hartford were dead. That amounted to the other forty percent of the company's shares.

For his part, Ralph Burger, like the man who had hired him, had little interest in the heirs. While he hired a few husbands for minor positions in the company, he did his best to bar them from the boardroom. "John and George Hartford discouraged any family member from participating in the business—and Burger figured he would be better off if they were out of the way as well," said Olivia Switz, granddaughter of one of the Hartford sisters.

The heirs considered Burger autocratic and arrogant; they were especially enraged when he sold *Woman's Day,* which the grocer had launched, to Fawcett Publications without mentioning it to them. (They were right to be furious: the magazine, now owned by the French company Hachette, brought in $115.6 million in advertising revenues in 1988, the thirteenth highest in the industry.) And so it was that seven cousins—Hunt Hartford the most vociferous of the lot—signed a voting trust, in an effort to consolidate their shares and retain a united voice in the A&P. They sealed their agreement with a pledge:

> If [we] remain divided and unorganized and fail to consolidate [our] strength through the creation of a voting trust, the Foundation will completely control the A&P. This means in fact that the directors of the Foundation will control the A&P . . . something utterly different from control . . . by John and George Hartford which the existing trust was established to assure. The Foundation is under the domination of employees of the A&P, and therefore, if the Foundation controls the Company, the Company will be under the domination of these same employees. . . . It is unthinkable for the owners to abdicate to a group of salaried executives.

The heirs' concerns were real. Although the A&P had successfully defended itself against the Justice Department, the grocery giant had become vulnerable on another front: it was losing its competitive edge, and Ralph Burger was responsible. So long as John was alive he retained effective control. George remained in charge of operations, and Burger's position was primarily titular. But after John's death in 1951, all that had changed. And while John Hartford had left Burger a legacy of power (not to mention a closet full of suits), he could not, unfortunately, pass on his business acumen.

Burger, an inexperienced manager, proved a rigid, frightened leader, unable to accommodate the changes in the food-manufacturing industry. He suffered from strategic myopia, and he demanded to be involved in virtually every corporate decision, no matter how minor. Not only did each lease and renewal have to be approved by an administrative committee, but Burger also demanded that new leases conform to the old rules: no more than five years, with rentals not to exceed $2 per square foot. As property values and building costs increased, developers required longer leases and higher rentals to finance their shopping centers; with the A&P refusing to flex its standards, rivals were obtaining the prime locations. A&P sales growth shrank to half of the industry average.

All the while, George Hartford kept up appearances, showed up for his quotidian coffee tastings. Then one day in September 1957, he felt too ill to go to the office. The doctors came and discovered that the old man was critically ill with uremia. He lingered for two weeks, then died.

Three hundred people attended George's funeral. Most were A&P employees. Ten executives, including Burger, were honorary pallbearers. Members of the family were there as well, but none took a position of honor.

Of the Hartford family, Hunt's sister probably felt her uncle's loss most keenly. Josephine, who shunned publicity as avidly as her brother sought it, lived a quietly patrician life centered around her racehorse stables near Saratoga Springs. In the late thirties, she had managed one foray into the business world with a clutch of high-class hot-dog stands called Swanky Frankie's. The business survived only a year or two, though, after which Josephine confined her fiscal ambitions to her horses. She achieved a fair measure of success, and through the fifties and sixties her Mill River Stables produced a score of champion thoroughbreds.

Although Josephine handled her family life with considerably more discretion than her brother, her relationships were not much more stable. For Josephine, like her brother, the troubles traced back to childhood. She had never had much in the way of familial ballast: her father, despairing and withdrawn, had provided his daughter with little warmth; her mother had rejected her altogether. By the late fifties, Josephine Hartford O'Donnell Makaroff Douglas Bryce was on her fourth marriage and had been largely estranged from her younger brother for years. She had found what family she had in her uncles' company. "Uncle George had been very kind to her at times," recalled her cousin Olivia Switz. "She used to spend summers with him in Spring Lake."

Now, in order to retain control of the A&P, Burger needed Josephine's support. Family allegiance was the most powerful argument Burger had, and he launched it when Josephine was most vulnerable: at George Hartford's funeral. Michael McIntosh, a descendant of one of the Hartford sisters, recalled seeing Josephine getting into Ralph Burger's Cadillac at George's funeral and driving off. It was there, McIntosh believed, that she was offered a position on the board of the John Hartford Foundation. Within weeks of George's death, Josephine joined the board and persuaded another ten-percent cousin to do the same. Thus Burger gained control of sixty percent of the A&P voting shares.

More than thirty years later, Hunt Hartford still bristled at the memory of his sister's defection. "That ensured the company would be run by mediocrity," he recalled. "Burger had control and he wanted to keep it. He was afraid that if he lost that power he'd get thrown out."

In December 1958, the battle between Burger and the dissident members of the Hartford family blew onto the front page of *The Wall Street Journal*: "HERMIT KINGDOM: The Isolated A&P Eases Its Border Guard After a Subtle Struggle; President Burger Is Prodded by Family Heirs but Gets Support from a Charity."

In the course of that "subtle struggle" the family had won a few victories. After George's death, the cousins talked Burger into including some outsiders on the A&P board, which had long been composed exclusively of company men. Just as important, they finally persuaded Burger to give voting rights to shareholders of the A&P common. But because the dissident Hartford heirs now controlled only forty percent of the shares, they couldn't achieve what they wanted most: Burger's ouster.

They did, however, attain the next best thing: liquidity. Two years after George died, the family offered its voting shares to the public. On March 25, 1959, within minutes of the opening bell, Hunt Hartford sold nearly half of his legacy. He netted more than $40 million—and he needed the money.

Once again, the bills for Hunt Hartford's profligate projects were threatening to run ahead of his income. In June 1956, he had announced plans for an art museum on the south side of Columbus Circle in Manhattan. The site, then occupied by a six-story office building, cost $1 million, and he planned to spend $1.5 million on constructing his new edifice. The idea was for a simple off-white structure, designed to blend in with the New York Coliseum, just across Columbus Circle.

The museum would have a restaurant on the top floor and as much gallery space as the Museum of Modern Art, which had opened seventeen years before. Hartford announced that he planned to start construction immediately, but the owner of the Regal Shoe Store on the office building's first floor put a crimp in those plans. The store's lease extended until 1964, and its owner had no intention of leaving. He sued, and Hartford was forced to delay construction.

But a lawsuit could not contain Hartford's fiscal free-for-all. In 1957, he finally willed *The Master of Thornfield*, his overwrought adaptation of *Jane Eyre,* to life.

Although Hartford intended the play as a vehicle for Marjorie, she refused to appear in it. "It was hard enough being an actress with the mantle of Mrs. Huntington Hartford," explained Marjorie. "If I [had done] *Jane Eyre*? Can you imagine anything more damning to my career?"

Hartford went off to London to cast his lead. He ended up with Jan Brooks, an unknown twenty-one-year-old ingenue whose chief virtues were her fresh looks and fine accent. Her acting ability, all agreed, was wanting.

As Rochester, Hartford cast Errol Flynn. It was supposed to be the first part of a deal with Flynn for two plays, *The Master of Thornfield* and Flynn's pet project, his own adaptation of Edward George Bulwer-Lytton's *Richelieu,* a historical play written in 1839. Hartford figured Flynn could help sell his nineteenth-century tale to a twentieth-century audience.

"I was just as conscious as anybody that *Jane Eyre* was the most old-fashioned thing you could probably find," Hartford said. "Flynn was still a big name. He had lots of stage presence, and I thought it would be wonderful to get him in the play."

"Huntington Hartford has always wanted to do something important," Flynn said at the time, "and now I feel that I would, too, so perhaps this is a good marriage." As it turned out, the union more closely resembled *Who's Afraid of Virginia Woolf?*

At first blush, Flynn, the storybook hero of the screen, seemed tailor-made for the role. He was Robin Hood, swashbuckling his way through Sherwood Forest, carrying Maid Marian off in his arms. He was Captain Blood, the young British surgeon who turns to piracy in the Caribbean after being wrongly condemned for helping colonial rebels. But those roles were over twenty years gone, and the Errol Flynn of the late fifties was an out-of-control alcoholic, with little regard for himself and even less for the A&P heir who was supporting him.

Not long before Hartford signed him to play Rochester, Flynn had been forced to forfeit his estate on Mulholland Drive as back payment on alimony to his third ex-wife. After he paid her off, the government came to call, claiming he owed hundreds of thousands of dollars in back taxes.

Initially, Flynn had been reluctant to take on the role of Rochester. But he was virtually broke and homeless, and Hartford had offered several powerful incentives. First, he gave Flynn free rein at Runyon Canyon. The house had been mostly empty since Hartford had fled to New York to escape the paternity suit, and Flynn used the estate to full advantage. In 1957, at the age of forty-eight, he began a two-year love affair with a precocious, postpubescent blonde, fifteen-year-old Beverly Aadland. She had met Flynn on the Warner Bros. lot, where she had a bit part in *Marjorie Morningstar.* The movie's designer told the teenager that Flynn wanted to meet her, and she obediently went to his dressing room. There, Flynn asked her to read for a play, the reading to be held at Hartford's estate. The reading led to dinner, which in turn led to seduction (her first, she told him afterward) on a thick bearskin rug on Hartford's living room hearth. Aadland wandered naked through the wild foliage; Flynn nicknamed her "Woodsie."

The heir also advanced the actor $85,000 to appear in *The Master of Thornfield*, $10,000 for the run of the play, the rest for a planned screen adaptation plus the promised *Richelieu* project. But even $85,000, more than double what any other stage actor was making at the time, was not enough to contain Flynn. He bellowed his disdain for Hartford's play in his autobiography, *My Wicked, Wicked Ways*: "The lines were unbecoming to me . . . a love line like: 'Now my little sparrow, I'll never let you go.' I just can't call a woman my little sparrow—not even for money."

Even if Flynn had been happy with Hartford's writing, it was unlikely he could have performed. Alcohol had rotted his memory; he not only was unwilling to learn his lines, he was unable. "I can't remember my own name, let alone a line in a play," he told a friend, and he used his dissatisfaction with the quality of the script to mask his own eroding talent.

Nothing ever starts out with disaster scrawled all over it. There is almost always a precise moment, a specific absurdity, that propels a merely mediocre production into the abyss of the irretrievable. For *The Master of Thornfield*, that moment came at one of its first performances, in Cincinnati.

"Hartford thought Errol would behave," said John Ireland, the actor who understudied Flynn's Rochester. "After all, he had gotten Errol out of a jam, he had put Errol up."

Hartford had seriously miscalculated. "Errol decided he was going to make it as hard on Hunt as he could. 'The dialogue is just so bad, I can't learn it,' " Ireland recalled Flynn saying. " 'I want a fireplace stage left, and another stage right, or something that looks like a fireplace, and inside the mantel I want a TelePrompTer.'

"So he got a TelePrompTer on either side of the stage. He would lean on the mantel, pretending he was looking at a portrait on the other side. He'd learn a couple of lines, walk across the stage, and lean again and look into the other TelePrompTer."

Even with all that, Flynn was impossible. At his first entrance, two hounds barked offstage. Flynn walked onstage, heard the dogs, then pronounced, "Down, Huntington; down, Hartford."

"It was terrible," Ireland said, laughing. "Hartford was furious but helpless. Then Errol had a couple of lines with Jane. He said to her, 'Jane, I'm just a poor man, perhaps you should marry a chain-store heir.' He had no shame."

Hartford watched the farce, tight-lipped, from the front row.

He did not have to suffer Flynn's antics for long. During that run in Ohio, Darryl Zanuck offered Flynn a script for *The Roots of Heaven*. It was an altogether forgettable film about the preservation of wild animals, set in Africa, but for Flynn anything was better than *The Master of Thornfield*. On February 19, 1958, he walked out, and he didn't go quietly. "The play as it now stands has no more business being on Broadway than 'Jack and the Beanstalk,'" he told local reporters, predicting that Hartford's play would never make it to the Great White Way.

Flynn underestimated Hartford's tenacity. First the heir sued to recover the money he had advanced to Flynn (ultimately he settled with the actor's estate). Next he cast John Emery as Rochester; Emery, in turn, was replaced by Eric Portman, a reasonably well-known British stage actor, who opened the play in Philadelphia.

"I'm a Yorkshireman and was born only ten miles from the Brontë country," Portman told a journalist. "I have definite ideas about how a Yorkshireman should be played." Not very good ones, apparently. The play was panned, and there were reports that its run would end right there. But Hartford could not be stopped. On May 1, 1958, *The Master of Thornfield* opened on Broadway at the Belasco Theatre. Afterward Hartford and the cast went to his apartment to celebrate. "It was a big, posh affair," recalled a man who worked for Hartford. "He invited the world. *Tout le haut monde* of New York. Helen Hayes was there, and so was Diana Barrymore—dead drunk. And Marjorie was there, necking with someone under the table. His wife, necking publicly while her husband was shaking hands as people came in. It was a fiasco."

The evening got worse when the first copies of *The New York Times* came in at midnight. The critic Brooks Atkinson lambasted Hartford's production as "two parts *Jane Eyre,* three parts East Lyme. . . . The play is a scrap-pile of old fashioned stage machinery—the wind machine, hoof-beats, the fireplace bellows blowing up a fraudulent blaze. . . . The flaws in taste are fatal. The lurid scene in which Thornfield Hall takes fire and burns sensationally is the most damaging. . . . It looks like a diorama of the Johnstown flood."

Still, Hartford insisted the show go on; he kept the play running for six weeks in front of a mostly empty house. His Victorian epic ended up costing more than $600,000.

In the end, Hartford held Marjorie responsible for the debacle. "I wrote it for Marjorie, and if she had been in it Flynn would have behaved," he said. "Flynn loved her like they all did. . . . Marjorie was to blame for the whole thing. Once she decided not to do it, I should have quit."

In August 1958, a reporter for the *New York Post* tracked down Hartford's ingenue, Jan Brooks. Just two months after the play that was supposed to make her into a star had closed, she was living in a dingy furnished room in London, having barely managed to scrape together the fare back to England. She said that she planned to look for work in a repertory company in Windsor. "I'm down to my last couple pounds," she told the reporter. "Maybe somebody there will lend me some cash."

Brooks had long since given up on Hartford's promise of a London production of *The Master of Thornfield*. "I haven't heard from Mr. Hartford since [the play] closed in New York," she reflected. "He's a strange man. Tremendous enthusiasm one day for something, then the next day, he's off on something else."

11

THE ARTISTS' colony, the Broadway play, the museum, the Handwriting Institute, and the rest were only passing flirtations with fiscal profligacy—checks kited but not bounced. In June 1959, Hartford began his most ardent courtship with financial disaster. He purchased four-fifths of Hog Island, just five hundred yards from Nassau in the Bahamas.

The Bahamas are an archipelago of some seven hundred islands and two thousand rocks and cays strewn like confetti across the Caribbean. Hog Island, one of those seven hundred, drew its name from its colonial function: it was where the British kept their pigs until they were ready for butchering. Its 625 acres quickly became the most ambitious of the Hartford projects, the Bermuda Triangle of his ambitions as well as his fortune.

Hartford rapidly renamed the island Paradise; in just over ten years, it would become a nexus of corruption and depravity. It was there that Howard Hughes, nails curling to his palms, gray beard grazing his chest, drifted into dementia. It was there that the fugitive financier Robert Vesco lost his last shreds of legitimacy before fleeing into the Caribbean netherworld of drugs and black-market money. It was there that tens of thousands of dollars earmarked for Nixon's Committee to Re-Elect the President were said to have been laundered, shipped off the island as bound bills in brown paper bags.

But before all of that came Huntington Hartford, questing for fame, grasping onto the frayed ends of his second marriage. An island in the Caribbean, a place where Hartford could create the ultimate arts oasis and Marjorie could take center stage in an open-air amphitheater, held out promise for preserving the Hartford union.

They found Hog Island through Thor Ramsing, a Hartford relation by marriage who lived in Palm Beach. Ramsing, a real estate developer, was working with John Volk, the Palm Beach architect responsible for the resort's stuccoed Regency mansions and clubs, to market parcels of Hog Island, then owned by Axel Wenner-Gren, a Swedish industrialist and arms merchant.

Most of the island property had been in private hands since the eighteenth century, when the British government divvied up most of it among a handful of residents. The westernmost tip was kept by the government, which in the early nineteenth century used it as a public gallows for black Bahamians. Criminals were hanged and then decapitated; their heads were hoisted high on fence posts. That barbarism ended by midcentury; the gallows were torn down and a lighthouse replaced them.

A full century later, a few wealthy Americans began buying up parcels of land on Hog Island, creating a winter colony. They named their club the Porcupine, and until the beginning of World War II, some of America's best-known industrialists and yachtsmen dropped anchor at its slips—Andrew Mellon, J. P. Morgan, and Vincent Astor among them. One of the biggest plots of land, on the eastern end of the island, was pioneered in the 1930s by Edmund Lynch, a founder of Merrill Lynch. He built himself a magnificent mansion, complete with covered tennis courts, but he barely had time to enjoy it. Lynch died just a year after the estate was completed, and Wenner-Gren purchased the property from his heirs in 1939.

Had it not been for imperial intervention, Wenner-Gren's property would likely have remained an elaborate estate. But in 1940, the Bahamas were suddenly caught in the bright light of the British crown. In August of that year, the Duke of Windsor, the man who had abdicated his kingship "for the woman I love," was appointed governor of the Caribbean colony and took up residence in Nassau. His mandate was to push the Caribbean colony into economic self-sufficiency. He appealed to the wealthiest of the Bahamian real estate holders to nurture the nascent tourist business by developing their property. Wenner-Gren responded with a vengeance. He dredged a large swamp at the center of Hog Island, then cut two canals through, making the harbor accessible for tall-masted boats.

But World War II quashed Wenner-Gren's plans. The Swede had made his first fortune as an arms merchant, and his uncomfortably close ties to Hermann Göring, the number-two man in the Nazi hierarchy, landed him on the U.S. government's blacklist of forbidden trading partners. Ultimately the entire Hog Island project became suspect; the Allies were convinced (apparently wrongly) that the island's canals were actually entrances for German submarines, the harbor a place where they could refuel and take on new supplies. In the early forties, a group of Nassau-based Allied soldiers raided Wenner-Gren's estate in search of incriminating documents. Although they found nothing, Wenner-Gren still decided it was time to decamp. He left for Mexico and didn't return to the island to stay until after the war. By then, the development was long stalled, and the Swede, strapped for cash, took on Ramsing and Volk to market his Bahamian acreage.

Their plan was to mimic the community E. P. Taylor had opened that year in Lyford Cay, just across a sandbar bridge from New Providence, the most populous island in the Bahamas. Taylor, a Canadian home builder and racehorse breeder, had spent much of his $30 million investment to drain and fill the secluded mangrove swamp with bargeloads of sod and palms shipped over from Florida. He built a sturdy fence around his compound and invited three hundred friends to join, and sold off pieces of the property to offset his investment. Among the first members were Hartford's sister, Josephine, the publisher Walter Annenberg, and the investment banker Charles Allen.

Ramsing tantalized the Hartfords with reports of Taylor's development. Within days, the heir and his wife sailed off to see the island. "Like a damn fool, I bought the whole thing," recalled Hartford. On the back of a napkin (supplied by Wenner-Gren) he signed a contract for $11 million to purchase the island on the spot—no advisers, no lawyers.

The island, Hartford thought, would establish him as more than just a man with too much money to spend. He wanted to create a retreat where the architecture would be pristine, the talk smart, and the beaches and women beautiful, a sort of cross between Dumbarton Oaks and St.-Tropez. "We will expect people of all walks of life. There will be no automobiles, no roulette wheels, no honky-tonks on Hog Island," he told a reporter. "In that way I hope we can create an atmosphere of cultural enjoyment that will complement the island's rare beauty and climate."

The blueprints verged on the fantastic: eight hotels, tennis courts, seaside cabañas, a golf course, yacht docks, and a 2,200-seat auditorium to be called the Marjorie Steele Theater—divided into separate sections for dramatic, musical, and sporting events.

"What I want to do is create something like another Williamsburg," he told another reporter. "I don't mean an American Colonial restoration, of course, but the same sort of thing authentic for the Bahamas. As soon as Marlon Brando and MGM are done shooting their remake of *Mutiny on the Bounty,* if we can pick up their replica of the boat for $200,000 or so, we could anchor it in the bay and use it for a cocktail lounge, a restaurant, or something."

He also said he was bidding for the chariots used in *Ben Hur*; he wanted to re-create Roman spectacle in the Caribbean. "I think I know now where we can set up our [Circus] Maximus," he told a reporter. "We'll have a spectator sport without attracting all the touts, bookies, and compulsive gamblers and other types you usually find around racetracks."

"When he told me about the chariots, I told him he was out of his mind," recalled Sy Alter, who served as Hartford's aide-de-camp on the Bahamian development. "The horses would drop dead from the heat." Only after an insurance company convinced Hartford that the races would risk the lives of both the horses and their drivers did he finally scuttle the idea.

The rest of his ruinous fantasy, though, remained intact. But before ground had even been broken in the Caribbean, Hartford flew back to New York to attend to his many other ventures.

"He loved publicity," said Ramsing. "He needed it. He wanted to build, build, build, and he wasn't satisfied to do one thing at a time."

Back in New York, misadventure was just waiting to happen at Hartford's modeling agency, then about ten years old. The firm had struggled through the fifties, losing money year after year. The problem, according to Jerry Ford, was an excess of overhead and a shortage of talented management: "Hartford employed people who told him what he wanted to hear."

Still, Hartford held on, and in 1959, inexplicably, he made a $1 million offer to take over Ford's rival outfit, by then preeminent in the business. "Hartford told us we would have total control and he would stay out of it," said Ford. "We negotiated for a long time, but it didn't happen."

The problem was the New York City Department of Consumer Affairs, then responsible for licensing such businesses. "An inspector called a few of the girls down for an interview, then asked, 'Has Mr. Hartford ever propositioned you?'" recalled one of the men who ran

Hartford's agency. ''The girls started laughing and responded, 'Of course.' The city made it clear Hartford was to get out of the modeling game.''

At that point, Hartford's attorney approached Ford and said, ''Since he's not going to buy you, why don't you buy him?'' Ultimately Ford absorbed Hartford's business, which was then carrying roughly $750,000 in losses. (Ironically, by the time Ford acquired Hartford's outfit, his women's division had long since flagged, but his roster included the best male models in New York.)

Hartford, a man who weighed his worth by the number of projects that bore his name, barely felt the loss. Just before he sold off his models, Hartford made good on his plans to enter a loftier arena. In 1959, he held a press conference in New York City to announce that he had finally chosen the man who would realize his vision for a realist art museum: Edward Durell Stone.

Stone had started at the vanguard of the International style in architecture, the ''row after Mies van der Rohe of glass boxes'' that Tom Wolfe deplored in *From Bauhaus to Our House*. Stone designed the first International-style house built on the East Coast, the Mandel house in Mount Kisco, New York; when he put up his second, the community revolted and changed the building codes to stop the modernist blight.

In the mid-thirties, those impeccable credentials led the Museum of Modern Art to select Stone to build on Fifty-third Street, west of Fifth Avenue, where the townhouses of John D. Rockefeller and his son had stood. Stone had been chosen, wrote Wolfe, ''to devise the object lesson, the very flagship of Utopia, Ltd.'' And he built a museum that was a monument to sleek, near-anonymous uniformity.

But by the mid-fifties Stone had become an apostate to modernism. In 1954, he married Maria Elena Torchio; her father, an architect, was Italian; her mother was Catalan. Their daughter, Stone liked to say, was ''explosively Latin.'' And in his passion for his Latin wife, Stone renounced his previous style. He designed the American Embassy in New Delhi with terrazzo grilles of concrete and marble, and steel columns finished with gold leaf; he called it his ''Taj Maria.''

It was altogether too sentimental for the International establishment, which roundly condemned both the building and its creator. Thus it was only fitting that Stone be resurrected by the most antediluvian of America's patrons, a man, as Wolfe put it, who was building his museum specifically to challenge Utopia, Ltd. Who better for Hartford to enlist in his war against the modernists than a heathen who had seen the light?

During those years of prodigious building, Hartford lived in New York, but he mixed surprisingly little with the men and women who orchestrated the city's cultural scene. He had dinners at his house, but the guests were generally a fixed set of characters: Sy Alter, Larry Horn, and token members of the art world's fringe: Edward Stone and Salvador Dalí, eager to keep Hartford's company in search of commissions. All of which left Hartford especially susceptible to a personal plea from one of the most commanding powerbrokers in American history, Robert Moses, the man responsible for reshaping virtually the whole of New York City. Moses first proposed to Hartford that he build a baseball diamond in Central Park. Hartford wasn't interested in that suggestion, he wrote to Moses, then parks commissioner. Nor did he want to be a patron for something as minor as a marionette theater, Moses's second suggestion. Hartford would do for Central Park what Moses had done for New York City: he would rebuild it.

Hartford wrote to Moses suggesting that the park have a promenade of outdoor cafés, a small Champs-Élysées beginning at Central Park South and extending up to the Reservoir. He wanted to recast the park as New York's version of the Tivoli Gardens or the Bois de Boulogne. In June 1960, the heir announced that he would donate $750,000 for the first step in the Europeanization of Central Park: the Hartford Pavilion, a 10,000-square-foot two-story café, designed by Edward Durell Stone.

Although Moses championed Hartford's cause, Manhattan's citizenry did not. In one of the first battles waged against the overdevelopment of the city—battles now commonplace as residents strive to save Manhattan's singular silhouette—the 795 Fifth Ave. Corp., a group of merchants headed by Tiffany & Co., sued to keep Hartford from building. The group declared that implementation of the plan was an unlawful use of public space and that Hartford was destroying what little green was left in the city.

Not only were the merchants against him, so was *The New York Times,* whose influential architecture critic Ada Louise Huxtable blasted the pavilion in a column titled "More on How to Kill a City." She called the café "a good idea gone very bad" and assessed its sponsor as having "a gift for backfiring cultural gestures."

The case against the café took six years to drag through the courts. In the end, Hartford won the right to build, but his victory proved Pyrrhic. Months after the courts ruled in Hartford's favor, John Lindsay was elected mayor (no thanks to Hartford, who had donated some $25,000 to Lindsay's opponent, Mario Procaccino), and his parks commissioner, Thomas Hoving, announced that the city was rescinding its approval for the café.

The ascension of John Lindsay reflected the changed politics of New York City. The era of the Moses *geste majestueux* was over; the master builder had lost his mandate for revamping New York City.

"During the Great Depression, if Moses threw his support behind something, it was bound to get built," explained Hoving. "By the time Lindsay was elected, just about the reverse was true. If Moses favored a project, it was doomed from the start. The notion was that Hartford was giving a gift to the city, but it didn't look as if the café's revenues would meet its expenses. Even though Hartford was putting up the money, the city was going to end up supporting this structure with Hartford's name on it.

"Hartford thought he could make something happen because Moses was on his side, that [his money] made him a cut above, [that] he could do as he pleased with an aristocratic wave of the hand. It might have worked in the eighteenth century, or even the nineteenth century, but by then [the early sixties] we'd seen a lot of that in New York. Hartford simply had a total lack of perception of things that were changing."

Hoving compared Hartford with Nelson Rockefeller: "They were rich and powerful from the very beginning. They assumed because they said it, it had to be right. Their wealth enabled them to override all other concerns."

The New Yorker took its own sly jab at the heir: the magazine ran a cartoon showing a hunched-over hot-dog vendor pushing his cart along the sidewalk bordering Central Park. A policeman faces him, arms folded, holster on his side. The caption: "I recognize you, Mr. Huntington Hartford! Now move along!"

And in the end the newspapers had the last laugh. In March 1966, the city returned the $862,500 Hartford had donated for his café—plus interest. The headline in the *New York Herald Tribune* read: "Hartford Gets $22,000 Profit on Café Failure." Hartford, who was in it for everything but the money, came off looking like a profiteer.

Ultimately, the café, the artists' colony, the theater, even the promise of a tropical paradise, could not buy Hartford back his marriage. By 1960, Hunt and Marjorie's union had foundered beyond salvation. For Marjo-

The Hartfords' anniversary (George and Josephine Hartford, seated front left; Edward Hartford, standing left). By 1911 the family was awash in the revelry of new money. *(Courtesy of The Hartford Family Foundation)*

Huntington Hartford. He had an opulent, isolated childhood. *(W. S. Ritch)*

Princess Henrietta and Prince Guido Pignatelli (1937). Obtaining a title was another of Henrietta's passé attempts at establishing social legitimacy. *(AP/Wide World Photos)*

Mary Barton. Dozens of red roses surrounded her deathbed. *(Photo by Bruno of Hollywood. Courtesy of Wayne Headrick)*

The Huntington Hartford Theatre in Los Angeles (1954). Hartford, who wanted to bring culture to Babylon, received a special commendation from the city; years later, the city would strip his name off the building. *(Los Angeles Herald-Examiner)*

Hartford with Lana Turner (1946). The heir trailed a parade of evanescent beauties. *(UPI/Bettmann Newsphotos)*

George, John, and Huntington Hartford (1947). The uncles never wanted family members to work for the A&P. *(Courtesy of The Hartford Family Foundation)*

Cathy, Marjorie, and Jackie Hartford (1956). "I had the most beautiful mother and father," Cathy said, "but I never felt my parents were a part of my life." *(UPI/Bettmann Newsphotos)*

Ed Barton with Florence Brangenberg (1955). He sued so he could use his father's name. *(AP/Wide World Photos)*

Robert Moses welcoming Hartford's gallery to Columbus Circle (1964). *The New York Times* said the building "bordered on poetic grotesquerie." *(Jack Manning/ NYT Pictures)*

Hunt and Diane Hartford (center) with Salvador and Gala Dalí. Hartford became convinced that the surrealist was a genius. *(Paul Cordes)*

Hartford with Richard Nixon. The perfidy on Paradise Island touched everyone from the ex-president to Howard Hughes.

With Cathy Hartford on Paradise Island. "Just tell me that you love me," she begged him. *(Mort Kaye Studios)*

Juliet Hartford "was a little girl who wanted her father to be someone other than who he was," his nurse said. *(Courtesy of Juliet Hartford)*

"This is really like a prison, you know," Hartford said of his house on East Thirtieth Street. *(Annie Leibovitz/Contact Press Images)*

rie, the endless, anonymous retinue of young women who drifted through her husband's life had made her own existence unbearable. "The trouble was, she could not handle Huntington and his actions," recalled Sy Alter. "Hunt never [ended] them, though, they [did]: you don't divorce your mother."

There were endless parties at One Beekman Place, dinners where the action was in the bedroom, not at the dinner table. "If you went to a party, he wanted you to watch him with other people," explained John Ireland, a reluctant guest at the Hartford table. At one dinner, Ireland recalled, he was asked to exchange his wife for another guest. "That's when I stopped going," he said, and, as he saw it, he wasn't the only one reluctant to participate. "I don't think [his wife] was into that either."

At first, Marjorie perceived the relentless procession of girls as simply competition for her own role in her husband's life. "I was in a state of jealousy all the time," she said. But over time she came to see that her husband's inexhaustible flirtations had to do less with love than with a crazy search for an icon of physical perfection, a slim-hipped virgin that she, the mother of his children, could never be. "Finally I realized it would be impossible for him to find *the* one. Once I understood this I didn't have the jealousy, but I had the humiliation. I had to bodily push some of these girls out."

She recounted one typical incident in London. Although they were separated much of the time, Marjorie naively expected her husband would maintain at least the illusion of monogamy when she came to visit. "I was with my sister in the south of France," she recalled, "and we were going back to England to stay at Red Lion Yard with Hunt. Knowing him as I did, I called up in advance to tell him when we would be coming. He said, 'Marvelous, I'm delighted.'

"I arrived. I went into the house. I went into my bedroom and the whole room had been changed. I went into my closet; all my clothes had been taken down and thrown in a box, and another girl's clothes were there."

Hunt came in and Marjorie vented her fury. "I warned you," she said. "Why do you do this to me?"

"You know I love you," he answered. "I don't love these girls."

"That's not the point," she replied. "This is humiliating."

Marjorie started throwing herself at other men, perhaps in hopes of rekindling her husband's attention. And although Hartford responded to his wife's histrionics, his reaction was hardly the contrition she hoped for.

Robert Wool, then a young editor at *Look* magazine, told of calling on Hartford at his London townhouse. Marjorie was there, along with the tennis pro Pancho Gonzales and a teenager who was clearly Hartford's companion for the evening.

"Marjorie was drunk. She kept sitting in Gonzales's lap," Wool said. "Gonzales didn't know what to do. He and I went downstairs to get out of the scene, started to sit on the sofa talking." Hartford's girlfriend, meanwhile, became unaccountably furious. She charged downstairs and started heaving things—ink blotters, letter openers, lamps—at them in the hope that they, and Marjorie, would leave.

"Pancho finally said, 'I've had it,' and walked out into the courtyard," Wool recalled. "Marjorie came running out afterward screaming, 'Pancho, Pancho,' then dropped at his feet and passed out." Gonzales picked Marjorie up, carried her inside, and put her on the sofa, then began brushing away the glass from the broken lamps and muttering, "I'm through with this, I'm leaving."

The master of the house took in the scene from the top of the stairs, giggling throughout. Said Wool, "For him it was some kind of comic nightmare."

As Sy Alter put it, "That marriage had to end."

Hartford, of course, didn't see it that way. Indeed, he seemed altogether blind to the fact that there was anything wrong with their relationship at all. When Marjorie suggested divorce, Hunt simply patted her on the head and told her, "But we have the most perfect marriage."

"At this stage," recalled Marjorie, "I was hardly with him at all." Still, the charade continued for a few months more, until it all fell apart in an awful confrontation on Paradise Island. One spring afternoon Marjorie appeared, unannounced, calling from the Nassau airport to say that she had arrived. Hartford told her she couldn't stay in the house, that there wasn't any room.

"But we sleep in the same bed," Marjorie responded.

Hartford, trying to stall, told her to wait for him at the Mermaid Tavern, a restaurant in Nassau. He was there within an hour, but by then it was too late. Marjorie had lost patience and was getting ready to leave with a friend, a strapping skin-diver named Art Pinder. When the couple attempted to drive off, Hartford would not let them go. "Hunt got on the hood, holding onto the windshield wiper," recalled Marjorie.

When that proved futile, "he jumped in a local taxi with a huge native that looked tougher than Art. Art started to drive; Hunt followed fast behind. Art pulled off to the side of the road, and the taxi driver came over and started to open our door. Art slammed it and we drove off.

"The next morning I called the house and said, 'I'm coming over, we have to talk about this, it has gotten too ridiculous.' He was sitting on the porch with a young, silly little girl. I told him I'd had it, I wanted a divorce."

Cathy and Jackie Hartford, then about to turn ten and seven, had missed most of the domestic drama; they were on vacation in West Germany with their nurse. Now, her mind finally decided on divorce, Marjorie flew to Europe and brought them back to the States in secret, flying first to Newark, then to Miami. There, in a rented house, she spent the summer and fall, keeping the children from their father and from newspaper stories of the Hartford split.

On October 20, 1960, in New York City, she officially filed for divorce. "Mrs. Hartford Asks All the $ From A to P" broadcast the *New York Post*. "Mrs. A&P Asks $1,000 Daily for Groceries and Other Bills" the New York *Daily News* announced. What Marjorie actually asked for was an unprecedented $25 million, half of what she believed her husband's net worth to be (in reality it was probably closer to $70 million), plus $1,000 a day for expenses.

In 1960, adultery was the only grounds for divorce in New York, and Marjorie came to court loaded with evidence. "Says World Was Mr. A&P's Bedroom" read the *Daily News* headline when Marjorie's charges became public. She claimed that her husband had dallied with six different women; although the women went unnamed, the dates and locales of the assignations did not. Moreover, Marjorie stated, he often brought not only her but several other female companions to the same social functions.

Hartford, in London at the time, still persisted in trying to save his marriage. He didn't want Marjorie to leave him, he said, and he aired his misery to anyone who would listen. What did the millionaire want for Christmas? "Me? I just want my wife back," he told a reporter for London's *Daily Sketch*, one of the tackier British tabloids.

Christmas came and went, and in February the case was brought to trial. Marjorie, demure in a blue blouse and pup-seal jacket, her hair in a pert pageboy, spent six minutes on the stand. Two other witnesses supported her claims of adultery.

Hunt Hartford never countered Marjorie's claims; he had a paralyzing distaste for any kind of confrontation, and he was terrified of appearing in court. Hours before he was scheduled to testify, Hartford agreed to a settlement. His second marriage was over.

Marjorie received considerably less than she had requested: $385,000 outright, plus two trusts totaling $2 million for the children. In addition, there would be $60,000 in annual alimony. As Marjorie left the court-room, from which the press had been barred, reporters clustered around her. Was she satisfied with the settlement? "I did not marry him for his money," she told one reporter, "and I am not divorcing him for his money."

Marjorie proved her point within a year. In November 1961, she married her attorney's stepson, a struggling actor named Dudley Sutton, and thereby sacrificed her alimony. "Honestly, the money was an embarrassment," she told a reporter after her second wedding. "Put it this way—we had yachts. The yachts sailed away. So what?"

Just after the divorce, in a moment of sour serendipity, Ed "Buzz" Barton reentered his father's life.

After the paternity suit failed in 1955, Barton had drifted away. He quietly finished his last two years of high school, then moved on to Santa Monica City College, his ambitions as fuzzy as his father's before him.

Florence Brangenberg died in 1959 and left Barton with a trust fund that paid out roughly $50,000 a year. He had one close friend, Wayne Headrick, a handsome Californian who was more interested in sports than studies.

"We would cut classes together, go to parties together," recalled Headrick. "One afternoon we went bowling [and] drank a bunch of beer, and he told me the whole story with Hartford and all. Buzz said, 'Why don't you come back to New York with me and see Hartford? I haven't seen him in years. Let's see what happens.' "

With an impetuosity born of adolescence, the two teenagers climbed into a car and drove to New York in search of Barton's paternity. They checked into the Plaza Hotel and called Hartford. At first, all was friendly. Hartford met with his son and told him he would pay for the boys' stay in New York. But when Barton said that he was less interested in the money than he was in the Hartford name, things started to grow tense.

"The two of them together were so damn nervous they could hardly talk," Headrick said. "It got down to where they were talking about the weather." Age had only increased the resemblance between father and son: not only did they look alike ("dead ringers," said Headrick), they shared that fear of confrontation.

Barton and Headrick stayed in New York for perhaps a month, and Headrick became the intermediary between father and son. He joined the retinue that Hartford kept in attendance at Beekman Place. Some of the men in Hartford's paper-strewn living room were associated with projects Hartford had already bought into; even more were there with projects they were trying to sell. "There were always these girls, from all over the world," remembered Headrick. "Hartford had the pick of the prettiest girls around, and he would just keep them there, two, three weeks at a time. It was a real power thing, all these people hanging around trying to see him. He'd see someone for ten or fifteen minutes, then close down shop and tell everybody to go away and come back in an hour. He gave people a taste of power and money, the illusion that they might get it. It was like a cat tantalizing a wounded bird."

Hunt toyed with his son as he did with all the others. He told Headrick he wanted Buzz to stay close, in New York. "He sent me back to tell Buzz that he wanted to give him a good education—Harvard, Princeton, Yale. Hunt promised he would eventually give Buzz the name and let him come into the family. . . . I couldn't wait to get back to the hotel room to tell Buzz."

But Ed Barton had little faith in the promises of a man who invited him to social functions at Beekman Place, then introduced him as "my good friend." "He's lied to me my whole life," he told Headrick. "I can go to school or do whatever he wants me to do, but I want the name now."

Headrick returned the next day and told Hartford what Buzz wanted. Hartford refused. "[He] would include people in his life, then turn them off completely—that's what he did with Buzz," Headrick said. "Money gave him the power to manipulate people like that; it was a hurting game."

Finally, Barton instructed Headrick: "Tell him I want the money out of my trust fund, and the hell with it." Hartford said the boys would have to see the trustee, who in turn told them liquidation was impossible. And so, temporarily stymied, the pair went back to Los Angeles.

Hartford started calling within days of their return. Buzz told his father that if he would not give him the Hartford name he did not want to speak to him. Hartford then called Headrick and asked to meet him in London in order to discuss his son. This time, Barton had instructed Headrick to tell his father that if he couldn't have his name, he wanted more of his money. "Have him give me fifty thousand in cash," Barton said.

Hartford agreed but, determined that the settlement not be publicized, insisted on a clandestine meeting in Little Rock, Arkansas, chosen for no other reason than its relative obscurity. Hartford's attorneys came armed with documents, papers in which Barton gave away everything, promising never to change his name to Hartford, never again to lay claim to the name.

Edward Barton put his signature on the papers and took his father's dollars, but he still held onto the hope of winning the Hartford name.

12

"*H*E WAS like a young sultan in a seraglio, his mind spoiled by women and overindulgence from a very young age," said one of the many men Hartford hired to realize his many projects. "Still, he honestly wanted to do something about the arts."

By the fall of 1961, Hartford's amorphous "something" involved a gaggle of ventures, all in varying degrees of development. There was the museum, the café, the island, and the Handwriting Institute. There was even an automated parking garage in midtown Manhattan, Speed Park, a mad scheme to solve the urban parking crisis by means of a computerized elevator system run by a single employee. Hartford's foundation and theater were still limping along in California, although their creator had not been there to see them in more than six years. "I'm inclined to think, after doing a lot of things, that their meaning evolves and becomes apparent eventually," he explained.

Hartford was constructing a random aesthetic conglomerate, a jerry-built machine whose continued existence required incessant infusions of cash. "The more Hunt builds," explained his second wife, "the more he has to build." The trouble with all the building was that precious little proceeded according to plan. Over on Columbus Circle in New York City, the museum plan was foundering. The difficulties started when the Museum of Modern Art sued Hartford, claiming that his calling the projected museum the Gallery of Modern Art would "dilute the distinctive quality" of the collection of the established museum, potentially diverting goodwill and donations and certainly confusing the public.

Hartford finally reached a settlement with MoMA: he would include his name on the new museum's façade. The recalcitrant shoe store owner on the first floor of the old building proved less tractable. He brought the museum construction to a dead halt, before finally agreeing to give up his lease in 1961.

And then, that May, the director of the museum project, Winslow Ames, quit. He had been hired four years before, to take the project from blueprint to ribbon-cutting. But when he tried to advise Hartford on the inadequacy of gallery space in the museum, his employer would hear none of it. Differences over interior design weren't the only source of friction; Ames found Hartford's scattered mien intolerable. "You never knew when he would appear," complained Ames. "He was utterly unreliable." Worse, Ames said, Hartford's acquisitions seemed bound up with his appetites. "The only way he shopped for art was to go out with some babe and use the purchase as a way to impress her. Hartford would regularly call up from somewhere a thousand miles away and say he had just seen some painting or another with a girl he was with and was desperate to buy it. I would say, 'Send a photograph'—they never came. Then he would turn up with some third-rate painting that he would insist on putting out for show."

One of the biggest sticking points involved Marjorie's paintings. Despite the divorce, Hartford remained a strong proponent of her talent, and he ordered Ames to devote a gallery to her work.

Ames finally ran out of patience with a museum that couldn't get built and a patron who was more interested in the taste of the teenager on his arm than the judgment of the man he hired for the job. With such demands for fiscal and creative control as he had, Hartford would spend three years trying to find a replacement.

Stymied in his efforts to build a place where New Yorkers could go to absorb culture, Hartford style, the heir decided he would bring culture into their homes, with his own magazine. The idea was born during a dinner-party conversation with John Crosby, a television writer for the *New York Herald Tribune* and one of the first critics to take the medium seriously. Hartford wanted Crosby to lead the project, but the critic instead recommended the young editor at *Look,* Robert Wool.

Wool and Hartford met one morning at Beekman Place. Hartford was in a robe and the trademark leather slippers he wore virtually everywhere. (Society photographs from the fifties and sixties show Hartford, black-tie immaculate, his feet in backless slippers more fitting for a flannel-robed Robert Young in a breakfast scene from *Father Knows*

Best.) Hartford described to Wool his loose vision: a chronicle of culture, a latter-day *Vanity Fair,* whose first incarnation had folded a quarter-century before. Wool accepted Hartford's propositions almost instantly. "When a man as rich as Huntington Hartford wants to start a magazine, you are obligated," he explained.

Hartford told Wool that he should work out the specifics of the magazine's finances when his attorneys, Aaron Frosch (an entertainment lawyer who represented, among others, Marilyn Monroe) and David Sher, arrived. The two men entered within the hour. Hartford first announced he was about to leave for England, then introduced his new employee. "This is Robert Wool, and he's going to start my magazine," Hartford told Frosch and Sher. The meeting that followed, Wool recalled, was terribly awkward; it rapidly became apparent that the lawyers, hired to hold the reins on the heir's empire, had no prior notice of his publishing ambitions.

As Wool told it, Hartford was like a naughty child, abashed at being found with his hand deep inside a cookie jar. And although Frosch and Sher made their disapproval known, it had little effect. Hartford departed for London, leaving Wool to begin development on the magazine, christened *Show.*

Hartford pumped in $1 million over the first year, enough to buy the best talent in the business. Henry Wolf, an Austrian-born art director who had made his reputation as a photographer for *Harper's Bazaar,* was taken on initially free-lance, then full-time. The first issues were a sort of cadenza on *Life.* But where that weekly hewed to the core of America, *Show* danced on the coasts.

The choreography was impeccable. The cover of the inaugural issue, dated October 1961, had an outlined numeral 1 framing a collage of cultural icons of the day: Louis Armstrong's trumpet, a television screen surrounding Gene Autry's shotgun, opera glasses, and a contact-sheet clip of Marilyn Monroe's Cupid's-bow lips, aflame with red lipstick. Inside were Martin Mayer on the ABC television network, Robert Kotlowitz on Arthur Rubinstein, and Kenneth Tynan on Orson Welles. Helen Hayes and Anne Bancroft contributed essays on the art of acting, while the critic Harold Clurman weighed in with a dissection of the essence of glamour.

As with his other projects, Hartford dabbled from afar He hired Helen Lawrenson, a flamboyant journalist who flaunted her Communist Party membership and covered everything from Hollywood to oral sex ("Why Latins Make Lousy Lovers"), as shepherd for his ideas. Hartford's most insistent notion was what Lawrenson described as the "girl feature," a

clutch of pages showcasing "talented" (for Hartford, virtually synony-
mous with nubile) young women. Here were Hugh Hefner's Playmates
without the raunch, a curiously chaste carnal fantasy.

Lawrenson was assigned to interview the candidates, then arrange to
have the most promising photographed. There was a compulsive method
to the madness of the chase. According to Edward Collins, who had
moved from the modeling agency to become a general public-relations
man for Hartford, his boss never left home without a size-ten envelope
in his jacket pocket, along with a couple of pencils. "At parties, he
would write down girls' names and numbers, and draw a line under
them. Then there would be a code under each one to jog his memory.
'YCV' meant 'young Catholic virgin.' He'd come in at night after two
or three parties and he might have filled the backs of one or two enve-
lopes; he'd leave them on his desk, and in the morning secretaries would
copy them so there would be a record.

"He wasn't sleeping with most of them," Collins added. He wanted
their acceptance, their approval. "There was a desperation about him,
a sadness, for these young girls."

Hartford lent legitimacy to his chase with his business cards. They
were embossed "Hunt Hartford / *Show* Projects Editor," and Hartford
used them as currency to buy the attention of any young woman who
caught his eye. They were handed out at parties, in restaurants, on the
streets of New York—he didn't shy away from stopping a cab in traffic
to push one through the window.

"I remember walking up Madison Avenue with him," said Collins,
"and in mid-conversation he spotted this girl taking off across the street,
ducking between buses and cabs. He was back a few minutes later and
said, 'Bitch. Wouldn't give me her name.' "

Hartford would return from his annual trip to Europe with a list of
women's names; Lawrenson had to contact all of the women. Further,
she was to request nominations from selected girls' schools; she cased
the forty-two female guides at the United Nations, checked out the win-
ners of music contests, surveyed every possible field that might include
pretty young women.

"I felt like Florence Reed playing Mother Goddam in *The Shanghai
Gesture*," Lawrenson wrote in *Whistling Girl*. Pretty young women filed
through the office by the score. "He had them sent in like swatches for
his approval," she recalled.

Hartford's first subject for "Double Exposure," as the "girl feature"
was titled, was discovered in the pages of *Bride's*—an exquisite brunette
in a virgin-white gown. Hartford pursued the woman, Diane Brown, at

a photographer's party and invited her to an interview. Brown, then nineteen, told Lawrenson she came from a mining community in Pennsylvania. Trying to prove some connection with the arts was difficult, Lawrenson recounted. Brown had no ambition for a career in theater or film. "It's too hard work," she told Lawrenson.

Did she paint? Lawrenson asked.

"No."

Play a musical instrument or sing?

"No."

She was a model, wasn't she?

"No. Not really."

Finally, in desperation, Lawrenson asked, "What can you do?"

"I can milk a cow," Brown answered. "It was," Lawrenson noted wryly, "a talent few of us at *Show* could boast."

But while Diane Brown lacked even the pretense of ambition, she was a breathtaking beauty; Hartford insisted she be used. On one page the teenager was shown with her hair tousled, face freckled. On the facing leaf she was bare-shouldered, a beehived sophisticate. Diane Brown may not have had a future in Hollywood, but she did have one with *Show*'s publisher.

For much of the next year Diane was at Hartford's side, accompanying him as he dashed from New York to London to the Bahamas, where he was becoming a one-man Marshall Plan—building roads, dredging a yacht basin, refurbishing a public beach, and erecting the island's centerpiece, a fifty-two-room hotel called the Ocean Club, a two-story colonial building surrounding a gracious courtyard.

Hartford's insistent idealism was omnipresent; etched on every glass door opening onto the central courtyard was the single word PEACE, and just across from the hotel rose a hill that Hartford had landscaped into a stepped series of gardens. Each of the first few levels was marked by a single sculpture, while an unlikely pair of bronzes graced the penultimate rise. One was a massive David Livingstone, the explorer; just across the green lawn, Franklin Delano Roosevelt stood with cape and cane, just as he did in Grosvenor Square in London. And perhaps five city blocks from the hotel, Hartford constructed a cluster of columns and arches, topping his Tivoli Gardens off with a nunnery. The latter was a monument to Hartford's overindulgence, a medieval cloister bought from the estate of William Randolph Hearst. Hartford had it shipped over from Florida, where it had been taken apart stone by stone. It took a European mason a full year to reconstruct the building.

There was much, much more. A mile from the main club Hartford built the Café Martinique, a three-star French restaurant. The details were impeccable: the men's lavatory had silver fixtures, the women's gold. The ashtrays mimicked the jockeys standing in attendance outside the "21" Club in New York, small brass servants holding trays for the guests' cigarettes. (Most were gone after the first weekend gala.)

Hartford briefly considered building a bridge to Nassau, but he ultimately dismissed the notion, concerned that making the resort more accessible to the public would also cheapen it. Instead, a regular ferry ran the five hundred yards to Nassau; for guests who cared to dock their own yachts, Hartford had a score of slips built just outside the Mermaid Tavern. For transportation on the island there were a dozen surreys, drawn by Nova Scotia horses.

Tennis courts were overseen by the great Pancho Gonzales. The golf pro Dick Wilson designed a nine-hole seaside course, where nature was everywhere to be overcome; sand would ravage the greens so badly that they required constant resodding. All told, 130 gardeners were on staff to keep the golf course and the rest of the island properly landscaped.

The price tag for the development was more than $20 million. Hartford told one reporter he hoped the resort would move into the black after five years, but that had more to do with boundless optimism than financial sense. Paradise Island was a fiscal fantasy, built without a business plan. Had there been one, the bottom line would have been all too apparent: there was no way revenues from a fifty-two-room hotel could support the kind of development Hartford was backing. "We could charge twenty dollars a drink and still lose money," said François Masari, one of Hartford's Paradise Island employees.

But Hartford had no desire to see his money quietly accrue interest in a bank; clipping bond coupons and collecting stock dividends left him cold. Profits, he felt, were not the province of one who had a fortune to tend; the bottom line debased the ideology of his aesthetic empire. "You see," Hartford told a reporter, "the idea is to give as much as you can and not worry about the returns."

Even his attorneys knew their client's story could not possibly have a happy ending. "I remember once sitting down at the Ocean Club," recalled Phyllis Sher, "and Hunt told my husband that he wanted to die broke. And my husband sighed, then said, 'But Hunt, you may have to live broke.' "

▲

Back in New York, *Show* chugged along, establishing cultural credibility. The November 1961 issue, for example, featured "The Soft Mythology of Jazz," by Nat Hentoff, then gaining a reputation as a writer for *The Village Voice,* and S. J. Perelman's war stories from the filming of *Monkey Business* with the Marx Brothers. While the magazine was making editorial strides, commercial success proved elusive. *Show* was failing to meet its circulation guarantees, and the 102-page December issue had an abysmal eight pages of advertising.

Hartford decided that the problem was the editor, Robert Wool. In early 1962, Hartford asked Frank Gibney, who had just launched a similar magazine for Hugh Hefner, what he thought of *Show.* "It's like a beautifully gilded dead fish," Gibney told him. "It looks lovely, but there's no life in it."

Hartford invited him to take over the publication. When Gibney accepted the invitation, he discovered the party a shambles. "It was a bombed-out shelter with no circulation to speak of and seven pages of ads," said Joe Coleman, the advertising manager Gibney brought along from Hefner's *Show Business Illustrated.*

Coleman and Gibney came up with a notion for boosting *Show*'s flagging circulation: they urged Hartford to buy Hefner's competing publication. It was easy to persuade Hefner to sell; his magazine was hemorrhaging about $75,000 an issue, and although *Show* was losing $25,000 more, Hartford had far deeper pockets than his Chicago competitor. On February 2, 1963, Hartford announced that he had arranged for *Show* to absorb *Show Business Illustrated;* he paid Hefner just over $250,000 for the privilege.

While the purchase goosed circulation, it didn't do much for what Gibney (along with every other *Show* editor save Lawrenson) considered the magazine's biggest problem: "What we couldn't buy was an owner with any sense of judgment," he said. "Hartford liked dealing with extreme situations. Doing business became a matter of scripting a drama. I'd say, 'We desperately need money.' Hartford would say, 'How many pages can you bring in?' I'd say, 'I'll stake my professional reputation that we can bring in twenty-five.' Then Hartford would turn to his lawyers and say, 'See, Frank is basing his professional reputation on twenty-five pages, so they're going to have twenty-five pages. Give them the money.' "

Successes had to be turned histrionic in order to catch Hartford's attention. "You couldn't just tell Hartford that you got an extra ten pages of advertising," explained Gibney. "You had to say, 'Well, maybe we'll get five,' then . . . come back and say, 'Oh, we've got seven,' and so on. It was cuckooland. Hartford didn't have his feet on the ground, and no one had a professional reputation at stake to make sure that they were.''

While Gibney professed to prefer Hartford's company to Hefner's, the heir's erratic management drove him to distraction. "At dinner with Hefner there would be a few comments about *la dolce vita,* but after that there was nothing. You could always raise Hartford up to some level,'' reflected Gibney. "Hartford had a vested interest in maintaining social norms, perhaps all the more because he was smashing them to bits with his social behavior. Hughie was and is a kind of animal.'' Still, it was those carnal qualities that fed Hefner's success. As Gibney saw it, Hefner, unlike Hartford, "was a good publisher because he had a vision of what he wanted to do with his magazine. He was a modern version of the Methodist preacher who sold liquor to the Indians on the side. He understood the basics of business.''

Hartford, even as he was publishing a high-minded journal of culture, insisted that the "girl feature'' be included in every issue. And those pages became bargaining chits in his unending battles with the editors of the magazine. If Hartford could get his young women in, he was willing to give ground to abstract art; he even allowed a feature on Henry Moore. "I'll let you have Moore, if you'll let me have four pages for the girls,'' he told Henry Wolf. The deal was struck: in the March 1963 issue, there were six pages on Henry Moore's studio in Hertfordshire, with photographs by Irving Penn; there were also four pages on Ingrun ("Call me Inkie'') Moeckel, a German fashion model.

"I was born with long legs and a marvelous digestive apparatus,'' Inkie commented in one caption. "I am wooed by so many men and boys,'' she said, in a remark seemingly directed at *Show's* publisher. "I know they think I can be made to topple. But I know what I am doing. I can make them feel very small, make them desperate.''

Hartford had other story ideas for the magazine, fits of aggressive nostalgia that were at sharp variance with the avant-garde notions of the editors. He wanted—and got—an article about a British poet who wrote "India Love Lyrics'' ("Pale hands I loved beside the Shalimar'') under the pseudonym Laurence Hope; a spread of pictures of old cowboy stars (William S. Hart, "Broncho Billy'' Anderson, Tom Mix); and even Enrico Caruso's account of his experience in the great San Francisco earthquake and fire.

Once, when the magazine was running short of cash, Hartford promised a $1 million infusion if Gibney would run a gatefold reproduction of the 145-by-195-foot crucifixion mural at Forest Lawn Cemetery, and an article on the Polish artist, Jan Styka, who had painted it. "As a young man, [Styka] often painted during the day and spent the nights drinking and dancing the mazurka until dawn," wrote the unnamed author who profiled the artist, who finished his mammoth work in 1895. The piece went on to describe the crypt where Styka was buried, which was in the Memorial Court of Honor, a mausoleum Forest Lawn's founder grandiosely called "the American Westminster Abbey." Styka's tablet bore a color reproduction of an artist's palette, and a tribute written by Billy Graham. According to the *Show* article, one of the privileged few elected (by the Forest Lawn Council of Regents) to share Styka's eternal sanctum was Carrie Jacobs-Bond, composer of the songs "I Love You Truly" and "Just A-Wearyin' for You." "Everyone except Hartford thought [the article] was hilarious and high camp," remembered Gibney. "And it did save the magazine."

In spite of Hartford's occasional folly, his journal was making a bid for intellectual consequence. And the heir made good his intentions to use Paradise Island as a cultural retreat; he held an "Inter-American Symposium" on the island, designed to bring North American artists and intellectuals into closer contact with their Latin American counterparts. Hartford not only agreed to cover everyone's travel expenses but also put up the participants for the length of the five-day conference. The North Americans were better known than the Latin Americans: Norman Podhoretz was there, as were Gore Vidal, William Styron, Arthur Schlesinger, Jr. (*Show*'s film critic), and Aaron Copland. The Latin American contingent included the Chilean playwright Luis Heiremans, the Colombian composer Guillermo Espinosa, and Alfredo Pareja, a historian from Ecuador. The symposium turned out to be more St.-Tropez than Dumbarton Oaks. The quality of the conversation could not keep up with the halcyon surroundings; the participants were lulled by the same euphoria that had dulled Seymour Krim at Hartford's California artists' colony.

As Podhoretz wrote years later in *Making It,* he finally understood "what it meant to be rich . . . to stretch one's arms out idly by the side of a swimming pool and have two white-coated servants vie for the privilege of depositing a Bloody Mary into one's hand, to sign checks (which we had to do, though of course we would never have to pay them) without giving money a second thought. . . . It meant that a serene self-assurance had been injected into the spirit to combat the uncertainties and anxieties which, to be sure, remained, but no longer had the field to themselves."

The conference and the magazine, like the foundation and the play that came before them, were bids by Hartford for immortality, bids that were destined to fail. "Hartford wanted the public to say he was a great man, and he always thought every project he started—and this was by no means the first—would make him a star," explained Henry Wolf. "Each project was like a romantic love he couldn't get. As soon as he came close to attaining it the bubble burst, and he wanted to move on to the next."

By Saturday, February 17, 1962, the bubble had expanded to gargantuan proportions. On that sultry evening, Hartford officially opened Paradise Island with a no-expense-spared party for two thousand. He chartered a Pan American jet to fly celebrities and other guests down from New York, and hired hostesses for the launches that brought the guests over from Nassau. Hartford also picked up the tab for the visitors who filled the fifty-two rooms at the Ocean Club and spilled over into hotels in Nassau. "When you arrived they personally escorted you to a horse-drawn carriage. Nothing was left out—the caviar and champagne were flowing," recalled Phyllis Sher.

Hartford flew in fireworks experts from Monaco to light the winter sky. The guests danced to the Meyer Davis Orchestra, which introduced the "steel twist," a variation on Fats Domino's standard. Zsa Zsa Gabor came, along with the Tony Randalls, the Clyde Newhouses, and Christina Paolozzi (the model who made her fame as the first to expose her breasts in a fashion magazine, *Harper's Bazaar*).

New York society columnists raved. In the *Journal-American,* Igor Cassini, who had replaced Maury Paul as "Cholly Knickerbocker," headlined his column "Hartford's Party the Most." In the *Daily News,* Aileen Mehle weighed in with similarly lavish praise, seduced by the white roses in her bedroom. "What's he going to do for an encore," she asked, "Versailles?"

While society columnists scattered billets-doux before the heir, the general press was losing patience with his slatternly spending. *Newsweek* was among the first to pop the Paradise mystique:

> George Huntington Hartford II . . . likes beautiful women, racquet games, traditional art, Monopoly, casual clothes, Fig Newtons, handwriting, London, and show business. As he puts it, he is also "a creator." Last week Hartford put on display his latest, greatest creation, Paradise Island, an exotic $25 million resort in the Bahamas. . . . As the night wore on, white and flamingo-pink fireworks

. . . blossomed in the sky, drawing Oooooos! from bishops and
British earls.

Seated on garden steps, unobtrusively watching the fireworks, the
fifty-year-old host sighed gently. "I'm pleased," he said. This is
less than surprising. Paradise Island would stir the envy of mad King
Ludwig, the castle-building buff of Bavaria.

Hartford waxed especially eloquent on the subject of Paradise Tennis,
a game of his own invention played with a tennis ball on an enlarged
Ping-Pong table. The morning after the Saturday gala he organized an
exhibition—Don Budge, former U.S. tennis champion, against Pancho
Gonzales. Of the hundreds of guests browsing around the Ocean Club,
only twenty watched. But the sorry turnout didn't matter to the game's
inventor. Noted the *Newsweek* reporter: "Hartford was happy, creating."

Diane Brown was quite visibly by Hunt Hartford's side when he
opened Paradise Island, and a month later, he started referring to her as
his fiancée. For Diane, who at eighteen had been given a ticket to New
York by her father and instructed to find her way in the world, Hartford
was an excellent catch. With his Bahamas tan, gleaming white smile,
and full head of silver-streaked hair he cut an elegant figure. And as
Diane herself later noted, "There weren't that many good-looking heirs
around."

"I guess she was looking for a rich man, there's no law against that,"
said Edward Collins, Hartford's former public-relations man, "and
Hartford certainly fit the bill."

While Diane may have been a bit of the adventuress, she wasn't driven
solely by dollars. Indeed, it was Diane who insisted that she and Hartford postpone their wedding until after her twenty-first birthday so that
she could sign a prenuptial agreement limiting her access to his fortune
should they divorce. "I didn't want anyone to think I had married him
for his money," she said.

The beginning of Hartford's third marriage had the unpleasant resonance
of his honeymoon with Marjorie. As Sy Alter told it, things went amiss
from the moment the couple went to get the marriage license. "I'm
driving the Cadillac, and I pick up Hunt, Diane, and the two lawyers.
Hunt is sitting in the passenger seat next to me. Diane is in the back, a
lawyer on either side. My intention is to drive to the East River Drive,

go up to the George Washington Bridge, and proceed on to New Jersey. When I'm standing on Fifty-seventh Street, waiting to make a left on York to get onto the highway, Hunt kicks me with his knee, which means, 'I've spotted a girl.'

"Remember, we're going for a marriage license. I grit my teeth and I whisper to him, 'No.' I just sit there, quietly waiting for the light. He purses his lips and says, 'God damn it, stop the car when you make the turn.' The light changes, I make the turn. He hits me again with his knee. I figure, Screw it, and stop the car. Well, Diane's no fool. She says, 'What's he dashing out for?' She looks at him running down the street and says, 'That's it, let me out of the car.' You should have seen the two lawyers holding onto her. He comes back, he says nothing, which means the girl wasn't attractive. And after that we can't stop because we're on the highway."

Diane forgave Hunt that transgression, and on October 6, 1962, she joined the Hartford parade, convinced that she was the one who could make the heir behave. They were married at Melody Farm, in what was the most traditional of Hartford's weddings. Diane wore simple white wool; a local judge presided. Sy Alter's wife was Diane's matron of honor; Hartford's nephew, Columbus O'Donnell, served as his uncle's best man. A few other relatives turned out—Diane's parents; Hartford's niece, Nuala Pell, with her husband, Claiborne (the senator)—as well as the Kennedys' pal Lemoyne Billings and Mr. and Mrs. Edward Durell Stone. Hartford's two legitimate children attended: Jackie, then nine, behaved well; Cathy was more of a problem. Diane permitted her new stepdaughter three glasses of champagne during the reception. The twelve-year-old proceeded to drink every unfinished glass she could find, and passed out long before the party ended.

Taking on the role of stepmother to an almost-adolescent did not come easily to Hartford's twenty-one-year-old bride. Nor did Diane, a very pretty young woman from a very small town, smoothly assume the role of Mrs. Huntington Hartford. In the first months after her marriage, she did what very young wives of very rich men often do: she quickly, and awkwardly, assumed all manner of social pretensions. She took on an Anglified accent ("Pennsylvania British," the newspapers called it) and gave a literary retort when a reporter asked where she had learned how to marry a millionaire. "Balzac," she told them. "I read his marvelous book on marriage." Doubtless she was alluding to *The Physiology of Marriage,* in which the French writer discussed the impossibility of monogamy and the importance of friction in maintaining a union. "The day when a wife behaves nicely to her husband,'' he wrote, ''all is over.'' That lesson would serve Diane well.

When news of Hartford's third wedding hit the press, a London reporter stopped in on Marjorie to see if she had any thoughts on her ex-husband. She had plenty. ''I couldn't help feeling like one of his projects, a show-piece,'' Marjorie said. ''You become a sort of child of his—a spoiled child, not a wife at all. . . . With all that money you are supposed to get a sense of complete freedom, but you become caged in by unreal values. . . . He has so many projects planned and unfinished that his life [is] lived at an unbelieveable pace. He could cope with the telephone jangling every ten seconds and rise above it. . . . I've met Diane Brown; she is a sweet girl. She should get him to cut down on some of his projects. If I was going to give Diane any advice, it would be this: Don't become just another project.''

13

*I*T SEEMED only reasonable to believe that Huntington Hartford, the
heir who paid for culture to come
to Hollywood, who bought an island and turned it into Paradise, and
who promised to build a museum to immortalize his own sensibility,
had the wealth of Croesus. Columnists dubbed him one of the world's
wealthiest men. *The Saturday Evening Post* spelled out specifics, naming
Nelson Rockefeller and J. Paul Getty as Hartford's fiscal peers. A United
Press International reporter dubbed him ''an intellectual Howard
Hughes,'' and added, ''While Hughes is busy making money, Hartford
is spending his.'' Even *Esquire* joined the game, moving from fact to
hyperbole, reporting that there was some $500 million in the heir's cof-
fers and attributing the figure to the august *New York Times*. But that
number was off, by a factor of seven—and the exaggeration irritated
Hartford more with each incantation. Hartford was no Donald Trump,
reveling in exaltations of his wealth; he bristled at the overstatement,
oddly protestant in his descriptions of his fortune.

''Madness,'' he told a London reporter when asked whether he was
really worth $500 million, ''absolute madness. If you press me, I suppose
I'm worth . . . let's say $70 million. Everybody sees me as a bottomless
well. I'm not a bottomless well. Have we got that straight now?''

The Hartford relatives had it straight—and most of them were mysti-
fied. ''I can remember these wonderful figures floating around *The New
York Times*,'' recollected his cousin Michael McIntosh. ''Mr. Hartford
spends seven million on this, eight million on that, and [the money
added] up. We all knew how much each of us had, and when we saw
that we kept saying, 'Golly, where's it all going to come from?' ''

By the middle of 1963, Hartford's bankers started asking the same questions. Although he had started selling off his A&P stock as soon as it went public, the money from that was used primarily to maintain his seven households, settle his second marriage, and establish a charitable trust designed to provide him with income as long as he was alive and ensure that his projects survived even longer. Marjorie took the credit for persuading Hartford to set aside that fund. "When he bought the island, I asked him to set up a proper trust for us," said Marjorie. "I told him, 'You're going to go straight through your money.' I said, 'Put nine million away, that way you'll never be poor.' "

The millions used to launch his ventures came from Morgan Guaranty Trust in a loan collateralized by his A&P shares. "He didn't have enough cash to do the things he wanted to do, so he started taking on debt," recalled the Morgan banker who handled Hartford's account. The A&P shares were as good as money in the bank, the bankers thought; after all, the A&P was the biggest grocery chain in America. Even if Hartford's projects didn't work out, all the bankers had to do was cash in those stock certificates.

What neither Hartford nor his bankers had anticipated was that the heir's fiscal foundation, those supposedly bedrock-solid A&P shares, would erode. "Hartford assumed those shares would keep going up in value," his banker said. But in his years at the helm, Ralph Burger, the corporate secretary turned corporate chairman, had begun to undo the century-old grocery empire and Huntington Hartford's fortune along with it.

During the four years ending in 1962, the A&P's after-tax profits continued to climb upward, averaging over $57 million a year. A&P stock, which traded for $58 a share when it first opened on the New York Stock Exchange, had climbed to $70 by November 1961. But the market failed to consider that nothing was being reinvested in the company. Indeed, of the $57 million in annual profits, an incredible $52 million was distributed in dividends, forty percent of which went to the John Hartford Foundation. Burger had balanced the A&P's future on the teetering fulcrum of its past. By late 1962, the outside directors finally realized the flaws in Burger's strategy and pushed him to retire; reportedly, they threatened to resign en masse unless he turned operations over to another chief executive. But even that could not prevent the stock's free-fall. By 1963, it had slipped to under $40 a share.

Hartford was too busy with his own projects to pay much mind. His bankers, however, were all too aware of the grocery chain's woes. There was no money coming in on the $20 million or so they had loaned Hartford, and so they did what bankers will do when a loan is in trouble.

They called in another banker, Lehman Brothers' Benjamin Buttenweiser, to assess the damages.

Buttenweiser took some months scrutinizing Hartford's books, then pronounced the outcome grim: a cash shortfall was not only inevitable, he concluded, but imminent. "He was," said Buttenweiser, "among the most reckless spenders there ever were." In an effort to ward off disaster, the banker drafted a prescription to cure Hartford's financial woes, one that appealed as much to Hartford's paternal responsibilities as to his fiscal ones:

> Surely you must see . . . that your financial condition demands drastic action. I submit in earnest objectivity that you must avail yourself of what may well be your last constructive opportunity. Your only choice as I see it is to:
>
> 1. Liquidate your non–income producing assets in an attempt to stabilize your situation.
>
> 2. Shut off all non-essential expenses, business and personal, ending or at least drastically curtailing many of your personal expenses.
>
> I cannot overstress the gravity of your situation if you continue to conduct your affairs as you have been doing. If you fail to heed the advice contained in this letter, if you agree only to halfway measures, if you persist in living as you have been at present, far beyond your income scale, if you do not squarely face the gallery situation, if you do not abandon the Central Park café idea, if you fail in any of these respects, you will I fear fail altogether. Not only will you suffer through such failure, but so too will two innocent victims of your present procedure, your daughter and your son.
>
> Surely as from one father to another you must appreciate that in this letter, though I write it as a financial adviser whom you engaged, I speak also for Catherine and John. . . . As a final word, let me emphasize that in your own interest this letter is for your eyes only and should be kept strictly confidential.

Never before had Hartford been forced to think about money, never before had he been forced to consider that his seemingly limitless flow of funds could come to an end. Contest though he might misstatements of his fortune, Hartford always assumed that his money would be there when he needed it. He may have been past fifty, but he treated his wealth as nonchalantly as a strapping youth regards his physique; he assumed it would last forever.

If he had taken Buttenweiser's advice to sell, Hartford could have salvaged much of his fortune. But for him such a prospect was unthinkable; he devoutly believed that any one of his projects could be the one that would lift him from celebrity to fame. Who could tell whether in selling one venture he might be pawning his chances for immortality?

"It was almost like *Death of a Salesman*," recalled Phyllis Sher. "Hartford was always going to have the great day, the success. . . . The island would pay off, the magazine would make money, he'd really make it, if only he hung in [there]." And so, instead of following Buttenweiser's advice, he defiantly had the letter framed and put it in a cabinet with his various commendations.

Almost from the time Christopher Columbus first landed on the island of San Salvador, Bahamian commerce had been a tangle of perfidy. The Spanish had never considered the Bahamas worthy of colonization, and by the time the British did, their attempts were complicated by the swarms of pirates who had already staked out the Caribbean.

Outright piracy had died out by the end of the eighteenth century, but local business practices remained rather sordid. Since the islands were scattered through one of the Atlantic's main sea-lanes, and since the prevailing winds and currents were hazardous for sailing ships, accidents were frequent; salvaging became one of the staples of the economy. When nature wasn't enough to rely on, the Bahamians helped it along, luring vessels onto the reefs with moving lights on the shores, making bargains with unscrupulous captains who could be enticed to wreck their ships for a share of the spoils.

The American Civil War provided the first big business boom in the colony. Nassau became the primary chink in the Union's sea blockade of the Confederate states. Having spotted potential profits in the Confederates' adversity, the merchants on Bay Street, Nassau's main thoroughfare, started running arms to the South and shipping its cotton to mills in England.

With the States reunited in 1865, the Bahamian economy reeled, and it remained depressed until the coming of Prohibition. Nassau became the distribution center for British whiskey, which was shipped off to bootleggers and racketeers on the mainland. With the repeal of Prohibition in 1933, the Bahamian economy once again lagged. There was some revenue from tourism, but by the mid-forties even that income was in trouble as a result of the Depression and World War II. The tourism business finally started looking up again in the 1950s, thanks largely to a politician, Sir Stafford Lofthouse Sands, newly named chairman of the Bahamian Development Board. He encouraged hotel construction and allotted funds for a new airport to accommodate the growing parade of tourists, mostly Americans, flush with success from the postwar boom.

Like the rest of the men who controlled the Bahamas, Sands was a member of the United Bahamian Party, a white ruling class controlling a poor black populace. These men, called the Bay Street Boys, were colonial pragmatists, industrialists who made sure that the government was a well-oiled bureaucracy, benefiting the businesses they controlled. And so great was their power that getting ahead in business almost invariably meant making sure that the venture was in the interest of the Bay Street Boys. This was a lesson Huntington Hartford would learn the hard way.

The titular top man among the Bay Street Boys was the premier, Sir Roland Symonette, who ran virtually all of the major construction businesses in the Bahamas. But the real power resided with the tourism minister, Sir Stafford; bald and white-linen-suited, he was Gutman, the Sydney Greenstreet character in *The Maltese Falcon,* incarnate. He was descended from a Tory who left the American mainland during the years after the Revolutionary War, and was an epic character down to the smallest details of his daily life: he chain-smoked so heavily that even the swimming pool behind his mansion (called Waterloo) was equipped with a floating ashtray. Sands was nothing if not given to the grand gesture. "At a dinner party for four," said one friend, "he would order caviar for a hundred." His favorite sport was shooting pigeons.

Sands was also a lawyer, and his government position and legal practice together made him a formidable figure. He was the man to hire to get business done in the Bahamas, but he was never hired by Huntington Hartford. The heir could not use Sands for the purchase of Paradise Island because the Bahamian kingpin represented Axel Wenner-Gren, the island's original owner, but even afterward Hartford's attorneys never saw fit to put Sands on their payroll. While Hartford's lawyers used a perfectly respectable Bahamian counselor, he lacked Sands's clout. And as if that were not enough, in an act of extraordinarily bad judgment, Hartford's advisers urged their client to make a political donation to the mostly black opposition, the Progressive Liberal Party. Hartford followed their advice, and gave $15,000 to a party run by men determined to overthrow the white colonialists who would determine his fate.

Word of Hartford's misguided beneficence quickly got back to the Bay Street Boys. "He was incapable of confidentiality. He'd tell the next broad he picked up," explained Howard Schneider, a dapper young associate at Stroock and Stroock and Lavan who worked with David Sher handling Hartford's affairs. "The Bay Street Boys . . . could not countenance the fact that Hartford could pin [payoffs] on them."

Sands didn't like Hartford's politics, and he found the way he conducted his private life equally abhorrent. The tourism minister had a British sense of respectability: the appearance of propriety was at least as important as its practice. Hartford, with his oceanside pickups—"Hi, I'm Huntington Hartford and I own this island," he'd say as he stopped by the towel of some sunbathing teenager—was thoroughly unacceptable.

"When you go down Bay Street stopping every attractive girl, some of those girls are going to turn out to be the daughters of the ministers," explained Schneider. "They go home and say, 'This man, Mr. Hartford, wanted me to come to Paradise Beach,' and those ministers would get very upset."

Despite his tense dealings with the Bay Street Boys, Hartford still had hope for his Bahamian investment. If he was willing to turn just a bit pragmatic, everyone told him, the island could be profitable. And so it was that in 1963, three years after declaring that he would never build a bridge, never permit wagers to be made on Paradise, Hunt Hartford began petitioning the Bahamian government to grant him bridge and gambling permits.

Over the next months, Hartford's attempts to obtain a gambling license grew increasingly desperate. The heir met at the Fontainebleau Hotel in Miami with Sam Golub and Alvin Malnik. Golub was a Florida businessman known to have good connections in the Bahamas, particularly with Sands. Malnik had a more tarnished reputation: he had made his name as Meyer Lansky's attorney. Hartford signed a contract with the two men, agreeing to pay a substantial fee if they could secure a gaming license. But when the contract expired sixty days later, Hartford was no closer to a permit than he had been before.

In the fall, Hartford told *The Miami Herald* he would close down his resort in December unless the Nassau government granted him a license. "The club at Paradise, one of the most lavish in the world," noted the reporter, "is having some financial problems. For example, the Ocean Club has only fifty-two rooms, yet Hartford keeps a staff of four hundred around the place."

Just days later, at a press conference at *Show*'s offices in New York, Hartford announced drastic alterations in his original plan. He told the Bahamian government that he would build a thousand-room hotel—if it would grant him the bridge and gambling permits. Then, in an act of wholly misguided philanthropy, he pledged to make gambling part of a broader change in the Bahamian economy. He offered half of the entire net profit of a Paradise Island casino to the Bahamian government for the specific purpose of improved housing, medical care, social welfare. Sands, who had yet to receive his tithe from Hartford (and who was already angry over Hartford's donation to the black opposition party), was, predictably, unimpressed by this new manifestation of Hartford's beneficence. Sands's portfolio was tourism, not social welfare.

Finally, Sy Alter approached Sands on Hartford's behalf. "Give us a break," he told the tourism minister. "Let us have the license, and Hartford might be able to come out from under."

"Mr. Alter," Sands boomed back, "I am convinced that if I gave Mr. Hartford a license, he would go broke with the license."

While Hartford battled the Bay Street Boys for his gambling license, another drama was unfolding, over another Bahamian casino operation. And although Hartford was not yet directly involved, those players eventually became his own ruination.

The Cuban revolution had set the stage for a gambling revolution in the Bahamas. When Fidel Castro took over Cuba and closed the casinos in 1959, he left the American mobsters who controlled them shopping for a new venue. One of those racketeers, Meyer Lansky, a man who had close ties to the deposed Cuban dictator Fulgencio Batista, sought to form a similarly close bond with Sands. Lansky visited Sands in 1960, and the man known as the Mafia's accountant came armed with a proposal to bring big-time gambling to the Bahamas. He enumerated the benefits: increased tourism, higher revenues, and of course, $2 million in "legal fees" for Sands himself. Although Sands later testified before a Royal Commission of Inquiry that he told the Miami-based mobster to return to the mainland, subsequent events indicated that relations between the two continued.

Until the 1960s, there had been only two exceptions to the law that forbade gambling casinos in the Bahamas. A couple of small "clubs" were allowed to operate during the high tourist season. One was on Cat Cay; the other, the Bahamian Club, was in a white-painted stucco mansion just outside Nassau. Local sentiment ran against adding more casinos, but Sands lobbied heavily in their favor, arguing that the increased income outweighed any opposition. By the early sixties, Sands finally seemed likely to succeed. The beneficiaries of that success would be Louis Chesler, a Canadian real estate developer, and Wallace Groves, a convicted American stock swindler. They had a third partner who remained discreetly behind the scenes: Meyer Lansky.

In the twenties, Groves had been called the "Boy Wonder of Wall

Street.'' He was done in not by the crash of 1929 but by a 1941 conviction involving a $750,000 stock scam, for which he was sentenced to two years in prison. Some thirty years later, in *The Grim Reapers,* a book about Caribbean corruption, Ed Reid would say of Groves: ''There is one area in which Groves's friends and enemies agree: He is shrewd, quick and perceptive—a 'natural genius at making money.' '' He claimed to have extrasensory perception when it came to business deals, explaining that he had ''vibrations'' during business negotiations.

In the mid-forties, the earth must have moved for Wallace Groves. Having been paroled after serving five months of his jail sentence, he went to the Bahamas, where, he was convinced, he could begin anew. He started with a lumber business, then moved into hotel development. Over the next ten years, with the help of two associates, Groves built up a 150,000-acre empire on Grand Bahama Island.

Groves's two associates were Chesler and Lansky. Groves, naturally, would provide the land for the casino project; Chesler, through his Canadian connections, would help with the financing and handle the construction of the 250-room Lucayan Beach Hotel. Although his involvement was, of course, never official, Lansky would provide the gambling expertise.

In March 1963, maintaining that the financial lures were now irresistible, Sands proposed to the Bahamian parliament that a gambling permit be issued to Bahamas Amusements, a new Groves–Chesler entity. The two men were so certain that Sands could push the permit through that they had actually begun construction of the Grand Bahama hotel-casino in the fall of 1962, months before Sands brought the permit question to a vote. Still, they were careful about their plans; on the architectural drawing, the huge space by the front door, earmarked for the casino, was labeled ''Handball Courts.''

Lansky and his crew were involved almost from the start. In late 1962, Chesler and Groves held a meeting at the Fontainebleau Hotel in Miami to discuss the Bahamian casino. Lansky and his brother Jake were there, as was Dino Cellini, the man responsible for teaching every croupier in Havana the business. Lansky himself met with the architect of the hotel to discuss the ''handball courts.'' When the equipment, including roulette and craps tables, arrived in the Bahamas, Lansky would direct their placement.

On April 1, 1963, a week and a half after Sands presented their application, Groves and Chesler were officially permitted into the gambling business. Sands benefited handsomely from the venture. Chesler and Groves paid him at least $500,000 in return for his ''legal services.''

▲

As Chesler and Groves forged ahead, Hartford's attempts to win a gambling license were going nowhere. When Hartford learned—from a newspaper article, no less—that Groves and Chesler had received permission to open a casino, he was furious. And when it came out that one of the lawyers working for Maxwell Rabb, one of the partners in the Groves–Chesler deal, belonged to the same firm as Hartford's attorney, David Sher, Hartford became convinced that they were all in cahoots and that he was the odd man out.

"Stroock never told me they were trying to get a casino license for anyone else," complained Hartford. "The first I heard that they were building a casino on Grand Bahama Island was when I read about it in the Miami paper. . . . The thing I resented was that Dave Sher had been my counsel and my mother's counsel all my life. And he never mentioned a word about a casino going up on Grand Bahama." Still, Hartford was never certain whether Sher knew about Rabb's relationship with Groves and Chesler, and he never filed any malpractice charges against his law firm.

Some months after Groves and Chesler received their permit, Sands sent word that Hartford could have a permit, but only under the most circumscribed conditions: He would have to bring in a financial partner. Complying with the fat man's terms would cost Hartford the better part of his fortune.

While Hartford struggled to bring gambling to Paradise, the resort had some curious guests. In November 1962, Richard Nixon, fresh from defeat in the California gubernatorial ("You won't have Nixon to kick around anymore") election, went to the Bahamas to lick his wounds. As Nixon later recalled, "After I was defeated for President in 1960 and for Governor of California in 1962, he welcomed me to Paradise Island. . . . Most of the media pundits didn't believe I had a political future after those two defeats—an assessment, incidentally, which I shared."

Nixon left his family at home, but he did bring along a close friend, the Florida banker Charles "Bebe" Rebozo. The two stayed nearly a month, and although they were the only guests, the Ocean Club was fully staffed. "I was given orders by Hartford that they were to pay for nothing," said Sy Alter.

Nixon generally dined with Hartford and Diane, and the two men golfed together. According to Alter, the former vice-president was not particularly convivial. "He was so morose," Alter recalled. "I pride myself on being a pretty good amateur comedian, but I couldn't get a laugh out of him.'' As Hartford was also exceedingly reserved, the two barely spoke. ''I guess neither of us was interested in getting to know the other,'' reflected Hartford. ''If I'd known he was going to be president, I would have probably paid more attention.''

Still, Nixon never forgot Hartford's generosity, and after he was elected president in 1968, he appointed him to the National Council on the Arts. Alter, much more of an opportunist than his patrician patron, struck up a friendship with Nixon and Rebozo that would eventually thrust him into the middle of one of the biggest scandals in American history.

Huntington Hartford may have been a constant source of anxiety to the Bahamian government and his New York bankers, but to the American public he was still the millionaire, with endless resources at his disposal. In February 1964, the *New York Herald Tribune* ran a profile of the heir by a young journalist named Tom Wolfe. The article, entitled ''The Luther of Columbus Circle,'' previewed the Columbus Circle museum, finally scheduled to open in March. And the social critic deftly took a measure of Hartford's madness. Hartford, regarded as a kook in a city of radical-chic conformists, finally thought he had found himself a champion. ''[He] has been suffering because for thirteen years now the New York intelligentsia has been taking his works lightly,'' Wolfe wrote. ''[Hartford has] the most flagrantly unfashionable taste anybody in New York has ever heard of.''

Wolfe described Hartford's two essays as ''religious tracts,'' 1950s equivalents of the ninety-five Luther had nailed up in the sixteenth century.

> Like Luther, he calls for a reformation, a return to a simpler and more blessed age. He has an age in mind: Victorian England—which the cultural religicos regard as the most reactionary phase of cultural history. . . . He has devoted himself to his chosen field—the religion of Culture—with a zealous and enduring disdain of the cultural Establishment. And if the culturati still do not fathom his Luther role, even with this white marble tower on Columbus Circle to illustrate it, Hartford will not be downhearted.

Wolfe closed his piece with lines from a Kipling poem Hartford had had cast in bronze and installed next to the elevators on the first floor of his gallery.

> When Earth's last picture is painted
> and the tubes are twisted and dried,

When the oldest colours have faded,
   and the youngest critic has died,
We shall rest, and, faith, we shall need it—
   lie down for an æon or two,
Till the Master of All Good Workmen
   shall put us to work anew.
And those that were good shall be happy:
   they shall sit in a golden chair;
They shall splash at a ten-league canvas
   with brushes of comets' hair.
They shall find real saints to draw from—
   Magdalene, Peter, and Paul;
They shall work for an age at a sitting
   and never be tired at all!

Some thought the essay a lampoon of Hartford, a Swiftian hoist into the realm of the mock heroic. But Hartford read Wolfe's piece and ignored the derision, the cries of "mama's boy," the insinuations that his sensibility was born of a patrician arrogance. The article became Hartford's bible; he gave copies to visitors, made reference to it whenever he was asked to speak: "I have always wanted to be a crusader for that religion known as culture," Hartford would say. "I even talked about starting up a new religion." Thanks to Tom Wolfe, Hartford had a compass point for his ambitions. Finally someone had recognized his efforts. Finally, he thought, he had Fame.

The gallery opened in March 1964, four years late and with a price tag approaching $10 million—nearly five times more than the original projections. Hartford guided two television crews through the collection before opening day, sat for a score of interviews with magazine and newspaper reporters, then put the museum's façade on the cover of *Show*. Proper attention *would* be paid.

This time, Hartford's connoisseurship was more than a paid advertisement in the nation's newspapers; it was a body of art, an oeuvre that the heir hoped would do for the Hartford name what the Morgan Library and the Guggenheim had done for their founders. "I am disgusted with contemporary art in general," he said. "Ethics, morality, and art are all related, but today ethics are unfashionable." His museum, he promised, would redress the problem.

When it came to the museum's design, adhering to that visual realism proved exceedingly problematic. The tiny, lopsided lot required all manner of architectural gymnastics. Edward Durell Stone, though, happily obliged. His museum looked like a punched railroad ticket; it was a rectangular shape distorted to a curvilinear trapezoid. What should have been four right angles ranged from 114 to 69 degrees, with building-code requirements—fire stairs, fire tower, elevators, and mechanical equipment—jammed into a central service core and galleries wrapped around them. Standing alone on that concrete island, Stone's nine stories of white Vermont marble looked like a citadel in a state of siege. What might have been perfectly appropriate for a sun-drenched square in Riyadh looked terribly misplaced in midtown Manhattan, orphaned in a swarm of traffic.

In the world according to Hartford, a museum was "really like a church." He installed a twenty-three-and-a-half-foot-high Aeolian-Skinner pipe organ; its music pulsed through the galleries. Except for the bamboo-lined penthouse restaurant, the Gauguin Room (cuisine: Polynesian), the museum was virtually windowless. "We needed the wall space for paintings," Hartford later explained.

The gallery furniture was upholstered in supple leather; floors were either parquet or covered with thick red-and-gold carpets. The effect was of a nineteenth-century drawing room—sumptuous, rather overwrought, not unlike the collection the galleries housed.

Architecture critics weighed in with denigration rivaling that heaped on *The Master of Thornfield*. Ada Louise Huxtable of *The New York Times* described the building as "a die-cut Venetian palazzo on lollipops" with an effect that "borders on poetic grotesquerie." The *New York Post* described the downstairs arcade as resembling a row of "boudoir hand mirrors."

The first show was a three-hundred-work exhibit of the Russian surrealist-symbolist Pavel Tchelitchew. His most popular painting, *Hide and Seek,* depicting a tree with foliage and branches that blossomed with children's faces, was, ironically, borrowed from the Museum of Modern Art.

Hartford's own collection, on the fifth floor, included some Corot and Courbet oils, an early Degas copy of Poussin's *Rape of the Sabines,* and works by Mary Cassatt, John Singer Sargent, and Reginald Marsh. Between the fourth and fifth floors were two immense Dalís, *The Battle of Tetuan* and *The Discovery of America by Christopher Columbus.* The latter, commissioned especially for the museum, was typical of the artist's later work: a technically superb monument to kitsch. It was an expansive steel-blue canvas, twenty feet across, with a forest of crosses in the foreground. Front and center was a huge figure Dalí called the "Immaculate Conception"; Dalí used his wife, Gala, as the model. Just beneath the Gala-cum-Christ, Columbus led his troops through the water, all of them nude but demurely sheathed by the froth of ocean waves.

The architecture critics may have been dubious; the featured artist was not. "This museum," Dalí told a reporter, with a sweep of his tooled silver-headed cane, "is magnificent. This museum is the vindication of the Dalínian prophecy of art. This is a historical event, because now the people of the world will start discovering the outstanding painting of the world.

"Dalí," added Dalí, "has never been presented better."

His praise was not echoed by the rest of the art world. "[There is] not . . . even a single other picture whose master is not better represented, providing he deserves to be represented at all, in another American public institution," wrote the reviewer for *ARTnews*. "With the avowedly anti-modern pictures for his museum, Mr. Hartford has labored like the greatest of mountains to bring forth, what, on his own avocational Broadway, is called a turkey."

The New York Times had never been particularly enamored of Hartford's philosophy, and the review of his collection was no exception. "It won't jell, no matter how long you keep trying to boil it down to some kind of essence," wrote John Canaday. "What in the world unifies a collection that includes Frederick Waugh's painted photographs of waves, a standard dustbin item for many years; a sub-dustbin photo-revival Bouguereau nude . . . and a powerful semi-abstract Orozco, *The Slave*?" Canaday blamed the confusion on the gallery's patron and credited Hartford's curators with "putting things into the best possible order."

While the members of the staff ably arranged their employer's artworks, there was little they could do about his haphazard managerial skills. Hartford held a series of black-tie openings to inaugurate the museum; the first was intended to honor the Police Athletic League. A handful of New York's finest were there, along with their New York society benefactors, among them Princess Lee Radziwill, the publisher Samuel Newhouse, Astor heir Ivan Obolensky, and a new name on the New York scene, Andy Warhol. They expected a lavish meal; Hartford's invitation had promised dinner. But the heir had told his staff to prepare only for cocktails. "We had to send out to Dover Deli for corned beef and tongue at the last minute," remembered Margaret Potter, an assistant to the curator. "It was just slapped onto trays—and we had to pay a fortune."

IV

❖

THE SELLING OF AN EMPIRE

The Caribbean Catastrophe

There is not a fiercer hell than the failure in a great object.
JOHN KEATS, *Endymion*

Hunt and Diane Hartford on Paradise Island. With his
Bahamas tan, gleaming white smile, and multimillion-dollar
fortune, the A&P heir seemed a great catch.

14

THE FIRST PUBLIC SIGNS that Hartford's finances were amiss came within a month of the museum's opening. On March 31, 1964, in a *New York Herald Tribune* article by Tom Wolfe, Hartford's attorney, David Sher, announced that *Show* was for sale. The reasons cited: the magazine's $6 million in losses and the "need to retrench somewhat after spending almost fifteen years of founding expensive and often financially risky projects."

But Hartford, a man who found it easy to build and easier to buy, balked. Within weeks, he backtracked, telling *The New York Times* and *The Wall Street Journal* that his magazine was *not* for sale after all.

The men who put out Hartford's magazine were finding it increasingly difficult to deal with their erratic owner. As editors are wont to do, they had become attached to their creation, and they were convinced it could thrive under new ownership. Frank Gibney took it upon himself to shop the magazine around New York in hopes of finding a savior. "I saw the only way to keep us above water was to sell," recounted Gibney. "By 1964 we had a sixty-percent renewal rate. I could finally see the promised land."

And there were men willing to finance *Show*'s journey to prosperity. Ralph Delahaye Paine, Jr., publisher of *House & Home,* voiced interest, as did Harry Sherman, founder of Book-of-the-Month Club. But Hartford turned a cold shoulder to all suitors. "Whenever I brought anyone in, Hartford would say he wanted to think about it, and start complaining about the losses," recalled Gibney.

Unable to finance *Show* but unwilling to sell, Hartford finally told the editors they would have to reduce the magazine's size and eliminate color pages. "I decided I would rather let it go than take away from its character," said Gibney. So, on May 21, he quit, leaving the magazine to a newly named managing editor, Selig Adler (in Gibney's words, "a perfectly nice man who didn't know a damn thing about magazines"), a onetime managing editor of the New York *Mirror* and, equally important, a cousin to Sy Alter. What's more, Hartford announced that he was taking over "personal direction" of the magazine himself.

"I had an umbrella that kept Hartford away," explained Gibney. Adler, without so much as a paper parasol, was caught in the deluge. "When I came on, Hunt had fired everybody," said Adler. "It was a dying thing. The magazine was purely his project, an excuse for Hunt to put juicy sixteen-year-olds between the covers, that's all."

That was only a bit of an exaggeration: the journal of the arts that had had so much promise just two years before was quickly devolving into a glorified girlie magazine. In October, for instance, *Show* devoted two of its precious color pages to a then (and evermore) unknown French actress named Annie Farge. She posed as a variety of famed French performers, the only common theme being her increasing state of undress. In one shot she was a scantily clad Josephine Baker; in another a Folies-Bergère dancer dressed in nothing more than a grass skirt and a pair of butterfly pasties.

In the same issue, Hartford, with his nineteenth-century sensibility and twentieth-century vices, included a dense excerpt (act 1, scene 4) from *Nan Bullen,* a turgid drama about Anne Boleyn and Henry VIII by Francis Hackett, who had adapted it from a best-selling biography he had written in the late thirties. There was an odd preamble to the piece; the play's publication, it seemed, was the product of Hartford's guilty conscience.

Hartford had met Hackett six years before at his artists' colony, where he read the play and optioned it. He had approached Elia Kazan, Elizabeth Taylor, and Orson Welles, among others, but was unable to find either a director or a star. Finally, Hackett, who was almost eighty, sent a letter to Hartford's lawyer, condemning the heir for failing to produce his play.

A week after Hartford received the letter, Hackett was dead. Now, wrote Hartford, "this drama will live when the rest of us are dead and forgotten." Hartford's three-page excerpt, of course, was the last anyone ever heard of *Nan Bullen.*

Show's prestige was eroding along with its editorial integrity, but Hartford pressed on. He tried to woo Madison Avenue's confidence with an ad of his own. On August 6, newspapers in New York, Chicago, and

Detroit carried a half-page in which Hartford declared that "my personal and financial commitment to *Show* magazine is projected two years ahead."

But even as Hartford was, temporarily at least, unwilling to sell *Show*, his lawyers told him that he had to start selling something. "The outflow was enormous, and nothing was producing anything. It was clear a tourniquet was required," explained Howard Schneider, one of the lawyers. "But every time we told him things were looking bad, like the boy who cried wolf, he never believed it would happen. You would tell him arteries [were] hemorrhaging, and he would pick a capillary."

Hartford was persuaded to let go of a number of employees on Paradise Island and to shut down Diane's stables on the island and at Melody Farm, but it was Schneider who had to give Diane the bad news. "I told her over lunch at '21,' " he recalled. "She started crying." By the end of the day Hartford countermanded the order, and the horses remained.

Finally, in May 1964, not two months after he announced he would not be selling *Show,* Hartford announced that he would be liquidating some of his properties, although he insisted he was under no financial pressure to do so. "I'm really doing this," he told *Business Week,* "to be able to concentrate my energies and resources on a few key . . . projects." In truth, however, he had run through roughly $40 million of his bankroll—not counting the millions lost on the sagging stock price of his A&P shares.

He shut down the Handwriting Institute, a $600,000 drain; unloaded his interest in Speed Park (the automated parking garage in midtown Manhattan), for a $1.8 million loss; and put the For Sale sign out on the East Fifty-seventh Street building that housed the *Show* offices. And once again, he announced that the magazine itself would be sold.

He had a buyer within two months: Gilbert Kraft, owner and publisher of *Playbill,* who met with Hartford for the obligatory graphology test, then reconnoitered with the attorneys. "I said, 'You guys ought to pay me to take it,' " recalled Kraft, and they practically did. No money changed hands; instead, Kraft promised to invest $500,000 in the magazine; Hartford would invest an equal amount if the new owner kept the magazine alive for a year.

"We had a provision that Hartford had a right to review the content that went into the magazine, but not to change it," said Kraft. "The trick," Kraft explained, "was to pry it loose from his grips, without letting him believe he had lost anything."

But after four months and nearly $1 million in losses, Kraft realized he couldn't keep *Show* going on his own. "I skipped an issue. I tried to find other funding." Nothing came through. Finally, after less than half a year, Kraft told Hartford he had to shut the magazine down.

Hartford did not take the news well; according to Kraft: "He would call and say, 'I understand you're going to close down. You'd better not.' Hartford told me that he would take me to the cleaners. He said that he was going to throw me in jail because I wasn't keeping my word."

Hartford's warnings notwithstanding, Kraft closed the magazine, leaving Hartford in possession of the title, free to publish again should he find the funds. And like so many of the men with whom Hartford did business, Kraft walked away from the whole affair with a sour taste in his mouth.

"He was the inheritor of the A&P fortune in every sense," reflected Kraft. "He sold people like you [sell] a can of pork and beans off the shelves."

Even as Hartford fought his futile battle to save *Show* in New York, he was quietly dismembering his California empire.

The theater was the first to go. Through the fifties, it had seen a smattering of notable productions: *The Diary of Anne Frank, The Chalk Garden, A Raisin in the Sun.* Bette Davis had played there, as had Tallulah Bankhead, Yves Montand, and Vivien Leigh. But the theater ended up dark nearly as often as it was lit—a consequence of both its size and its owner's negligence. With just two thousand seats, it was not large enough for most touring companies, and Hartford had long since lost both the interest and the resources to mount original productions.

At the beginning of 1964, James Doolittle, a local impresario who had been producing plays at the Greek Theater high up in the Hollywood Hills, offered to buy Hartford's theater for $1 million. Hartford responded with a reflexive refusal. But within six months, he had David Sher contact Doolittle with the message that his client was ready to deal. Sher wanted cash; Doolittle cut his original offer to $850,000. "[Sher] called right back and said, 'Let's close the deal,' " recalled Doolittle.

The change in ownership happened so quickly that Doolittle did not even take the time to change the marquee. For twenty years more, HUNTINGTON HARTFORD still blazed across the theater's face, giving his Hollywood fame an undeserved half-life. (But even that was slightly illusory. Most Angelenos assumed that the theater was affiliated with the Huntington Library and Art Gallery in San Marino, which housed the collection of Henry Huntington, a nineteenth-century railroad tycoon.)

▲

Despite Hartford's absence, the artists' colony had continued to function through the fifties and early sixties. Its reputation had been tarnished by its patron's reactionary philosophy, but the retreat still received three hundred applications a year from artists eager for a stipend, a studio, and six months of California sun.

But in May 1965, Hartford called the director of the Foundation, John Vincent, to tell him he was selling. Vincent first tried to persuade the University of California at Los Angeles to buy the property, but UCLA would take the colony only as a donation, and Hartford badly needed the proceeds from the sale. Throughout that summer, more potential buyers trooped through. Cary Grant was interested, then decided against it; while he wanted the real estate, he figured that turning those artists out on the street would be a public-relations disaster.

Eventually, the property was purchased by a local real estate developer, John Morehart, for $700,000; the last bungalow was empty by the fall. Morehart, though, was stymied in his attempts to develop the land, as was the next developer who bought the property. Today that land, a thorny blanket of brambles and tumbleweeds, is owned by the State of California. What is left of the artists' cabins is scattered rubble from their concrete foundations. Only the stables remain; their stalls are thick with shattered window glass and broken beer bottles.

"No man but a blockhead ever wrote except for money," said Dr. Johnson, who got it almost right. While money matters to even the lowliest scrivener, the quest for recognition can be equally potent. Huntington Hartford, bedeviled by his fortune, dogged by celebrity, and eluded by fame, turned to authorship as his avenue to public respect. "I'm sick of being dubbed a millionaire," Hartford told a reporter for London's *Daily Mirror*. "I would prefer to be regarded as one of the leading experts on contemporary art."

The publication of Hartford's treatise—*Art or Anarchy?*—was originally scheduled to coincide with the opening of his museum, but it was beset by delays, primarily because of the heavy editing required. Finally, in November 1964, the publisher, Doubleday, had bound copies, and Hartford threw himself a prepublication party in the Gauguin Room at his museum. As the guests lunched, Hartford offered them a sampling of his thoughts: "The most important thing I say in the book is that there has to be an ethical element to art as well as a positive, constructive view."

"Does anyone agree?" asked a guest in the crowd.

"I'll know better when the book is out," the author replied.

Art or Anarchy? was essentially a grand restatement of two arguments Hartford had been putting forth since the early fifties, a populist credo that melded the People's Choice with the Moral Majority. Art, he insisted, must embody morality, and its images ought to be accessible to the public. The book began with a confession that had less to do with critique than with its author's own unhappy childhood:

> As a friend of artists, as I hope I am, I have always hated the goose step. I hated it at St. Paul's School in Concord, New Hampshire, where I was forced to go to church in a blue suit and stiff collar on Sundays when I would have preferred to be out playing football. . . . In prep school and later in college I tried to avoid the science and math courses in which mundane and heartless logic prevailed. During the war I joined the Coast Guard because I had a feeling it might be slightly less regimented than some of the other branches of the service. And in recent years I have been fighting the philosophical battle, which will probably be going on till I die, to restore a creative middle ground to the world between the subjective miasmas of Stravinsky and T. S. Eliot on the one hand and the objective clichés of Dale Carnegie and Bishop [Fulton] Sheen on the other.

Art or Anarchy? wasn't just another restatement of the Hartford credo. It can be read also as an implicit attempt to defend the artistic sensibility, the deviant force that enabled Edward Hartford to create and then drove him mad, the nature that the son so strongly believed he shared. In one chapter, Huntington Hartford asked, "What makes the artist run? Is he often a psychopath, as he has been accused of being and as the widely publicized careers of Van Gogh, Cézanne, Gauguin and Lautrec might cause us to believe . . . ? If the artist is indeed sometimes a psychopath, as I believe he is, what are the excuses for the utterly miserable and obnoxious manner in which he often acts?"

Hartford then went into a description of the various transgressions of Benvenuto Cellini, Caravaggio, and van Gogh (who held his hand over a flame because a woman refused to see him). This was Huntington Hartford trying to justify his own behavior, trying to catapult his own egocentrism from the realm of the eccentric to that of the inspired.

Most of that plea for understanding, though, was lost in the book's shrill paean to yahooism. "I don't know anything about painting, but I know what I like," was the crux of Hartford's thesis, and he wasn't ashamed to say so.

> In the matter of taste and judgment concerning the arts, I believe that the average intelligent American can hold up his head with the

best of the critics, and it is high time that we stop apologizing for our amateur standing. If anything is to be done to halt the downward trend of aesthetic standards in America today, it must be done by the public.

Little wonder that most critics regarded Hartford's effort as an inept, inarticulate argument in support of the arrière-garde, a book, in the words of *Life* magazine, not to be missed by any connoisseur of the absurd:

> Huntington Hartford is an average millionaire who reportedly dreams of the day when someone will mention his name without immediately adding "A & P heir." . . . To remove this commercial taint he has devoted himself to the arts, a field in which millionaires traditionally have dreams of glory. He has made two solid contributions—*Show* magazine, which he has just sold to a theater program publisher, and the Gallery of Modern Art. . . . The main threat to both these successes is Huntington Hartford. He keeps giving them the benefit of his ideas. These ideas have free play in his new book. . . . Hartford making like a thinker is first-class entertainment, a disarming parable of incompetent goodwill.

Years later, Hartford would reflect wistfully on his venture into artistic "expertise." "I'm sorry I spent so much time caring whether paintings were good or not," he said. "I had so little effect."

Bad enough that the critics lanced *Art or Anarchy?*; far worse were the bankers' laments over the increasingly enfeebled state of its author's finances.

In October, the heir was forced to begin confronting the future of Paradise Island. He laid off about a hundred employees. The handful of men left tending the golf course fought a losing battle against the encroaching tropical vegetation. Finally Sidney Pines, one of Hartford's retinue of legal advisers, announced that his client would not be opening the resort for the winter season—it cost less to keep it shuttered.

Hartford's desperation had become regular fodder for the press. He announced to *The New York Times* that he could no longer shoulder the $600,000 a year it cost to keep the museum operating. "I hope to get some help," he told the *Times,* adding, "if I don't, there won't be any museum in two or three years . . . it will become an office building." *Newsweek* ran a story entitled "Hartford on the Rocks?," a précis on his evaporating cash flow.

But Hartford's attorneys remained publicly optimistic. "Once we get the whole drain from Paradise Island stopped," one of them said, "Hartford's going to be in good shape. I should have his troubles then."

The only way Hartford could generate profits from Paradise Island was with gambling and bridge permits, and the government refused to give him those unless he had a partner. Hartford's attorneys concluded that their client would be better served to remove himself from the venture altogether, and they urged him to put the island up for sale. The asking price for the property, which comprised the Ocean Club, formal gardens, and yacht harbor, along with a square-block site in Nassau that boasted a boat landing and restaurant (alone said to have cost in excess of $2 million), was $32 million. But even as the offer was announced, Hartford's realtor conceded that the price would likely be a bit less. It turned out to be a fire sale.

Scores of interested buyers turned out. Some were squeaky clean: Laurence Tisch, then chairman of Loews, looked at the property but decided he didn't want the problems of dealing with gambling. Conrad Hilton, apparently, came to the same conclusion.

Months passed, no bidders emerged. Then, in early 1965, Hartford told his problems to Richard Olsen, a Miami traffic court judge whom he had met while judging a Miss Florida pageant. Olsen told Hartford he might have a solution: one of his tennis partners, he thought, might be interested in the Paradise property.

His name was James Crosby, and although he was only thirty-seven years old and not yet a well-known corporate player—he headed a small-ish, publicly traded company, Mary Carter Paint—he proved to be far savvier than the man he would ultimately undo. Crosby was a hard-drinking chain-smoker who measured men by the power they wielded and the money they made. As one man who knew both Crosby and Hartford put it, "Crosby was very money-oriented; Hunt was pleasure-oriented." Small wonder that from the very first Crosby had nothing but disdain for an heir who was consumed with spending money and incapable of making it.

Crosby was the son of a Harvard-educated lawyer who had served as deputy attorney general in the Woodrow Wilson administration before taking over the family business, a Wisconsin foundry called Shaefer Manufacturing. The family summered in Spring Lake, New Jersey, the "Irish Riviera," where Hartford's grandparents used to spend the season more than a half-century before. There the Crosbys forged ties with another prosperous clan, the family of a New Jersey State Supreme Court judge named Charles E. Murphy. His son Charles, a rangy athlete who graduated from Dartmouth and Columbia Law School, would become Jim Crosby's chief adviser through the next quarter-century of empire-building.

Crosby moved into the business world within months of graduating with an economics degree from Georgetown; he went to work for International Paint. He then moved onto Wall Street as a stockbroker for Harris Upham, where he rose quickly to the meat of the business, making deals. After eight years on the Street, he went to work for a Washington, D.C.–based financier, Gustave Ring, who charged him with finding properties for acquisition. And although he spent only four months with Ring, he discovered two companies that proved to be the keys to his future: Unexcelled Chemicals and Mary Carter Paint.

By December 1958, thirty-year-old Jim Crosby was the chairman of Unexcelled, a small manufacturer of chemical fertilizers and a few other products that verged on the implausible, among them an advertising medium called a Skyjector, a high-powered projector supposedly capable of projecting images onto the sides of skyscrapers as well as in the evening sky. Two years later, Crosby sold off control of Unexcelled and became chief executive of Mary Carter Paint. Charles Murphy served as his general counsel; the president was Irving George "Jack" Davis, a Harvard graduate given to gold chains and a good tan. "He seemed like someone who had taken a Dale Carnegie course a little too seriously," recalled Howard Schneider.

By 1963, the Murphy/Davis/Crosby troika had built the company into a multimillion-dollar conglomerate with some thousand stores spread throughout the United States and the British West Indies. A subsidiary controlled the National Biff-Burger System, a fast-food franchise, along with a manufacturing plant that produced everything needed to operate a Biff-Burger drive-in, including the portable structure.

The company had acquired its foothold in the Bahamas in 1963 with the purchase of 3,500 acres of Wallace Groves's land that became a residential community called Queens Cove. In March 1965, Murphy, Crosby, and Davis had even bigger plans for the Bahamas. After Judge Olsen told them Paradise was available, they took off for New York to meet with Hartford at Beekman Place. It soon became clear the deal would be contingent on three factors: a gambling permit, a bridge permit, and an adequate water supply.

Unlike Hartford, Crosby and company had the good sense to put the Caribbean's most powerful negotiator on their payroll: Sir Stafford Sands.

Nor was Sands Crosby's only advantage. Midway through the negotiations, Sy Alter realized just how dire his boss's financial straits were and concluded that his own fiscal future would be better served if he aligned himself with the powers-to-be. In doing so, Alter proved himself another in the long series of flatterers who were interested as much in the Hartford money as in the man.

Hartford was surprisingly candid on the nature of those relationships: "People have always said to me, 'How in the world do you know who your real friends are?' I've always said, 'Look, these people are my friends as long as this is my life and these are the circumstances I live in. If I suddenly lost all my money . . . I wouldn't necessarily expect them to be my friends. . . . I wouldn't be sore at anybody if they drifted away.' "

Hartford had been Alter's sole source of support through much of the fifties, first with the modeling-agency job, then with a $250,000 "loan" to open a Manhattan liquor store. (That proved to be nothing but trouble. Alter was accused of bribing a judge in order to get his liquor license cleared and twice had his license suspended for selling below the fixed minimum price. Since one more suspension would have forced the place out of business, Hartford ended up selling the operation. As for Alter, he offered testimony to a grand jury in return for immunity from the charge.) Hartford paid for more than that liquor store; he covered virtually all of Alter's living expenses.

Still, for Alter, that wasn't enough. "He let me live as well as anybody could possibly live," Alter said. "But no cash. The reason for it was quite obvious. . . . Very wealthy people, when they get a person they could really enjoy being with and trust, . . . are constantly afraid that if [the person makes] enough money [he will] leave. So I had a very fine apartment, a car, a garage, a maid, and a credit card, but very little cash. I could live well, but I couldn't build up a bank account." Now, as Alter saw Hartford's fortune dwindle, securing that bank account became critical.

Hartford's attorneys tried to warn their client of Alter's shifting allegiance, but Hartford refused to believe them. Consequently, Crosby, Davis, and Murphy were constantly being updated on just how dire Hartford's financial straits were, and thus could maintain an upper hand in negotiations.

In mid-1965, Hartford and Crosby appeared to have a deal. The Crosby group agreed to pay Sands $750,000 in legal fees, and the tourism minister promised they would get a certificate that would allow them to open a casino. Sands had one additional demand: he insisted that Mary

Carter Paint take on a partner, Wallace Groves. (Groves came alone to the deal; earlier he had forced Louis Chesler out of the Grand Bahama operation.) Under the terms set by Sands, Groves's Bahamas Amusements would manage the casino, hold the gambling license, and own four-ninths of the operation.

Financing was the only roadblock, and it turned into a big one. Just before the deal was to be signed, Crosby's backers vanished. A panicky Alter leaked word of Hartford's troubles to Groves's ex-partner, Chesler. Perhaps he might be able to strike a separate deal with the heir?

Chesler then called Hartford, who agreed to meet with him in New York. "I said I'd have a drink with him at the Carlyle Hotel," Hartford remembered. And there Chesler offered Hartford $5 to $6 million for fifty percent of the island, with Hartford keeping the other half. The deal sounded good, Hartford told Chesler, but he had to have the money up front. He never heard from the Canadian again.

A few months passed and Crosby found new financing, but still the negotiations tarried on. As he had with *Show*, Hartford insisted on maintaining a relationship with the venture. Every time the deal came near closing, Hartford invented another demand.

"We took the [final] papers to Hartford," recalled one of his attorneys. "We talked for hours. At one point Hartford turned to me and said, 'I want a restriction on the size of the buildings. I don't want this to look like Miami Beach.' " Specifically, he wanted to make sure that no structure would be taller than the highest tree. And he had his lawyer dutifully take the request back to Charles Murphy, who was representing Crosby.

"How can you do that if the trees are growing?" Murphy wanted to know. Finally, Murphy agreed to establish an aesthetics committee to approve all building done on the island.

In early 1966, Mary Carter Paint came up with a deal Hartford had to live with. In return for the part of the island he had already developed, he received $3.5 million in cash and 250,000 shares in what would become yet another subsidiary of Mary Carter Paint. The company also took over a $9 million mortgage on the island. In addition, for another $750,000 and an agreement to loan Mary Carter $1.25 million more, Hartford would own 17.6 percent of the Island Hotel Company, which would own the high-rise Britannia Beach Hotel, then under construction. He would also receive an annual percentage of casino profits above $6.25 million. For his $30 million investment, Hartford would end up with a lot of promises—and just $1.5 million in cash.

Crosby and company were happy with the arrangement. And for his part, Hartford expressed little displeasure. "People are always trying to equate things in terms of present money value," he said. "They never consider future results."

In reporting the details of the arrangement, the gossip columnist Aileen Mehle wrote of the "nice fresh money" being brought in by Hartford's new partners. Thanks to the involvement of Mary Carter Paint, Hartford figured, the $50,000 a month he was losing on Paradise Island would soon be stanched. "[Those losses] are expected to stop," Mehle wrote, "because the new group has acquired the gambling permit once owned by Nassau's Bahamian Club. Now they can play with the big boys."

It would not be long before Huntington Hartford was dealt out of Jim Crosby's game.

15

*I*N JANUARY 1966, just as the deal with Crosby was closing, Hartford received a phone call in his New York apartment from a lawyer in the organized-crime division of the U.S. Department of Justice. His name was Robert Peloquin, and he wanted to know about Paradise Island.

Hartford agreed to meet Peloquin on the island several days later—since he didn't travel by plane, he would need the time for the train-and-boat journey. Hartford told Peloquin and his companion, another government lawyer, Robert Bancroft, that if they met anyone during their tour he would introduce them as reporters. Peloquin and his partner thought the gambit was rather absurd; they had met the Mary Carter executives and told them they would be interviewing Hartford. But Hartford insisted on the ruse, and the lawyers agreed to it.

Peloquin was unimpressed by Hartford's understanding of the island's intrigues. "My own reaction was that if I [had given] him a badge out of a cereal box he would have given me the island," Peloquin noted, and when he returned to Washington, he wrote a memo to William Hundley, his superior at the Justice Department.

> Huntington Hartford appears to be a bored millionaire with a childish outlook on life. Mary Carter Paint will be in control of Paradise Island, with the exception of the casino, which Groves will control. The atmosphere seems ripe for a Lansky skim.

Peloquin's prediction was already coming to pass, and just ten months later the whole world would know about it. In October 1966, *The Wall Street Journal* detailed the payments Sands and other members of the

Bahamian executive council had received in return for granting gambling licenses. The black Progressive Liberal Party accused Sands and the rest of the Bay Street Boys of grand-scale corruption and successfully demanded an investigation by a Royal Commission of Inquiry. In a special election on January 10, 1967, the PLP won nineteen seats in the government, one more than Sands's United Bahamian Party, and the PLP's leader, Lynden Pindling, a portly thirty-six-year-old London-trained lawyer, became the first black premier in Bahamian history. Sands ignominiously retired to Spain. (As it turned out, Hartford had figured right in making that $15,000 donation to the PLP; unfortunately, he made it too early to do his own cause any good. By the time the PLP was in power, Hartford, having sold the island, was no longer in need of its influence.)

But even a change in government did little to hamper Crosby's plans. By the end of 1967, the Mary Carter group had accomplished everything Hartford could not: a high-rise hotel, a casino, and a bridge from Nassau.

Crosby threw a bash in January 1968 to celebrate the reopening of the island. It was a glittering affair, full of society sorts and movie stars. Janet Leigh (a frequent companion of Jack Davis's) came, as did Ladies Astor and Sassoon. Norman Jewison was there, as were Dina Merrill, Cliff Robertson, and Henry Mancini. Carol Channing flew in from Hollywood. The guest of honor was a man most people still considered a political has-been: Richard M. Nixon. Even Hunt Hartford turned up. The columnist Earl Wilson crossed the bridge to Paradise. "The gambling casino was in full operation, jammed with people with fistfuls of chips," he wrote. "Las Vegas, take note. It's all run by James M. Crosby, head of Mary Carter Paint Co. . . . and they tell me there never was any Mary Carter, but this paint company thought it sounded like a sweet name."

For Wallace Groves, the party was brief. Within the year, his tawdry dealings on Wall Street and with the mob were revealed in exposés in *Life* and *The Saturday Evening Post,* and Crosby bought out his casino contract for $1 million. A few months later, Crosby sealed his commitment to the casino business, selling off the paint company and renaming his corporation Resorts International.

Sands was gone, Groves was gone, but the mob taint persisted. In December 1967, Resorts International signed a three-year management contract with Eddie Cellini, younger brother of Dino Cellini, Meyer Lansky's right-hand man. The elder Cellini had run Lansky's casinos in Havana and, after Cuba closed down, had operated a croupier school in

London until British authorities threw him out of the country because of his Mafia ties. Dino was not permitted to run casinos in the Bahamas; he had been deported from the islands after a number of complaints from American law enforcement agencies. His offense was mastery of the Mafia skim; his croupiers (who included his younger brother) had been carefully instructed to run their tables so that the mob was sure to get the best piece of the action.

Even though Eddie was officially clean, his presence created considerable controversy. For two years, Resorts withstood the heat, but in November 1969, despite Crosby's insistence that Eddie had done a scrupulously honest job of operating the casino, the Bahamian government ordered Cellini off the island.

Had he seen where his interests lay, Hartford probably would have appreciated the wisdom of the government's decision. Although the contract with Crosby called for Hartford to receive any casino profits over $6.25 million, he would never see a nickel from the operation. But Hartford's assessment of Cellini, the man in charge of making those profits, was incredibly naive. "I kind of liked him," Hartford would say later. "He was good-looking, businesslike, tall."

Hartford still spent time on the island (the deal with Crosby let him keep his house), but he was no longer a player in the unfolding scandal. Instead, he persisted in the demands that had made striking the original deal difficult. Those demands were so far removed from the matters at hand that they drove Crosby to distraction; finally he had Hartford barred from meetings of both the board and the so-called aesthetics committee, insisting on a proxy. The man Hartford selected was James Vanderpol, a soft-spoken Dutchman who was originally Hartford's accountant at Coopers & Lybrand and later became his full-time financial adviser. It was Vanderpol who would keep Crosby apprised of Hartford's demands: fresh, not frozen, orange juice had to be served (never mind that it was much more expensive to ship over to the island); a brass railing had to be installed on the top of the Britannia Beach tower so that the structure would appear more Bahamian.

"Because Hartford had a minority interest in the hotel, he would interfere in things where he thought he had a point to make," recalled one of his attorneys, Howard Schneider. "Hartford was interested in aesthetics. Resorts had an economic purpose, dollars and cents, and they viewed Hartford as a roaring pain in the ass."

Crosby, who was all business, perceived his minority partner as nearly all bothersome whimsy, and he wanted him out. He apparently resolved to follow the simplest strategy: Let his erstwhile colleague self-destruct.

▲

While Hartford was selling the island, Paradise became the set for a different sort of drama. The producer Kevin McClory used the Café Martinique as the set for a scene in *Thunderball,* the fourth James Bond movie. The scene showed Diane dancing with Sean Connery, then going off in a pique when the villainess, Domino, sleek in a black-and-white jumpsuit, cut in. "You should have told me your wife was coming," Diane snapped. It sounded rather like a scene from her marriage.

Hartford, as if determined to re-create the same bad marriage in each of his unions, would leave clues when he was with other women. Once he had a young woman stashed in the Ocean Club on Paradise Island (a second-floor room was kept vacant for his assignations). "He told Diane he was going to play golf," recalled Hartford's psychiatrist friend Herbert Smokler. "Then he left the telephone number of the hotel room at the pro shop. Diane called, got the number. Of course, the girl answered; it was not that hard for Diane to figure out what was going on."

That night, Hartford, Diane, and Smokler dined together at the Café Martinique in tense silence. As the plates were taken away, Hunt's hand crawled slowly across the table toward Diane; he wanted to make up. She grabbed her knife and stabbed at him, then stormed away from the table. He bolted to the restaurant window and rapped on the glass, holding up his wounded, napkin-wrapped hand. Diane ignored him and walked off into the night. Her husband skulked back to the table.

"He would probably deny it," said Smokler, "but he set himself up. Diane played the role all his wives played, the punishing mother."

Discretion had never been Hartford's long suit, and so when his marriage to Diane ran aground, he made public spectacle of his troubles. He dedicated *Art or Anarchy?* "to Diane, who refuses to read it."

Hunt Hartford was a difficult man to be married to under the best of circumstances—and these were anything but. By 1964, Diane was more interested in pursuing her own adventures than wallowing in her husband's fiscal difficulties. "I think Diane was genuinely fond of Hunt, but she found herself in the role of being his keeper," said Harry "Coco" Brown, a movie producer who traveled in the same circles as the Hartfords in the mid-sixties.

Diane met the Beatles when they were filming *Help* on the beaches of Paradise Island, and with three friends she decided to form a rock-and-roll group. The What Four?, as they were known, bought matching jumpsuits, hired a PR man, and sent out a publicity photograph. Diane, a press release noted, was married to Huntington Hartford, but "he has nothing to do with the group."

The What Four? toured a few college campuses and released a 45 during their short life span. They had a part-time manager, a young red-haired lawyer named Kenneth Klein. Hartford insisted to anyone who would listen that his wife was romantically involved with her manager, whom he dubbed "Uriah Heep," after the malignant clerk in *David Copperfield*. By fall 1965, Diane had left the Beekman Place triplex and taken her own apartment, and on November 5, the split turned into tabloid melodrama at a discotheque owned by Richard Burton's ex-wife. As the *New York Post* had it:

> HARTFORDS GO-GO AT IT AT ARTHUR
>
> Police called to break up a battle royal at Sybil Burton Christopher's celebrated discotheque left empty-handed when they discovered nothing was going on but an old-fashioned family dispute. . . . Had the yelling and pushing match taken place on the dance floor—where a program is necessary to tell the difference between a Frug, a Jerk, a Watusi, or bloody murder—it might have gone unnoticed. But Hartford and Diane had their spat in a telephone booth.

The Hartfords had gone separately to the club. Hunt was on his own; Diane was accompanied by Ken Klein and China Gerard, a model turned What Four? When Diane went to make a phone call, Hartford spotted her and gave chase; he pushed at the door to pry her from the booth. Klein jumped to Diane's defense, only to have Hartford go after him. The two ended up tussling on the floor while Diane, phone in hand all the while, called the police.

One of Hartford's attorneys, who had arrived on the scene before the police, persuaded them it was nothing more than a domestic dispute. But on November 18, Diane filed for separation, citing "cruel and inhuman treatment."

Within days her husband was begging her to return. "Diane is very, very mad at me," a contrite Hartford told Earl Wilson, who reported the conversation in the *New York Post*. "But I'm hoping the separation suit will be dropped and we'll get back together."

"What's she mad at you about?" Wilson asked.

"For being an SOB for about five years," Hartford replied.

"Are you willing to make up with her despite that fight at Arthur, where you pushed that fellow she was with down to the floor?"

"Sure," Hartford said, grinning. "If it hadn't been him, it would have been somebody else, the way we were usually apart. I don't know what I can do about him. I can't get in a fight with him.''

"And you are promising Diane that you will personally reform and be a devoted husband if she takes you back?''

"I am," Hartford insisted, "although I don't know whether she'll believe me.''

Apparently she did. By mid-December the columnists were buzzing about a reconciliation, and the two were back together at One Beekman Place.

As Hartford's say over Paradise Island diminished, his attention drifted to other concerns. When the Egyptian government announced plans to build a high dam at Aswan on the upper Nile, a project that would flood the ancient temples of Abu Simbel, Hartford led a group to raise $7 million of the $36 million needed to remove the antiquities and establish them elsewhere.

A few years earlier, Hartford might have put up the millions himself, but by 1966 he could afford only to act as a fund-raiser. Toward that end, he threw a black-tie party at the Gallery of Modern Art, a fine affair with belly dancers, shish kabob, and a recalcitrant camel named Loumi, which Hartford contrived to get into the building through the revolving door. Once inside, though, the normally docile beast spat and kicked all evening—then ended up relieving himself in the middle of the ballroom floor. To Hartford's credit—and despite Loumi's antics—the money was raised; one of the saved structures, the Temple of Dendur, was subsequently transported to the Metropolitan Museum of Art in New York.

In the summer of 1966, Hartford put up a $100,000 bond in a futile effort to help save the old Metropolitan Opera House from destruction. It was $100,000 down the drain: when the developers won the right in court to tear down the building, they also won Hartford's money to help defray their legal costs.

For nearly ten years, a decade of gathering losses, Huntington Hartford had given scant attention to the source of his wealth, his shares of the A&P. But in 1966, after three years of watching the value of the stock sink, Hartford's bankers persuaded him to start selling. On June 7, Hartford filed with the Securities and Exchange Commission to sell off 760,000 A&P shares, three percent of the total stock outstanding and just about all that was left of his stake in the family business.

Reason would dictate that the time to take on a company's management is when, as a significant shareholder, one can hope to press its executives into action. But pragmatism, never Hartford's forte, was in particularly short supply when it came to his dealings with the A&P. Not long after he had sold off most of his shares, Hartford decided to launch a noisy campaign against the grocery giant's management. To save the A&P, to rescue his beloved uncles' legacy, Hartford turned to one of his own failed ventures: *Show* magazine.

"The magazine was like a child to him," remembered Phyllis Sher, "only he didn't treat his children that well." Ever since it had folded, Hartford had been obsessed with reviving the journal. In 1967 Hartford got his wish. A new *Show* would be financed by the Longines Symphonette Recording Society, the entertainment subsidiary (records, radios) of the Longines-Wittnauer watch company. The plan, according to John Day, the Longines executive in charge of the project, was not just to publish a magazine of the performing arts; this *Show* would "let the American family in on the richer life that is all around them . . . things previously reserved for the multimillionaire." While Hartford would have only a small financial stake in the venture, his multimillionaire's sensibility would be on tap in his role as editor in chief.

The new *Show* was a K Mart version of the rich life, little more than a catalogue for Longines collectibles. Issues were glutted with ads for chess sets and cheesy stained-glass reproductions. On the editorial side, there was much ado about the occult—one piece tried to answer the question "Was Dracula a good guy?"—and there were articles on tarot, tea leaves, and Hartford's perennial favorite, handwriting analysis.

Shoddy though the new *Show* may have been, it still provided Hartford with a platform to attack the men he felt were mangling the company his uncles had built. He began his attack in June, at the A&P's annual meeting, the first he ever attended. That year, with his client no longer a significant shareholder, Hartford's proxy, David Sher, had quit the A&P board. But that didn't stop Hartford from running for election himself. In announcing his candidacy, he charged that current management consisted of "nothing more than puppets of the [John Hartford Foundation]." Hartford's criticism of the A&P was dead-on, but he had no effect on either the Foundation or management. He was overwhelmingly defeated by management's seventeen-man slate.

Hartford battled on. In the October 1967 issue of *Show*, he charged that complacent management had emasculated the grocery chain. He noted that the A&P's annual sales had been mired at $5 billion for eight years while its stock had plunged from $70 to a low of $27—all that "during one of the great booms of American history." A&P service, Hartford said, now made mockery of its motto: "We care about you." As evidence, he cited letters he had received from shoppers complaining about everything from tacky stores to rotten eggs.

Hartford's article, "Why the A&P Doesn't Care!," began with a description of a walk down First Avenue in Manhattan. Strolling along, he looked into a closed but illuminated A&P, and there he saw a clerk lying prone on a section of merchandise. Hartford was outraged. First he banged on the glass door to get the man's attention. Then he wrote a note and held it up to the glass for the clerk to see; the man shuffled over to read it. Only then did the clerk look abashed. He was sorry, he told Hartford, but it was his hour off, and he would at once retire to a less public resting place. What had Hartford written on the note? "I don't think Mr. John would have liked what you're doing." The piece went on to detail the accomplishments of the Hartford brothers, and the ruination of the company in the hands of John's former private secretary, Ralph Burger. Hunt Hartford called for a government breakup of the Foundation's control of the company.

"We take no part in management," Burger snapped to a reporter. And an A&P official pointedly observed that "Mr. Hartford's lack of knowledge about the company may be attributed to the fact that he has never been a part of management."

For the next several years, Hartford crusaded against the men who managed his uncles' empire. Belatedly carrying the family standard, he took his campaign to the air, telling Helen Gurley Brown on her daytime television talk show that by hanging onto the A&P stock and trying to keep control of management, the Foundation had destroyed the company and with it the price of the company's shares. He marched on to Washington, sending a letter to Congressman Wilbur Mills, chairman of the Committee on Ways and Means, that offered his support for a proposal to limit the stock a tax-exempt foundation could hold in a publicly held company.

When the Foundation executives learned of the letter, they were, predictably, outraged; the Foundation's law firm fired off its own letter to Mills, requesting an opportunity to reply "in view of the fact that the letter contains several errors and omissions." (The Foundation ultimately lost that battle; in 1969 a new rule was added to the Internal Revenue Service code prohibiting charitable foundations from controlling more than twenty percent of the shares of a publicly traded corporation; those that already did were given up to twenty years to divest.)

In September 1968, Hunt Hartford took his battle from the House to the street: the heir turned up at a picket line at A&P headquarters to support a United Farm Workers boycott of California grapes, announcing that he was "sympathetic with what they are doing."

The feeling may not have been entirely reciprocal. Just moments after he arrived, someone had the presence of mind to whisk away a picket sign that read "Huntington Hartford Gets Rich on Scab Grapes."

While Hartford was fighting his losing battle to right a company in which he had precious little financial interest, he was very quickly losing his grip on the investment that he had made the keystone of his fortune: Resorts International.

When Hartford sold Paradise Island, he loaned Resorts $2 million toward the construction of the Britannia Beach Hotel. Four years later, Jim Crosby wanted to remove that debt from his company's balance sheet. Hartford and his financial adviser, Jim Vanderpol, flew to Acapulco to negotiate with Jim Crosby and Jack Davis. Hartford asked for cash (needed to upgrade the newest incarnation of *Show,* he said), but Resorts offered only stock. Hartford ended up with 150,000 Class A shares of Resorts International, worth $28 apiece. There was a catch: Hartford's shares were not registered with the Securities and Exchange Commission. Resorts claimed that registering the shares would create an oversupply on the market and depress the price. As a result Hartford could not sell his holdings on the open market. He would have to wait for the registry of his shares, a lengthy process, or arrange for their private placement himself, which was equally time-consuming.

Hartford didn't like the tenuousness of it all; he asked Davis what would happen if he wanted to sell out, if he needed to raise cash in a hurry. Davis reassured Hartford that if Resorts failed to register the shares with the SEC within one year of the transaction, the company would provide Hartford with a $1 million bank loan and pick up the interest.

The year passed; Resorts never registered the stock. Meanwhile, the price dropped from $28 per share to $16, making Hartford $1.8 million poorer, at least on paper. But Hartford never seemed troubled by the market value of that stock; especially in October 1969, when Resorts fulfilled its obligation to provide him with a loan. The Bank of Commerce, a New York–based institution with close ties to Crosby, provided Hartford with a "demand note"; the bank could call it at any time. He took his comfort from the fact that Resorts promised to act as the note's unconditional guarantor. For the Bank of Commerce, though, Resorts' guarantee wasn't enough. Hartford put up the 150,000 shares of Resorts stock that he owned as additional collateral, and several months later, when the bank asked for the stake in the hotel as well, Hartford complied.

Years later, Hartford's advisers defended their precarious deal, saying that it was the only way they could get the bank to put up the money for Hartford, and that cash was key. But they conceded that the deal planted the seeds for Hartford's destruction. "We were always negotiating from a very weak start," explained Vanderpol. "He was insisting he wanted to launch another *Show,* and the overriding factor was that we had to raise cash. . . . We always had our backs up against the wall, that was the reason that we made deals that might not have looked that attractive. This was the best deal Hartford could get at the time. In hindsight, though, it looks like he was set up for a squeeze."

16

"*T*O START WITH, I have to say that my family has been a dysfunctional one." That was the way Cathy Hartford described her upbringing in an essay written in 1987 as part of her treatment for drug and alcohol addictions. "I started out with a wealthy father and an actress mother," Cathy wrote. "My father wasn't really a father and my mother was always on the road. . . . When I did see her she was usually drunk."

Just a year after her divorce from Hartford in 1960, Marjorie had found a new husband and a new life in England. The children generally spent summers with her and she tried to remain a force in their lives, but she and Hartford agreed that their offspring should be raised in the United States. For all practical purposes, Huntington Hartford had sole custody of his children.

He was a passive patriarch, fitfully vigilant at best. "At home he always had a whole lot of people going in and going out and whatnot, and that's not an atmosphere for bringing up children," recalled Phyllis Sher. "I don't know if he ever did anything with them. He just had no sense of responsibility—financially or any other way. His idea of being a father simply wasn't acceptable."

Concerned about the effect that her ex-husband's womanizing would have on her soon-to-be-teenage children, Marjorie urged him to send them away to school. "Mommy wouldn't let me live with Daddy, and I couldn't live with Mommy," explained Cathy. "So instead of becoming a ward of the court, I ended up in boarding schools."

After an unhappy year in Switzerland, Cathy persuaded her parents to allow her to live at her father's house. "There was one school that I knew of in New York where Daddy got most of his girlfriends," Cathy recalled. "So I wrote him a letter saying, 'I'm so happy to be coming back, I'd be happy to go to any schools except that one.' Of course that's where he enrolled me. So I'd bring home my friends, and he used to try to get me to pimp for him." By her own estimate, Cathy went to seventeen different schools.

Jackie too bounced from school to school; finally he ended up at Stockbridge, a boarding school in Massachusetts.

Both Hartford children were starved for parental attention, and for a time both turned to drugs as a way of getting it. When Jackie was about fifteen, his father found out he was shooting heroin. "Hunt found the needle, called Jackie, and gave him a real strong lecture," Marjorie remembered. "Then he handed Jackie back all this gear and said, 'Get rid of it.' To this day, Jackie can never understand why he gave him back the heroin. You would think he would have gotten rid of it himself if he didn't want his son to take it. You would almost think he was trying to keep him on heroin." No thanks to his father, Jackie gave up drugs before any lasting damage was done. His sister would be less fortunate.

Cathy began her pharmaceutical experiments on Paradise Island. The Hartford home was next door to the Mellon estate; living there were William and Peggy Hitchcock, sibling heirs to the Pittsburgh banking fortune and part of the group whose locus was ex–Harvard professor Timothy Leary, now an LSD guru. Cathy called them the psychedelic socials, and she was a regular at their parties.

As for her father, his involvement with the psychedelic experience was unintentional. Even if he was ineffective, Hunt Hartford was vociferously opposed to drugs, and Cathy knew it. But in July 1967, she was desperate to go to one of the Hitchcocks' parties on their estate in Millbrook, New York. "I called Billy [Hitchcock] and said, 'I really want to go—how am I going to do this?' He said to ask Daddy along and tell him there would be a lot of beautiful girls going." For Hartford, the potential discovery of a new Galatea obviated his qualms about hallucinogens. Hartford father and daughter trooped to Millbrook; both quaffed considerable amounts of the fruit punch. Unbeknownst to Hunt, it was spiked with LSD.

"I thought it was a big thing that Daddy should get stoned," Cathy recalled. "He started walking around the Hitchcock mansion and looking for this girl, and he was walking into [a] bedroom." When the couple in bed demanded to know what he was doing there, he resumed his search elsewhere. Afterward, Cathy asked him how the drugs had affected him. "He wasn't aware he had gotten high," she marveled. "He wasn't into drugs, he was into girls."

Although Hartford was but a distant spectator in his children's lives, he constantly tried to run the show from afar. "If they were late or they didn't tell him where they were going, he would spend all evening trying to track them down," recalled Jim Vanderpol. "He would hire detectives to follow Cathy, watch her. If he didn't know where she was, he would call the police, call a detective to make sure he was informed. He wanted control, but he didn't want to spend time with them."

For Cathy, the worst came in 1968, when she was celebrating her high school graduation. A group of young socialites had thrown her a party, complete with ample quantities of drugs. "All of a sudden there's a phone call from Daddy," Cathy said. "And he's furious at me . . . because I didn't invite him to the party." He ordered her to come home; she refused. "Eight in the morning came 'round. Then these policemen came running in and proceeded to bust all the adults. Now, I had a joint in my purse. They looked through it and said, 'Oh, this is nothing,' and they threw it away." Cathy was convinced that her father orchestrated the whole incident so that she would be frightened but not harmed.

Not long afterward, Hartford's sister, uncharacteristically, reached out to her niece, trying to pull Cathy back into the family fold. Josephine Hartford Bryce announced that she would have a double coming-out party for Cathy and her granddaughter, Dallas, daughter of Senator Claiborne Pell and his wife, Nuala. But the glittering debut never did come off. In the course of planning the party, Hartford asked his sister to return an heirloom necklace that he had lent to her years before; the jewels were part of the legacy that Henrietta had pointedly excluded from her daughter's inheritance. Josephine told her brother that if she was forced to return the necklace, there would be no party. But Hartford held firm, and his daughter was left standing at society's door.

By the late sixties, not only had Hartford lost his children, he was well on the way to losing his on-again, off-again wife. The relationship with Diane had foundered before, but this time the Hartford persona was no longer that of a reckless youth or even a graying libertine. The line had been crossed from aging playboy to cuckold.

"The thing about the relationship [with Diane] was that Hunt was always looking for her," recalled Harry Brown. "And when he pursued her, it had to be by train or boat, because he didn't drive [or fly]. When he finally did catch up with her, she would stay for a couple of days and be off again—and he would take up in hot pursuit.''

In 1967, a new man entered Diane's life: Bobby Darin, who had just divorced the actress Sandra Dee. Diane was on a solo trip to Los Angeles, pursuing, at her husband's urging, a career on the screen, when she first met the pop singer at Daisy, an exclusive Beverly Hills discotheque. On June 29, a paparazzo spotted them together at the premiere of *Woman Times Seven,* a dim-witted seven-episode sex farce starring Shirley MacLaine and Peter Sellers. ''Diane was looking at Bobby as if she could hardly wait to throw her arms around him,'' reported the photographer, Sylvia Norris.

Darin flew off to London for a singing engagement; Diane followed. Reporters trailed the couple throughout the summer: there were stops in Paris, Monte Carlo, and New York. By August, people were asking Hartford just what was going on between his wife and the singer.

Diane's relationship with Darin, Hartford assured one reporter, was ''just another fling.'' Nonetheless, he made it quite clear he was unhappy with the situation, and huffed that he didn't like Darin ''monopolizing his wife.''

All the articles, photographs, and fatuous comments somehow served to anchor Hartford's hold on history and deflect the humiliation he must have felt when he discovered his wife had run out on him. That summer, Marjorie's third husband, the writer Constantine Fitzgibbon, on a trip through London, visited Hartford at home and found him listening to one of Darin's recordings. ''Doesn't that make you feel a little uncomfortable?'' Fitzgibbon asked. To which Hartford responded, ''The publicity is sort of fun.''

In early September, Diane flew back to New York and filed for divorce, charging cruelty. Hartford immediately hit the phones. First he called Diane's attorney, Burton Monasch, to complain. ''I don't mind if she [sleeps with] him,'' he told Monasch, ''but does she have to divorce me?''

Next Hartford called the New York *Daily News* with his woes. ''She has no case,'' Hartford told a reporter. ''I was always good and considerate to her. As a matter of fact, I am hoping that she will come back to me, as she already has done several times.''

This time was no exception. At the end of October, Hartford and Diane were spotted first at the April in Paris Ball in New York, and then hand in hand at the revival of *Gone With the Wind.* In November, Diane was back at Beekman Place, and a month later she announced that not only was she dropping the divorce action but she was expecting a child.

According to newspaper accounts, Diane's reconciliation agreement with Hartford called for a $1.5 million trust for the unborn child. Said Monasch, "It has all been tidied up very nicely."

Just as Diane discovered she was pregnant, Ed Barton stumbled back into his father's life.

After signing the papers and agreeing to give up his claim to the Hartford name, Buzz had tried to break away from his father for good. But Hartford could not let his son go. In 1962, Barton's friend Wayne Headrick was drafted into the Army and shipped to Berlin, and Barton followed. Hartford, still unwilling to let the relationship go, tracked his son down in Germany, and called and asked what his plans were. He implored him to write, to come to New York, and promised his help in whatever Barton might want to do.

He told his father he might be interested in pursuing a career in drama. Hartford, in turn, offered his mostly shuttered Los Angeles theater as a forum for his son's aspirations. He summoned Barton and Headrick to the Bahamas to close the deal. But no sooner had they arrived than Hartford told them he had changed his mind: he could not, he insisted, afford to bankroll another venture.

Once again, Barton tried to pull away. He returned to Europe with Headrick, and the two spent three largely unstructured years there, with occasional stints at language school, before deciding it was time to get on with their lives. They went back to Los Angeles in 1965.

Even though Barton had legally signed away his rights to the Hartford name, he could not give up his quest for legitimacy. And now he reached out to his father, in a desperate attempt for recognition. "What's it going to be?" Barton said when he called. "I want the name and I don't want any more games of yours. It's not the money I want, just the name."

Hartford once again made vague promises, and once again he showed no signs of action. In the months that followed, Ed Barton grew increasingly disconsolate, drinking more and sleeping less. He dreamed up a fantasy romance with Sue Lyon, the actress who starred as the pigtailed nymphet in *Lolita,* and sent her crazy telegrams declaring his love. "He was really flipped out," remembered Headrick. "Just a matter of three weeks and he went totally haywire."

Headrick called Hartford in New York, hoping that, as Barton's father, he might take charge. "Hartford told me to call his attorney," recalled Headrick. "I said, 'What in hell does an attorney have to do with it?' " But that was all the assistance Hartford offered. When Headrick tried enlisting Hartford's lawyer, he told Headrick there was nothing he could do. And when Headrick called Hartford back, he was told to take care of Barton himself; Hartford was too busy. "You handle it, Wayne," Hartford said, "the best way you can."

Headrick checked Barton into the Westwood Psychiatric Hospital. "Buzz was in the hospital for about six weeks," recalled Headrick, "writing screwy things, doing screwy things." The psychiatrists diagnosed him as manic-depressive. Even so, Headrick was unable to convince them that Barton should be forcibly committed, that he was a danger to himself or anyone else. In the summer of 1967, Ed Barton checked himself out of the hospital.

After his release, Barton grew increasingly manic. He started a film company, Bardrick Productions, complete with a brochure intended to lure investors. At first glance, it looked slickly professional: Barton, the pin-striped executive, pen in hand; Barton, a Cannes Film Festival folder under his arm, seated on a desk with two pert actress-cum-secretaries in the background. The text sounded like pure Huntington Hartford: "We aim to combine incisive social and moral consciousness with imaginative and profitable film-making. . . . We are certain that there is a sizable market for motion pictures which present American values in a fresh, provocative way. . . . To achieve these goals, we propose films of initial impact, enduring artistic merit, and lasting appeal. We believe in happy endings."

For Ed Barton, the ending would come far too soon, and it was tragically unhappy.

Barton decided to go back to New York and, as he told Headrick, "settle this thing with my father for once and for all." He took a room in a hotel and contacted Hartford. At first, his father refused to see him. But each day Barton sent letters pleading to be given the family name. Hartford finally agreed to a meeting. Afterward Barton called Headrick with the good news. "He told me the deal was done, that Hartford finally agreed to give him the name," recalled Headrick.

The next day Hartford took Barton out to lunch with Cathy. Once more Barton pleaded, and once more Hartford told him that while he had not ruled out giving him the name, he still was not ready; he still did not think it was a good idea. "He always said he wanted him to accomplish something," remembered Herbert Smokler. "He said, 'I'll give him the name when he's making twenty thousand a year.' "

After the lunch, Barton confided in Cathy. All he wanted, he told his teenage half sister, was to "walk down the street and be your brother and have your name."

"I'll tell everyone you're my brother," Cathy answered. But that was nowhere near enough.

That night, Barton went to a neighborhood gun store and bought a pistol. Sometime in the next two days—no one knew just when—he put the muzzle to his head and sent a bullet through his brain. The suicide note, according to Headrick, said he "simply couldn't bear it anymore."

Several days passed before he was found; hotel employees, alarmed by the stench permeating the hallway, called the police, who broke the lock and found the body. In Barton's wallet was a card with the name and phone number of someone to contact in case of emergency: his closest friend, Wayne Headrick.

The police reached Headrick in California. "I called Hartford, expecting he would know," said Headrick. "He didn't. Then I called the morgue. They told me that if I didn't get the body out in twenty-four hours they would dispose of it themselves." Frantic, he called Hartford again. This time, Hartford started to cry.

"Listen," he told Headrick, "you come back here and don't mention this to anybody. Contact my attorneys as soon as you can so we can keep the publicity down."

Headrick did as he was told. He was met at the airport by one of Hartford's employees, who shepherded him from the hotel to the morgue. "Hartford made sure I didn't talk to anyone, made sure no one found out," said Headrick. "I felt the power of the situation I was in. They told me everything would be taken care of, and it was."

Headrick took the body back to Los Angeles and arranged for the burial. "Hartford kept calling," he remembered, "concerned that the news not get into the papers." It barely did: the only mention was a two-inch item in the *Los Angeles Herald-Examiner* titled "Was This Suicide Heir's Son?"

Hartford did not go to the funeral, but he demanded one final gesture. Headrick was besieged with calls from Hartford and his lawyers, who insisted that a stanza of "A Dead March" by a nineteenth-century Englishman, Cosmo Monkhouse, be inscribed on Barton's grave.

"He was interested in the headstone," said Headrick. "That baffled me. I said, 'Don't concern yourself with this. In life he didn't matter, why should he after he's dead?' "

Huntington Hartford's son is buried in an out-of-the-way cemetery in Inglewood, California, not far from the house where Hartford shipped the Brangenbergs back in the fifties. The grave lies just above a stagnant manmade creek. In the end, Headrick chose the inscription himself. A single unattributed line is chiseled into the shiny granite: "Love is the

morning and evening star.'' But Headrick could not give his friend what
he wanted most. The name on the gravestone is Edward Barton.

"If I had realized he was going to commit suicide, I would have given
him the name and everything," Hartford said later. "The thing was, I
was always nice to him, I wrote letters to him and kept in touch with
him. He couldn't think I was brushing him off. I had in my mind to give
him the name because he wanted it so much. I always said, 'Buzzy, I'll
do it, but I want you to get some respect, do something big.' "

17

On July 4, 1968, Diane Hartford gave birth to a baby girl. With that infant came a moment of bliss; it looked as if the Hartford marriage might be salvaged. The family took up residence at Beekman Place, and Huntington Hartford doted on the child, named Cynara Juliet and referred to by her middle name. He sat for a profile with *The Miami Herald,* his baby cradled in his arms, looking more like a graying father given one last chance at paternity than an aging playboy scrambling after lost youth. "We're terribly happy most of the time," Diane told the reporter.

It sounded too good to be true, and indeed it was. The fragility of their marriage was displayed in the spring of 1969, when both Hartfords were summoned to appear at the trial of an electronics expert named Bernard Spindel. There had been a crackdown on illicit eavesdropping, and Spindel was charged with installing a bug, at Hartford's request, in the apartment of Diane's onetime boyfriend Ken Klein.

Diane took the stand in April. As for her husband, she testified that he had taken off for Nassau to avoid a subpoena; she had not seen him since Christmas.

Spindel's attorney, Arnold Stream, questioned her about her relationship with Klein. "Did Klein visit you in your apartment at 500 East Seventy-seventh Street?" he asked.

"Yes, about fourteen or sixteen times," she replied.

"Daytime visits?"

"Yes."

"Nighttime visits?"

"Evenings," she corrected.

"What about overnight?"

Here Diane took the Fifth Amendment.

Stream moved on to Bobby Darin. Diane said that she had seen him in Los Angeles and two weeks later in San Francisco, and again in New York. In the summer of 1965, she said, they had both been staying at the Regency Hotel in New York.

"Did you spend any time in his suite?"

"Yes."

"Did he spend any time in yours?"

"Yes."

"Did you have sexual relations with him?"

"I refuse to answer, on constitutional grounds."

The prosecution also took testimony from Jonathan Connors, Ken Klein's roommate, who revealed that Hartford had paid him to assist in the bugging operation. Spindel was convicted in May.

Hartford returned to New York after the verdict, and by then Diane, exasperated with her absentee spouse, was almost gone. When she finally headed for the door in early June, Hartford did not make it easy. He stood at the top of the stairs, holding Juliet and screaming that he wasn't going to let Diane have the child. Only after calling the police for an escort was Diane able to leave, baby in tow.

This time there would be no reconciliation. "I could see things were going downhill," Diane said later, "and I had my child to consider." On June 10, 1969, she filed for divorce.

The attorneys negotiated for a year; Diane ended up with $2,500 a month in alimony and $6,500 more in child-support payments. On July 7, 1970, she arrived in Juárez, Mexico, to seal the split. "No, sir," she told a reporter who followed her to the courthouse, "I'm not getting married again for a long time to come."

Her departure destroyed the last semblance of stability in Hartford's life. As Cathy's friend Billy Hitchcock put it, "Diane was the only sobering voice in the wilderness. After she left, it was all downhill."

At Hartford's museum, the signs of decline had begun while Diane was still—more or less—by his side. The gallery had been in financial trouble almost from the moment it opened its doors, and by 1968 it was in danger of having to close them. True, it had held a few successful shows, most notably a retrospective of the works of Aubrey Beardsley, but far more typical were the embarrassing failures: an exhibition of Dwight Eisenhower's artwork and one entitled "The Challenge Is Freedom," a selection of self-important text and indistinguishable black-and-white silhouettes by Earl Hubbard, whose wife knew Hartford from the social circuit.

But the gallery's problems had less to do with art than economics. Running it cost more than $500,000 a year, a sum that Hartford could no longer afford. And so he was forced to start looking in earnest for someone who would take over.

He tried to interest several of New York City's leading academic institutions, Columbia, Fordham, and New York University among them, but he found no takers. He got furthest with Fordham, which proposed to acquire the structure as a center for its communications arts program, but the talks were scuttled when Hartford insisted that the building be retained as an art museum. Then a friend of Hartford's, Henry "Sandy" Williams III, son of the owner of a newspaper, the *Paterson Morning Call,* suggested he contact Peter Sammartino, the founder and retired president of Fairleigh Dickinson University in New Jersey. Sammartino was interested; the gallery would give his suburban university a potentially prestigious urban outpost. But finances proved problematic. The school, Sammartino told Hartford, could not afford to take on the entire burden of running the gallery.

Months passed. Then, while Sammartino was in London, he received a 1:30 A.M. phone call from Hartford. The heir had a new deal in mind: he would donate $1 million in working capital and subsidize half the museum's annual deficit, up to a total of $100,000. If the university kept the museum operating for five years, it would receive half of the charitable trust Hartford had set up in the fifties to fund his various projects— potentially some $5 million. This time Hartford struck a deal.

On August 13, 1969, the gallery officially became the New York City Cultural Center in Association with Fairleigh Dickinson University, its stated goal "to present the contributions of all races."

Hartford was circumspect about the loss. "It's a very difficult problem for one person to support a museum," he told a *New York Times* reporter. "It was probably foolhardy for me to try—but then fools rush in. Perhaps I should get one or two points for not selling it to the telephone company."

Hartford kept the title of president, but it was Sammartino and his wife who actually ran the place and raised the money. And cash was tight from the start. They kept the original name, "Gallery of Modern Art Including the Huntington Hartford Collection," inscribed on the building for the simple reason that they didn't have the money to change it, according to Sammartino, even though the name made it harder to raise money. "People didn't feel like going in and giving money and saving the Huntington Hartford museum, and Hartford certainly didn't have friends who were willing to step forward and help him."

Once Hartford's ownership stake slipped, his interest waned. "When we took over, I thought it would be nice if he wrote up descriptions of the paintings," Sammartino recalled. "I asked him and he said, 'Nothing doing. I don't do hackwork.' " The only time he became involved, said Sammartino, was when the center put on a show for Marjorie.

In 1971, the gallery finally hired a professional curator, Mario Amaya, fresh from a three-year stint as the chief curator of the Art Gallery of Ontario. Amaya was a habitué of the Warhol scene (while visiting Warhol's Factory in 1968 he was creased by a bullet from the same gun that almost killed Andy), and his curatorial taste reflected that very contemporary sensibility. In his four years at the center his more notable shows included a tribute to Max Reinhardt, "Blacks, U.S.A.," and "Women Choose Women," one of the first to focus solely on female artists.

Hartford was willing to take the glory at openings, but that was about it, said Amaya. "He never even came up with the $100,000 he was contractually supposed to contribute." Even worse, the curator said, paintings started disappearing off the gallery's walls. Amaya felt that the pictures bought for the museum should stay there, even though Hartford still legally owned them: "He took the pictures and sold them. Then he used the money himself." Amaya grew increasingly angry as he read of the prices the paintings fetched. In one auction, Sotheby's sold a Pre-Raphaelite Venus for $79,200 (a record for Pre-Raphaelite works). In another, the Dalí work commissioned especially for the museum, *The Discovery of America by Christopher Columbus,* went for $100,000, just a third of what, reportedly, it was commissioned for, but it was cash all the same.

"We never saw a penny of those proceeds," Amaya recalled bitterly. "Hartford claimed to be all for saving the museum, but he never came up with any money."

Amid the cacophony of failure, there was one Hartford venture that still had promise: Tosco, the venture founded to extract oil from shale. By the mid-sixties two establishment corporations, Sohio and Cleveland Cliffs, had invested millions for a prototype oil-shale plant. The first tests failed miserably; the cost of extracting oil from rock proved to be many times that of simply drilling it out of the ground. Rather than pump in more millions, the two companies decided to withdraw. Tosco shares took a dive, and Hartford, who was still a substantial shareholder as well as the titular chairman, panicked.

On July 17, 1968, he called a press conference at Beekman Place to announce his resignation as chairman. He was doing so, he said, because of "mismanagement" by Tosco executives, who had acted in a "high-handed and arbitrary manner" in their dealings with Sohio. In particular, he said, one director, Edward Kennedy, had made "derogatory statements at a board meeting about Charles Spahr [president of Sohio]." Further, Hartford planned to sue Tosco's upstart management.

Management had no comment about its wayward chairman. "We didn't have a lot of time to worry about what Hartford was thinking," recalled Morton Winston, then Tosco's president. Instead of trying to pacify Hartford, Winston focused on redeploying Tosco's assets.

His strategy proved astute. Hartford quickly lost interest in the Tosco imbroglio, although he would wait for a few years before he sold his stake in the company. And when he did, he ended up with a few million dollars in profit. It wasn't a terrific return on a twenty-five-year investment, but with Hartford's track record it seemed like a bonanza.

"The only role he missed was being a general in Vietnam," said one of Hartford's attorneys, marveling at his client's persistence in the face of constant failure. "Hartford saw the light at the end of every tunnel."

It seemed not to matter how long the tunnels were. In the mid-sixties, Hartford hinted to a gossip columnist at the *New York Post* that he was interested in running for mayor. That trial balloon never made it off the ground, but Hartford became more involved with the ill-fated mayoral campaign of Sanford Garelik, a former chief of the New York Police Department, in 1973.

Those political dalliances led a procession of new schemes, apparently motivated by little more than the pursuit of one more headline, one more grasp at the shadows of renown. Hartford announced plans worthy of Robert Moses to rebuild the Queens waterfront, just across the East River from Manhattan, but nothing much came of them. Then he started to downsize his ambitions; he put most of his efforts into two of his more eccentric notions: handwriting analysis and a hybrid tennis game.

In 1973, Macmillan published Hartford's graphology treatise, *You Are What You Write,* a history of handwriting analysis that was more interesting for its insights into its author than for its dubious science. In a chapter titled "Connective Forms," Hartford juxtaposed a sample from his "darling mother" with autographs from Charles Dickens and Leonardo da Vinci. He pointed out the series of "garlands" in his mother's script, looplike endings to *m*s, *n*s, and *w*s that he believed were a sign of both ambition and immaturity. "My beloved mother," he wrote, "who found a combination of finality and love an irresistible formula by which to guide her son, wrote with a continuous series of garlands that looked like an exercise in perpetual motion."

As a sort of parlor game, he included a celebrity sampler, a lifetime's worth of collecting: Ingrid Bergman ("highly creative writing with an unexpectedly conventional streak"), Salvador Dalí ("the persistent 't' bars betray the hard worker, the businessman . . . the good salesman whose worldly characteristics are usually blamed on his wife, Gala"), and Joe DiMaggio ("highly physical writing").

Then there was his exegesis on the publisher of *Playboy*: "My acquaintance with Hugh Hefner began around the time he merged his ill-fated *Show Business Illustrated* with the original version of my magazine *Show* in 1962. I was not particularly conscious of any intense reaction to Hef at that time except pure jealousy, of course, at his success." The heir was not enthralled with the publisher's taste in women. "After two or three visits to the Playboy mansion, I began to become terribly disappointed. The girls that one saw around seemed to be only window dressing for the VIPs, and they reminded me of flocks of geese which disappeared at the slightest movement in their direction."

Hartford was more impressed with Hefner's script than with his entourage. His penmanship, he wrote, reminded him of Kurtz, the ivory trader in Joseph Conrad's *Heart of Darkness*. According to Hartford, Hefner, like the jungle-bound trader, displayed "a genius for the commonplace and the unexpected in an arena where the theorist and the specialist could never have survived." It was the sort of worldly savvy that eluded the heir altogether.

There is nothing of Hartford's own penmanship in the book. When a *Daily News* reporter asked Hartford how he judged his own script he responded: "The small 'g's' and 'd's' showed a tendency toward the creative, with a weakness when it came to doing business." But he insisted that was changing, that the rhythm in his writing "shows better adjustment now than in earlier specimens, the pressure's heavier, too— a sign of materialism."

Did that mean he hoped his new book would actually make money? "Oh yes. I'm very anxious to make money," he said. "I didn't used to be."

▲

But when it came to divining money-making projects, his judgment remained unerringly bad. There was Surf-jet, a motorized surfboard for lake use (the equipment proved too heavy and too expensive to be practical). Then, in 1973, he took out a patent on Ten-Net, the hybrid tennis game he had first tried to launch when he opened Paradise Island a decade before. The "court" consisted of two Ping-Pong tables separated by a net; the players used three-quarter-sized tennis rackets and a foam ball as big as a tennis ball. The accompanying brochure explained the creation of Ten-Net as a continuation of the grand A&P tradition. Just as George Huntington Hartford had founded the first chain stores in the United States and Edward Hartford had pioneered the automotive industry, so too was their scion inscribing a new entry in the annals of American innovation with his newfangled tennis game. Hartford even tried to apply the lessons of Paradise Island to Ten-Net. Gambling—or rather the lack of it—had been the downfall of his Caribbean venture, and he wasn't going to let that happen again. There was a gaming element in Ten-Net from the start; a dielike cube enabled players to bet as they played.

He had grand plans of starting a company to manufacture the game. But although he kept Ten-Net brochures piled in the paper-strewn room that served as his library, and the prototype was set up in his backyard, he never found the money for a full-fledged operation. Still, he remained obsessed with the game and hoped that the eccentric novelty would finally provide permanence to the legacy of George Huntington Hartford II.

As Hartford fought his own waning battle to live up to the reputation of the men who had built his fortune, their very empire continued to come apart from within. A&P stock, which traded as high as $59 a share in 1960, had dropped to $9 by the late sixties. In 1972, the company lost $51.2 million on sales of $6.3 billion.

The men who ran the A&P stayed implacably smug. "They thought that they were the only people who understood the grocery business," said Wendell Earle, a professor of marketing at Cornell University.

Clearly, their understanding was woefully inadequate. In the sixties, much of America had moved to the suburbs. But the A&P had not followed. The chain remained overloaded with small, uneconomical inner-city stores, and the men who ran the John Hartford Foundation, which still had the majority stake in the company, refused to permit investment in better, more modern outlets. All of John Hartford's preaching on high volume and low prices seemed to have been forgotten; the A&P's managers were mesmerized by the teachings of brother George, who had sternly warned them to hoard cash as the hedge against the depression that was sure to come again.

Huntington Hartford owned virtually no A&P stock, but he remained, in the words of one Hartford cousin, "a lightning rod for publicity." In 1971, ever eager to help anyone who wanted to take on the giant grocer, Hartford was recruited by New York Operation Breadbasket, the economic arm of the Southern Christian Leadership Conference, which was urging a boycott of the A&P to protest what it alleged was racial discrimination in employment practices.

"There's an absolute obligation on the part of these [A&P] people who inherited this business from my uncles to get out or get involved," Hartford said at an SCLC-sponsored press conference. "There's a clique running the A&P, which is going steadily downhill, but I'll do anything I can as a small shareholder to change the situation." Hartford demanded the resignation of the chief executive, William Kane. "There's no difference whatever between Burger [secretary, then A&P president, then head of the Hartford Foundation] and Kane," said Hartford. "It's a round-robin, it's all the same group. What's needed now is a real leader—or else the company should be sold."

In fact, several suitors had already made their intentions known. For the A&P had all the marks of a classic takeover target: a good name, substantial assets, and abysmal management. The only stumbling block was the Foundation, which refused to sell.

The opportunities had begun as far back as 1969, when Nate Cummings, the former head of Consolidated Foods, assembled a group that included Henry Ford II, several Rockefellers, and a scion of Britain's Rothschild family. The group offered the Hartford Foundation $35 a share for its holdings, $6 more than its current range, but Burger would not even take the matter to the board of directors for a vote.

Burger died a year after that offer, but his legacy of intransigence survived. In 1971, Gulf + Western acquired five percent of A&P's outstanding shares on the open market and made a tender offer to purchase fifteen percent more at $20 per share, $3 above the current price. Burger's successor, Henry Adams, another longtime A&P employee, joined management in resisting the offer. William Kane instructed his attorneys to take whatever action was necessary to thwart the takeover and promptly filed for an injunction, claiming the acquisition would violate antitrust laws and the Securities and Exchange Act.

This time, Hunt Hartford wasn't the only family member who was furious with management's actions. The Josephine McIntosh Foundation, legacy of one of John and George Hartford's nieces and owner of some 250,000 shares, announced its intention to tender its stock to G+W. "We feel abandoned by A&P's management and by the Hartford Foundation," said the McIntosh Foundation's president, Michael McIntosh. In the end, the family's fury meant nothing. The courts ruled in favor of A&P management. G+W appealed, but the verdict was sustained, and the tender offer was blocked.

By then, Hartford took a perverse sort of glee in the grocer's foibles. "If I'd kept my money in the A&P," he told *The Wall Street Journal,* "I'd probably have less money than I have now."

By 1970, Hunt Hartford had gone through well over half his fortune, but he was happy to spend what he still had to try to re-create Hugh Hefner's tired dream. In March, he announced that *Show* would be back for a third run.

Hartford hired serious editorial talent: Dick Adler from *Life* magazine would be editor; Digby Diehl, who often wrote for *The New York Times,* would be in charge of West Coast coverage. And on New Year's Eve 1970, they had a party to welcome in the new venture. "We wanted to have it at Tavern on the Green," recalled Adler. "[Hartford] insisted on Inn of the Clock, a cheesy little hamburger joint on the East Side." There was much ado about who would be chosen as guest of honor. "We started out with Olivier, and ended up with Dame Edith Evans and Tiny Tim." The evening was a disaster. Despite the tatty surroundings, Hartford set up an elaborate security system; guards were instructed to bar anyone not in black tie. One possibly consequential advocate, William Paley, showed up in a business suit and was turned away at the door, as were Diehl and his wife, whom Hartford had flown in from the West Coast.

"I wore this fancy Edwardian jacket," said Diehl. "The guy at the door looked me over and said, 'You don't have black tie on, you can't get in.' I said, 'Get out of here, I'm the West Coast editor of this magazine; Mr. Hartford sent me all the way from LA.' The guard went in to talk to Hartford. The guard came back and told me that Hartford told him it was black tie or nothing. I said, 'Sayonara, pal,' and went off and played Monopoly."

Paley and Diehl didn't miss much. "Hartford was typically chintzy about food and drink," recalled Adler. "There wasn't enough of anything. It was a New Year's Eve party, and everyone left by eleven."

In the wake of this dubious launch, even the phone company seemed to conspire against publication. The wrong number was listed in the phone directory. Hartford filed suit against New York Telephone, claiming damages of $2 million; ultimately he ended up dropping the case, sans settlement.

In June 1971, he switched *Show*'s headquarters to the West Coast and replaced Adler with Diehl. But if anything, the transcontinental move made matters even worse. Hartford insisted on signing off on every single page, so each month Diehl, together with his managing editor and art director, would have to go to New York.

"He would install us in a hotel, and then we would wait," recalled Diehl. "He would say, 'Come over at three.' We'd get there with boards under our arms and find a party going on. He would say, 'Come in, have a drink.' Then he'd say, 'I'm not feeling well, let's do this another time.' We would take limos out to his house in the country, but he would be busy with some woman. It took days, sometimes a week, to get him to look over pages. It was absolutely maddening, because we were really trying to put out a magazine."

The magazine they put out was a cut above the Longines-sponsored *Show*, but it still paled by comparison to the original. The editorial content was perfectly respectable: Andrew Sarris on John Huston, Milos Forman on his first venture into American filmmaking, Alan Arkin on *Catch-22*. But without the money for lavish art, the design was merely serviceable; it lacked the inspired visual conceits that had vitalized the magazine's first incarnation.

Hartford's hand showed up in such features as an astrological chart of Marlon Brando ("The Stars' Stars") and a cover story on the photographer David Hamilton, whose soft-focus pubescent nudes were tailor-made for Hartford. And of course there was what Diehl called the "bimbo of the month"—the "Miss Soft Sell" feature, a page or two devoted to some model. But if these young women were vessels for Hartford's own visions, how those ambitions had been cut down to size. In the first *Show*, the "girl features" occasionally included some real discoveries, the actresses Elizabeth Ashley and Shelley Hack among them. Now there were a Miss Teen Pacific Coast and a blonde who shilled for Virginia Slims, women never heard from again. Hartford's dreams had shrunk to five minutes of commercial television time.

Typically, Hartford folded this latest version of *Show* on a moment's notice, dispatching his financial adviser, Jim Vanderpol, to the West Coast to tell the staff the publication was no more. "We had an issue ready to go that never got printed," recalled Diehl. As he had before,

Hartford shut down without paying his bills. The printer filed a $654,309 suit against Hartford; Diehl put in for $28,000. The printing company saw some fraction of the money it was due; Diehl never got a cent. In fact, the only person who managed to be paid in full was Harlan Ellison, who was owed $3,000 for his profile of the rock band Three Dog Night. And he had to resort to marching in front of the Huntington Hartford Theatre with a picket sign that read: "Huntington Hartford doesn't pay his bills."

Unbeknownst to his West Coast editors, Hartford was already working to publish another version of *Show* in the East. This version was considerably lower-rent than the last; Hartford was moving closer to Hefner's vision. "The Happy Hooker," Xaviera Hollander, smiled from one cover; on another was Marilyn Chambers, once an Ivory soap girl and now a porno queen, who regularly turned up on Hartford's arm. His friends assumed that he and Chambers were having an affair, and he did nothing to dissuade them. But appearances were deliberately deceiving. Chambers remembered Hartford as more interested in playing Svengali than in pursuing sex. "He thought I was going to be this new sex symbol, and he wanted to be seen with girls," she recalled. "The sexual part wasn't there anymore, but he wanted to make people believe that it was."

In November 1972, Hartford took his *Playboy* dream to the next level. He took over a restaurant, the Cork 'n' Bottle, and converted it into what he hoped would become the first of a chain of Show Clubs. The new club featured red plaid carpeting, red velvet upholstery, black tablecloths, and the ambience of a Louisiana bordello.

"It was, to put it mildly, bedlam," wrote Enid Nemy of *The New York Times* about opening night. "And, according to one guest who was delicately removing an oily lettuce leaf that had been jostled into her somewhat remarkable cleavage, the scene . . . made 'sardines look like pikers.' " The club could hold 350 people comfortably; three times that many showed up.

Hartford had no trouble luring hoi polloi—but they had come to see stars, and they were few and far between. Celeste Holm was there, as was Rudy Vallee, a relic from Hartford's Hollywood past. And on Hartford's arm was a statuesque blonde in a skin-tight silver dress. She identified herself to Nemy as "not doing anything really," and added, "I'd like to live a life of idle luxury, but don't say that."

Later on, Nemy reported, the blonde reconsidered. "Oh, I don't care if you say it. I just want everyone to have a good time. You can even make up things if you want." Noted Nemy: "It wasn't necessary."

Within two years, the club was out of business.

▲

Most of the men Hartford did business with simply gave up in frustration when it became clear he lacked either the skills or the discipline to see their projects through to fruition. His children did not have that luxury. Cathy was the most emotionally needy of his surviving offspring, "always trying to get her father's attention," said Herbert Smokler, Hartford's psychiatrist friend. Cathy bore the brunt of her father's indifference, and she suffered it noisily. "Hunt paid attention to Cathy when it suited him," said Smokler. It was "a whole Electra situation."

Linda Never, an aspiring singer who was a frequent visitor to the Hartford household, recalled one evening when that "situation" escalated to particularly uncomfortable heights. "This girl came in at five A.M. and started doing this seductive sort of dance. Hunt kept saying, 'Cathy, stop it, stop it.' I was appalled to find out that she was his daughter."

One of Cathy's more desperate plays for her father took place when the Show Club was still open. "Cathy was drunk all the time," said Donna Wilson, a friend of Hartford's who was a waitress at the club. "There Hunt would be, sitting in a booth, and these girls would be there, all vying for his attention. . . . They all wanted to be Hunt's number-one chippy."

One evening, said Wilson, Cathy came in, drunk as usual, went to her father's booth, sat down, and turned to him and said, "Daddy, tell me you love me." He said, "Oh Cathy, will you stop, just stop." She said, "No, Daddy." Wilson remembered that Cathy "was getting ready to go away, to school or something like that. She said, 'Please, Daddy, tell me you love me, just once, tell me you love me.' He said, 'Cathy, you're embarrassing me. Will you just stop it?' And he kept pushing her away. She said, 'Daddy, I'm serious, just tell me you love me, just one time. Tell me you love me.' The girls just kept looking at Hunt and one said, 'Would you just get rid of her. . . . Get this girl out of here.' They all knew it was Hunt's daughter, but they couldn't be bothered. Finally Hunt did get up and they all got in a limousine, and Cathy was up there and she was falling down, hanging onto the door of the limousine, calling out, 'Daddy, Daddy, tell me you love me.' She was crying. And he said, 'Cathy, would you just stop it.' And they drove off."

"Hunt was very, very bad to [Cathy]," said Marjorie. As Cathy herself put it: "I don't think [my father] has been crueler to anyone else in the world."

18

"THERE ARE two ways of looking at the things I do," Hartford told *The Wall Street Journal* in 1973. "One way is the American way, to look at how much money they make. The other way is, what is it that I'm doing? What have I accomplished? You can't judge everything by its dollar value. . . . For the survival of capitalism, business can't just be business. It must have social awareness of the area in which it operates. Take somebody like Getty or Howard Hughes or H. L. Hunt. What are they doing with their money? They've missed the boat, in my opinion."

The article trilled the usual litany of Hartford failures: the magazine, the museum, the theater. Even then, Hartford was hopeful about the future; he estimated his remaining fortune at $25 to $30 million, most of it tied up in Paradise Island. "Potentially," he added; "not in ready cash."

The Bahamian culture that had existed on Hog Island when Hartford had purchased it had ceased to exist by the early seventies. The casinos had destroyed the last vestiges of the colonial aristocracy; the postlapsarian Paradise was all crass commercialism, a big-business dream machine. In the casinos, the venality came formally attired: men were required to wear black tie, women ball gowns. But the veneer was thin.

"All morals are gone down there," said one woman who spent the late sixties and early seventies on the island. "The girls from the Midwest on their honeymoons would be totally taken with the dealers. After all, here is this guy that has power over their husbands and the money that they were saving for their mortgage or station wagon, and these dealers are making it or breaking it. They're completely poker-faced, and it's intensely seductive.

"Then there is the husband, the poor sap trying to win his money back, and he gets a little engrossed. These young wives end up at the bar, and then these nice-looking dealers come over and chat them up, tell them how pretty they are. 'Would you like to see the porpoises?' they ask—that's the big line. They take them to the tennis courts, bend them over, and screw them. . . . The girls get star-struck. I remember one girl down there screaming in the streets, 'I'm not going back, I'm not ever going back.' Every married couple I've known has split up down there."

There were two worlds that mattered on Paradise Island: the crowds in the casino and the oligarchy that ran it—the men of Resorts International and the men behind the banks that were nothing more than mail drops on Bay Street. It was this second caste that was responsible for making the Bahamas the international capital of sleaze finance.

In 1968, the Bahamas lured the biggest name in the financial world: Howard Hughes. He had spent some time there in the 1950s, and when he was trying to decide where to settle, he vacillated between Las Vegas, where he owned the Desert Inn, and the Bahamas, where he was considering purchasing Resorts' holdings: the new casino, the 270-room Britannia Beach Hotel, and the fifty-two-room Ocean Club. He wrote to his lawyer, Gregson Bautzer, asking him to look into the casino's profits, the cost of maintaining the island—and most of all, whether the place was still swarming with rats. Not much came of the bid. Bautzer's talks with Jim Crosby's contingent proceeded for several weeks, were abandoned, then started and were abandoned once more.

While Hughes never did invest in the island, his concern about the rodents apparently abated. In November 1970, the reclusive billionaire was spirited out of the Desert Inn in Las Vegas and installed in the ninth-floor penthouse of the Britannia Beach Hotel on the island. There, with his clawed nails and scraggly beard, Hughes kept to his bed. He watched Agatha Christie movies in a codeine-induced stupor; the painkillers he had taken after an airplane accident long before had resulted in a powerful addiction.

Hughes was too addled to pay much attention to the island's political goings-on, but other businessmen grew worried that Prime Minister Pindling would start nationalizing the private industry that had invested tens of millions of dollars in the islands. Crosby feared for his hotels; others were anxious as well. Even Sy Alter had acquired property on the island, a small gift shop in the Britannia Beach tower.

No one, after all, wanted another Havana.

▲

Donna Wilson had close ties to all the men who had the most to lose. Hartford met the leggy blonde first, and she had drifted in and out of his life since the early sixties; he was the one who had most recently paid her way from New York to Paradise Island. Once there, practically penniless, she quickly fell into Crosby's camp. She became his lover and Alter's proxy in the casino. Alter was a compulsive gambler, and since Resorts employees were forbidden to play in the casinos, Wilson played his hands in exchange for a small percentage of the winnings.

But gambling, according to Wilson, was the least of what Alter wanted her to do. "In 1970," she said, "I met with Sy and some Bahamians I didn't know at Crosby's house [on Paradise Island]. Sy told me they wanted me to go to the Jockey Club in Miami, pick up a package, then book a round-trip spot on a cruise ship to Freeport and get on the boat with the box." Cruise passengers, explained Wilson, went through customs only on the return trip. They wanted Wilson to get off in Freeport and leave the box on the boat.

"Sy, do you want to tell me something about this box?" Wilson asked.

"It's none of your business," he told her.

"If it's a bomb and it blows up and I get killed I'm going to be very upset. . . . It's guns, isn't it? You're going to shoot the prime minister."

"We have to," Alter replied.

But the assassination never came off. "I was supposed to leave at seven in the morning," said Wilson. "Sy told me to wait for his call. I waited and waited and waited; then Sy called and said that the Bahamians couldn't get their act together. I thought, 'Great, they can't get their act together now, what's going to happen then?' " Eventually Alter phoned and told Wilson that the plan has been canceled.

Years later, Alter denied that the incident had ever occurred. But he did manage to turn a tidy profit on his gift shop, selling it for $315,000, ten times what he had paid for it. The buyer was a Detroit high school dropout turned financier named Robert Vesco, and he had his eye on much more than that hotel gift shop.

On January 7, 1972, Howard Hughes held his first press interview in more than fifteen years. Its purpose was to reveal Clifford Irving's so-called Hughes autobiography as a hoax. For Vesco, who apparently was afraid that Hughes would interfere with his plans to purchase Paradise, that interview, coming after so many years of seclusion, created the perfect climate of attention.

By then, Hughes's residency permit had long since expired. More-over, few members of his entourage had Bahamian work permits. Enter Robert Vesco, who wanted the reclusive billionaire off the island. Re-portedly, Vesco urged the opposition party to use that information to embarrass Pindling's Progressive Liberal Party, in power at the time. Fearful that he might appear to be giving the billionaire special treat-ment, Pindling sent immigration officers to the Britannia to investigate Hughes's situation. When they arrived and asked to enter the penthouse, the request was summarily denied. While Hughes's guards stalled for time, several aides carried the billionaire to a fire escape on the floor below. Finally the officers left, and the guards walked Hughes back to bed. Two days later, Hughes left his Britannia Beach hotel suite for good. He was once again carted down the fire escape, then slipped onto an eighty-three-foot luxury yacht headed for Key Biscayne, and Vesco was free to bid for Paradise.

In February, Vesco offered Crosby $58 million for the island. Talks broke off in April, then resumed in the fall. This time, they agreed on a deal, which was scheduled to close at the end of November. But the deal fell apart, for reasons having nothing to do with Resorts: Robert Vesco was named as the central figure in what was then one of the largest civil fraud complaints ever filed by the Securities and Exchange Com-mission. He and forty other individuals, corporations, mutual funds, and banks were accused of having bilked Investors Overseas Services, the mutual fund empire built by Bernard Cornfeld and later purchased by Vesco, of $224 million. Vesco fled to Costa Rica, leaving his deal for Paradise a shambles.

Robert Vesco was just one piece of the Paradise puzzle. The island also figured in the investigation of the Senate committee looking into the Watergate scandal. There was speculation that Paradise Island was the nexus of an operation in which contributions to Richard Nixon's infamous Committee to Re-Elect the President were laundered along an elaborate daisy chain that linked Crosby, Nixon, Bebe Rebozo, and Al-ter. The friendship among Rebozo, Nixon, and Alter dated back to 1962, when Nixon went to the Bahamas after his failed California gubernato-rial bid. At a party in Miami in 1967, Alter introduced Rebozo to Crosby, and later that year he introduced Crosby to Nixon. Not long after, Crosby donated $100,000 to help fund Nixon in the 1968 New Hampshire Re-publican primary. All of that was perfectly legal.

What appeared a bit more suspicious were the bundles of bills that Alter transported from the Bahamas and deposited in several different banks on the mainland. A good bit of that money ended up in the Key Biscayne Bank, which belonged to Rebozo. Alter claimed that cash came from his hotel gift shop on Paradise Island, but Martin Dardis, an investigator in the State Attorney General's Office in Miami, suspected otherwise. He had heard that Alter was the "bagman" for Resorts and he wanted to find out whether Alter's cash deposits had come from the company, skimmed off casino operations.

Dardis suspected a connection between Alter's deposits and a series of $100,000 certificates of deposit that had floated in and out of an account held by Nixon at Rebozo's bank. In the summer of 1973, ABC News reported that the Senate committee investigating Watergate was also examining reports that illegal Nixon campaign funds had been laundered through gambling casinos in the Bahamas, with the cash then routed through Miami. An ABC affiliate in Miami reported that the Watergate committee was searching for "ties" between Rebozo's bank and the Paradise Island casino. Did Nixon receive money (via Rebozo's bank) taken from Resorts' Bahamian operation, money brought over by Alter? The Watergate committee never found proof of that, and the government investigation was dropped after Nixon resigned from the White House. The Bahamian connection remains one of the many unresolved questions from the Watergate scandal.

Back into this world of perfidy stepped a man who had never balanced a checkbook, a man who, by his own admission, knew nothing about business. As Thor Ramsing, a Hartford relation by marriage, put it, "Hunt was a goldfish in with a bunch of sharks."

In 1973, Hartford decided it was time to unlock that potential $25 to $30 million he believed he had locked up in Paradise Island. The reason was painfully simple: he needed the money. He had shut down both *Show* magazine and the club, but he still was supporting four houses and five or six servants, and paying out alimony and child support to Diane. If he sold off the last of Paradise, he figured, he would no longer be forced to scramble for cash.

Instead of using his attorneys to negotiate, he decided to go directly to Crosby. And so, one afternoon in the spring of 1973, Huntington Hartford went to the house that Crosby had built next to the Ocean Club. It was a magnificent residence with sculpted gardens and an uninterrupted view of the beach from nearly every room. Crosby and Alter were playing backgammon when Hartford entered. He waited for the game to end, then popped the big question: What would Crosby pay to buy out his minority position?

"One million dollars," Crosby answered coolly. Hartford reeled. That was for his unregistered stock, his piece of the Britannia Beach Hotel, the golf course, the Hurricane Hole harbor, the Café Martinique—everything. That was $1 million for properties that had cost Hartford thirty times that to buy and build, properties he figured were worth vastly more.

After six years, Crosby finally had Hartford exactly where he wanted him.

Hartford did nothing. But in June, Crosby alerted Hartford that Resorts would be removing its guarantee from the $1 million loan at the Bank of Commerce, a loan that was collateralized by virtually everything Hartford had on Paradise Island. Hartford was close to apoplectic. He knew the bank would call the loan, and there was no way he could raise the cash to pay it off. So he went to court in search of a temporary restraining order to keep Resorts' guarantee in place. Crosby, Hartford charged, had tried to "ruin me financially," by conspiring with Vesco to buy out his holdings for far less than they were worth. Much to everyone's surprise, the judge granted Hartford's request.

"We lucked out," said one of his attorneys years later. "I couldn't believe that we got it." Emboldened by that first victory, Hartford took his case a step further. On October 8, he filed a shareholder's suit against Resorts, alleging that Crosby had plundered the company by improperly keeping profits from bridge tolls and skimming casino profits that rightfully belonged to Resorts shareholders. According to Hartford's claim, it wasn't just Crosby who profited from the bridge and the casino; Nixon's buddy Rebozo also had a piece of the action. Hartford demanded $10 million in damages.

Resorts had appealed the initial restraining order, and by December, Crosby once more had the winning hand. An appeals court overturned the first judge's decision, and the Bank of Commerce was free to liquidate Hartford's holdings. In the meantime, Hartford's attorneys had worked out a settlement—$1 million. It wasn't any more than Crosby had offered him over that backgammon game on Paradise Island, but now it seemed the best he could expect.

But that settlement was not to be; it was derailed by Hartford's current girlfriend, Elaine Kay, a Carroll Baker look-alike not much more than twenty, who would prove as disastrous to Hartford's personal affairs as Resorts International had been to his fiscal ones. Everything came apart on a freezing December night when Hartford's attorneys came calling at Beekman Place. "Elaine was there in a see-through dress with nothing on underneath," recalled Howard Schneider. "So was Sandy Williams [the newspaper publisher's son who had helped arrange the deal between Hartford and Fairleigh Dickinson for the art museum]. We explained to Hunt what the deal was. Then Elaine got into the act. She told Hunt he shouldn't do it, the island was worth millions. Williams chimed in that he didn't think Hunt should do it either.'' And the deal was off.

(Over time, Williams's business judgment would prove exceedingly questionable. In 1980, he would be named as an unindicted co-conspirator in the Abscam investigations. Williams owned a substantial stake in a mining company that promised shares to New Jersey senator Harrison Williams—no relation to Sandy—in return for granting federal contracts.)

Elaine Kay (she had changed her last name from Kokinakis) had walked into Hartford's life three years earlier on Paradise Island. As a teenager, she was already making regular trips from Fort Lauderdale to the Bahamas; it was the sort of place bored and beautiful girls her age went looking for adventure. Elaine found it with a vengeance. Just before she met Hartford, she had fallen for a swindler named Victor Danenza, whose unctuous charm was as thick as his dark, curly hair. Danenza introduced Elaine to Hartford, and the triangle was set: Elaine wanted Victor, Hartford wanted Elaine, and Victor apparently wanted Hartford's money. As Schneider recalled, not long after Elaine and Hartford became seriously involved, she unsuccessfully tried to persuade Schneider to put Victor under contract, so that the two of them could handle Hartford's affairs.

Elaine continued to divide her time between the two men, even though in 1974 Hartford had started introducing her as his fiancée. The couple turned up in Earl Wilson's column that February. Said Hartford: "She's a beautiful blonde and very creative; I've known her two or three years. She has a brilliant personality."

Elaine was also fearsomely self-destructive. She liked to compare herself to Errol Flynn, explaining her life away as a gorgeous wreck. "I have such a zest for living, but twice an urge to die," she responded when asked about her future; she added that she owed the phrase to the boozy actor. But while Flynn drank himself to death, Elaine was developing a prodigious drug problem.

"I can put my finger in my nose and touch my skull," she used to say. And it was in these years that Huntington Hartford, more than six decades into a lifetime's worth of disappointments, began to use drugs himself. It was an unlikely but somehow inevitable match. For Hartford, the partly pleasant, partly paralytic world of infinite possibilities offered by expansive wealth was giving way to its weak sister—the illusion of potential induced by pharmaceuticals.

Sleep became one of his most pleasant experiences; when he awoke in the morning he became frighteningly conscious of his circumstances. Frequently he would lie in bed in a comatose state until late in the afternoon. And for the first time in his life he began to drink and try out assorted amphetamines and barbiturates, anything that might keep reality at bay.

During one of his jags, he visited his sister. He mentioned to her that his financial affairs were hardly in good shape. Her only comment came in the form of a question: "Are you taking drugs, Huntington?"

Through the years, Marjorie had stayed in close touch. There were, of course, the children, but more than that Hartford had remained one of her staunchest champions as she pursued a career first in painting, then in sculpture. She credited Hartford with starting her artistic career, and she remained loyal to the memory of the vital young man she had married decades before. When she looked at her first husband after he took up with Elaine Kay, she saw an aging and suddenly deteriorating man, and she blamed his latest girlfriend for his decline. "He was an easy target," said Marjorie. "He wasn't used to drugs. He was getting older and wanted to feel young and gay."

On May 21, 1974, Hunt Hartford made a last desperate bid for youth: he married Elaine Kay at his Beekman Place apartment.

Hartford had made a score of last-minute phone calls to invite relatives to the wedding. "He called about three in the afternoon to invite me," Thor Ramsing remembered. "He told me he was getting married that night; I said I couldn't go, that I had a dinner engagement. He said it [wouldn't] take long."

As it turned out, Ramsing was virtually the only family member in attendance. "There were all these strange people standing around. And then this old family retainer came over to me, saying, 'Oh, don't let him do this.' "

There was a half-hour delay while Elaine gave her husband-to-be a haircut. The trim was serviceable—despite the fact that, according to Cathy Hartford, then twenty-three, she and Elaine both took LSD the morning of the wedding.

Elaine wore a low-cut white gown to the ceremony, gilded straps crossing between her breasts. Her husband presented another image altogether. Huntington Hartford, the milk-drinking heir who always used to look so much younger than his age, was starting to show his years. He wore a mottled green velvet dinner jacket, an ersatz Edwardian outfit that might have lent a certain panache to a much younger man. Hartford, pushing sixty-five, looked simply shabby—an overgrown Little Lord Fauntleroy outfitted by the Salvation Army.

Victor Danenza gave Elaine away. The Unitarian ceremony was mercifully brief. "The minister finished with 'As long as you both shall love each other,' " recalled Ramsing.

The wedding reception was held, fittingly, at Danenza's apartment on Fifty-fifth Street. The food might have been ordered up from the corner deli: cold cuts, potato salad, cole slaw, rye bread. "It looked like a low-class bar mitzvah," said Anita Brooks, who was doing public-relations work for Hartford at the time.

News of the wedding appeared in *The New York Times* as a small item in the "People" section, relegated to a spot behind the news that the Maharaj Ji, the baby-faced leader of the Divine Light Mission, had married his twenty-four-year-old secretary.

The morning after the wedding, a reporter from the British newspaper *The Guardian,* Linda Christmas, called the Hartford residence to arrange an interview. Elaine answered. "Come on over for breakfast," she insisted.

"She sounded so friendly that I went right on over," Christmas reported. She entered to typical Hartford disarray. "Everywhere there are photographs. Photographs of Hartford with the Duke of Windsor, Eisenhower, Nixon, Bobby Kennedy, Peter O'Toole, and so on. There are also a number of suggestive cartoons alongside some fine paintings and some not so fine paintings done by his former wife Marjorie. The red staircarpet is threadbare."

The place was teeming with hangers-on. Finally Hartford appeared, in a deep-red dressing gown, shuffling past in scruffy slippers. He seemed dazed, Christmas reported, then left the room—to get dressed, she presumed. But when he returned he was still in his gown, which "was designed to stay open. Underneath he wore Y-fronts."

Christmas figured she would show the heir her handwriting. She scrawled her sentence and the analysis began. Hartford told her she had the most exciting *g*s and *d*s that he had seen in a long while. Her well-rounded consonants signified her creativity and "instinctive understanding of people and situations."

"I was enjoying this when Elaine Hartford entered," Christmas recounted. "She was barefoot and wearing a diaphanous negligee which could have been made of silk but seemed to be made of nylon. Her hair was not so much tousled as torpid and she was carrying a packet of Kool cigarettes and a gold cigarette lighter.''

Elaine greeted neither her husband nor the reporter. Instead, she ordered Hartford to take his feet off the table. He obediently did so, then put them up again and continued with the handwriting analysis.

''Hunt, don't ignore me,'' Elaine said, and grabbed Christmas's handwriting sample. ''Hey, look at those *g*s, aren't they weird?''

''Hold on, baby,'' Hartford said, then went on with his discourse. ''A strong personality,'' he told Christmas. ''A strong personality.''

''You know,'' said Elaine, ''your handwriting is a little like mine.'' Then she accused her husband of flirting with the reporter and went upstairs.

Christmas tried to continue the interview. How did Hartford come to be so interested in handwriting?

''Look,'' he responded, ''would you do me a favor? Would you go and interview Elaine for a few minutes? She's a bit of an actress offstage and I think she feels left out.''

Hartford followed Christmas upstairs, where Elaine was lying on an unmade bed. The curtains were closed, the television was on. Hartford asked her to turn it off; she said no, and pulled a gun from the side of the bed.

''Is that real?'' Christmas asked.

''Oh, wouldn't you just love to put that in your article,'' Elaine answered, and squirted water all over her.

There the interview continued, with Hartford lying on the bed beside his wife, from time to time caressing her back. Christmas asked about their first meeting. ''It was love at first sight,'' said Elaine. ''By the way, what did he say to you downstairs? How did he describe himself? Did he say he was a writer? He isn't. He is a professional Pygmalion. I was thinking of becoming a bookie before he married me.''

Christmas tried to ask about *Art or Anarchy?*, about Tosco, about anything that would make sense of the interview, but it was impossible. Then the telephone rang.

''Elaine, answer that for me,'' Hartford ordered.

''I'm not your secretary,'' she snapped.

Finally Christmas went for the final question. What was Hartford hoping to do next?

''The most important thing right now is for me to make a success of my marriage,'' he responded. ''Isn't that right, Elaine?''

Elaine, though, would not be tamed. "Why are we talking in front of her?" she demanded. "The press never has anything good to say about us anyway." She turned to Christmas. "I have never met anyone who asks such nosy questions. Who are you? I don't believe you are a reporter. Where are your credentials?"

Christmas apologized for upsetting her and rose to leave, Hartford following. When he got to the bottom of the stairs, he yelled for Elaine, but she simply ignored him.

Hartford may have married into a whole new set of problems, but the old financial woes were still with him. There was even a bill for $10,000 from the detective who had prowled the Bahamas for months in a futile search for proof of a Crosby/Rebozo/Vesco conspiracy to squeeze Hartford off the island. Hartford made panicky phone calls to anyone he thought could help him out of the Resorts fiasco. He talked to Rebozo to see if he could correct matters. "He was thrilled to hear from me," said Hartford. "He said he'd get right back to me. The next day I called, and they told me he had gone off indefinitely, that he couldn't be reached.

"I'm sure he talked to Nixon, and he put him off. That's Nixon for you. That's gratitude."

He found a more sympathetic ear with Bernard Cornfeld, the financier who had sold to Vesco. Unfortunately, Cornfeld had no luck when he tried to intervene. "I called Crosby," he said later, "but his attitude was that it was a business deal and he had met his end of it. Hartford ended up getting massacred."

Once the court stay was lifted in late 1973, the bank started selling Hartford's collateral; first to go were the 147,600 shares of Resorts stock. The price: $2.50 a share. The buyer: Resorts International. Then, in April 1974, the Bank of Commerce sold the hotel company stock to Resorts for just $20,000—then immediately marked it up to nearly $800,000 on its own books.

By the fall, it was clear that Hartford would have to settle his lawsuit, and he would have to work out a deal with a new group of lawyers. When Hartford rejected the deal Resorts offered in December 1973, his attorneys and advisers decided they could do no more for their client: not only was he impossible, they felt, but at the rate he was going through his money he would not be able to afford them. Jim Vanderpol was gone, and even his mother's law firm, Stroock and Stroock and Lavan, had all but ceased taking his calls. "Hartford owed the firm hundreds of thousands of dollars, but David Sher decided it was easier simply to [drop] him than collect," recalled Howard Schneider.

The deal Crosby offered this time around was even worse than the one Hartford had rejected the year before. Crosby would pay Hartford $50,000 on signing the release and $250,000 more six months later; he would also pay off the balance of the bank loan and cover a portion of his legal fees. The only sticking point was a 1966 contract in which Hartford had agreed to give Sy Alter a twenty-year pension of $25,000 a year.

Neither Alter nor Hartford would budge, and Hartford didn't have the financial resources to hold out. He had no choice but to sign. He also agreed never to sue again, but the agreement was signed with prejudice. If he could prove fraud, the contract would be nullified, and he could take on Resorts again. He searched for proof of conspiracy for years, but he never found enough to take the case to court.

"I was naive," Hartford reflected. "I had a tendency to think more about what it would look like and not enough about money. I didn't know anything about the stock market. I would sign whatever pieces of paper my advisers put in front of me. I thought Davis and Crosby were nice fellows. The stupid thing . . . is that I have always trusted people."

"We tried to accommodate him," Jack Davis, president of Resorts International, insisted fifteen years later. "We tried to keep him happy. But the fact is, we made smarter business deals than he did. And we made them very legitimately, very aboveboard, and we won the game."

Needless to say, the $50,000 Hartford received on signing the deal did virtually nothing to relieve his fiscal crisis. Almost all of the income he had left was being generated by the trust Marjorie had forced him to set aside two decades before, and those monies were being attached by his creditors. He rarely picked up the checks anymore if he could avoid it—even his own. There was the printing company in California that wanted the money from one of the last versions of *Show*. Then the board of his Beekman Place cooperative apartment building charged tenants $40,000 apiece to reduce a mortgage. No problem for his neighbor Blanchette Rockefeller, but for Hartford it was a near impossibility. Hartford's new attorney, William Eaton, even instructed Hartford's secretary not to pay bills of $25 or less. Apparently, he thought creditors would be unlikely to go to small-claims court for such minor sums.

Hartford was even forced to put his cook on a budget—lunch guests had to make do with creamed spinach as a main course. But the funniest thing to the publicity-conscious heir was that no news of his dire financial straits had leaked out to the press. He concluded that there had been so many reports of his losing money that rumors of his being on the verge of bankruptcy—this time, accurate—simply were not taken seriously.

Richard Nixon's people, it seems, never got the word to his successor that Huntington Hartford had become persona non grata; Hartford received an invitation to dine at the Ford White House on May 8, 1975. The dinner was to honor Lee Kuan Yew, the prime minister of Singapore. "I am not entirely sure that I would have gone if Elaine had refused to accompany me," Hartford said, but his temperamental young wife made the appropriate concessions.

They took the train down to Washington. It was running late, and to make matters worse, Hartford was hobbled by a swollen ankle: a relic of a push Elaine had given him when he tried to read a love letter she had been writing to one of her boyfriends.

They arrived at the White House just at eight, when the dinner was supposed to start. Elaine was placed on the arm of a uniformed escort; Gerald Ford entered as "Hail to the Chief" was played. The 114 guests were seated around tables for ten. It was an eclectic crowd: the artist Larry Rivers, Eva Gabor, Red Skelton and his wife, and the chairman of the Union Carbide Corporation. Hartford's table included corporate chieftains and journalists, as well as Edward Villella, scheduled to perform with Violette Verdy afterward. Hartford opened the dinner discussion with a woman to his side, asking what her husband did.

"He's the attorney general," replied Mrs. Edward Levi.

And so Hartford proceeded to complain about his problems with Paradise Island. Mrs. Levi reacted with a rather pointed silence, and started up a conversation with Singapore's foreign minister, seated at her left.

After a short speech by the president, in which he stated that "our commitments in Southeast Asia and elsewhere are honored and will be honored," the dinner party retreated into an anteroom, for the Verdy–Villella duet.

Hartford began to doze off. His recent crises had left him increasingly inept at small talk. His solution was to imbibe a Nembutal and a strong cup of coffee. The combination, he said, made him a much cheerier dinner companion.

The White House visit called for such a solution. Which was fine, recounted Hartford, except for one thing. By accident he discovered a half of a leftover Quaalude in his tuxedo pocket, which he ingested along with the other remedies. That Quaalude had a not exactly salubrious effect. As Hartford was dropping off, Elaine took note. She jabbed him with a powerful fist in the ribs. The ballet performance over, Hartford and Elaine were escorted to a waiting taxi. Hartford offered an impromptu lecture on Washington architecture. Elaine responded with a barrage of expletives.

V

❖

AFTER THE FALL

All human evil comes from this, man's being unable to sit still in a room.
BLAISE PASCAL, *Pensées*

The wedding of Hunt and Elaine Hartford (1974) "looked like a
low-class bar mitzvah," said one guest.
(UPI/Bettmann Newsphotos)

19

IN MAY 1971, Hartford was one of a dozen New Yorkers who offered up their abodes for the New York City House Tour, the proceeds to send two hundred blind children to summer camp. The 750 voyeurs trooped through the miniature jungle of Mr. and Mrs. Belmont Towbin on Central Park South and the nearly all-white townhouse of Mrs. Albert Lasker on Beekman Place, which boasted two Braques above a bathtub.

While Hartford had the same tony address as Mrs. Lasker, his triplex was more bohemian than Brahmin. He lived amid a clutter of books and papers; most of his twenty-one rooms looked like a boarding school dormitory. The living room was chock-a-block with collectibles: a silver tray presented to his uncles by grateful A&P employees; a sterling cigarette lighter inscribed to him from Richard and Pat Nixon; a note from Joan Crawford, who was connected to Hartford by divorce, for Crawford's first ex-husband, Douglas Fairbanks, Jr., was married to Hartford's first ex-wife:

> Dear Huntington:
> Wherever you are, I'm also in the same position—broke, that is.
> Bless you,
> Joan

"I hope nobody steals anything," he fretted to the *New York Times* reporter who accompanied the crowd. Hartford had little to worry about from those carefully corralled strangers, but his so-called friends were another matter altogether. Over the next several years, Hartford's Beekman Place spread would be pillaged by the men and women he greeted as they stepped off the elevator into his foyer. Carpets were hoisted out the window, books were carried out by the crateload.

Through the mid-seventies, Hartford still made regular trips to London and his house at Red Lion Yard. While he was on one of those trips, his New York triplex became the scene of a high-class garage sale. The gossip columnist turned boulevardier R. Couri Hay, who was a regular guest at Beekman Place, remembered one afternoon he spent there with Cathy and Jackie, who were both still living with their father. As the three of them watched, Elaine escorted an antiques dealer through the house; in a matter of minutes, two valuable Chippendale chairs and a table were appraised, paid for, and carried away. "She got $25,000 for those chairs," recounted Hay. "We called Hunt in London to tell him what was going on. He said 'God Almighty' when we told him." But according to Hay, Hartford did nothing. He stayed in England and let Elaine have the run of the house and his possessions. The Hartford children, though, decided to find other living quarters.

In August 1973, Hartford's lawyers forced him to make a list of his major assets; it was time to determine just what could be used to raise cash. It became all too apparent that the once far-flung Hartford empire was down to a few shabby city-states. Some of it could be promptly liquidated, and it was: Melody Farm went for $200,000 (a few years later, when Hartford had a bit more cash, he bought back the house and a mere fraction of the land for $475,000), and he unloaded a house and acreage on Long Island's East End for $700,000. The London house he kept, for the time being.

Then there was the matter of the museum, now the New York City Cultural Center. In August 1974, Hartford's five-year management agreement with Fairleigh Dickinson University expired. Peter Sammartino recommended that the museum be sold. "It was an exhilarating time, but skyrocketing costs made it [impossible] to maintain," according to Sammartino, and the university was already entitled to half of Hartford's trust fund.

So it was that Hartford's museum, already stripped of its name and much of its art, landed on the real estate market in November 1974; asking price: $6 million. Those were desperate hours for New York; the city was flirting with bankruptcy, the middle class was fleeing to the suburbs. It was not a good time to be selling a trapezoidal marble highrise on a busy traffic circle, and the building languished.

After years of indifference to his gallery's fate, Hartford made a last effort to find new patrons. At the top of his list were a wealthy manufacturer and his wife. Hopeful of encouraging their involvement, Hartford arranged to be at a cocktail party that the couple was sure to attend.

The problem was the woman on his arm: Marilyn Chambers. Inexplicably, he decided to take the notorious star of *Behind the Green Door* and *Insatiable* with him to the party, where he introduced her to the manufacturer and his wife.

"Thank goodness you are not that awful Marilyn Chambers we have been reading about," said the wife, whereupon Chambers, with what seemed to Hartford unnecessary alacrity, confessed her true identity. With that, the gallery's potential saviors vanished. Hartford tried to reach them for weeks, but after a notable lack of success he finally gave up.

The end came quickly. In September 1975, nearly five hundred mourners gathered at Columbus Circle for what was billed as a "museum cooling." The event had a desperately festive air. "You just can't be sad about this," said Mario Amaya, the museum's last director, who stood by the entrance accepting condolences. "You have just as much fun as you can with a corpse." The guests speculated as to the center's future. The art critic Gregory Batcock suggested it be turned into a disco; the painter Alice Neel thought it might be a decent site for an A&P. Another guest proposed that it might make a snazzy funeral parlor.

Hartford turned up at the wake, his Paradise tan faded to a dissolute pallor. As his museum closed, he mourned what might have been. "What bothers me is that I got together one of the greatest collections of paintings ever seen here," he told a *New York Times* reporter as he surveyed the bare walls. "I sold them because I thought they were ignored. . . . There was no recognition. My God, you get discouraged."

Still, there was that dim light up ahead. "I feel optimistic," Hartford declared. "I don't think this will be the end of the gallery. Something good will happen. I have enough confidence in the huge public for art in America to believe that it won't be torn down."

And in the end it wasn't. In 1977, Gulf + Western, headquartered across Columbus Circle, purchased the building for just over $1 million; the company put $1.5 million more into renovations and in 1980, in an act of corporate beneficence, donated it to New York City.

Today the building houses, among others, New York City's Department of Cultural Affairs and the city's Visitors Information Center. Altogether, it is a testament to bureaucratic ennui. The carpets are stained, the paint is peeling. On the ground floor backpacking tourists line up for subway maps and brochures about the Bronx Zoo and the Statue of

Liberty. Upstairs, sullen civic workers have taped travel posters on the rich ebony walls that were once a backdrop for Dalís and Courbets.

On the building's façade, under the brass lettering that now marks the building as the home of the Department of Cultural Affairs, one can still see the palimpsest with Hartford's name in the once white marble, now gray from the exhaust of passing cars.

As for *Show,* Hartford shut down the last version in 1973. Over the next few years, he periodically threatened to start it again but was never able to come up with the cash. In 1977, his lawyers told him it was time to sell, and he finally listened. The buyer was Stephen Saunders, who published *Genesis,* a girlie magazine.

Saunders's *Show* was a twin of his other publication, essentially a collection of bosoms and bottoms. "I saw a copy of something called *Show* on the newsstand, and it was nothing more than a skin book," commented an outraged Frank Gibney, who had edited *Show* in its brightest period. He phoned Hartford, with whom he had not spoken in years. "I got him out of bed and asked how he could do an appalling thing like that. He said, 'Well, I'm sorry. What could I do? They offered me some money.' "

Another lingering trace of the Hartford legacy was erased a few years later when the name of the Los Angeles theater was changed to honor James Doolittle, the man who had run it longer than the man who had rebuilt it. Hartford fought a pathetic battle to salvage that scrap of fame, pleading with Doolittle to leave his name on the marquee. "He told me that even though he had had nothing to do with the theater for years, many people still associated him with it, and he basked in its success," said Doolittle. "He said it would help him if the name was left alone."

Hartford even recruited some old California friends to lobby for his cause. "He was desperate to keep that name on," recalled Joseph Perrin, the real estate investor who had known Hartford since his early years in Hollywood. "It was something that he wanted, something that he created, something that he did. We did what we could for him. We even called Governor [Edmund] Brown, but the decision had been made to change it. I was hoping they would at least give him a plaque—but there's nothing."

In 1978, Huntington Hartford was sixty-seven years old. During his waking hours, he maintained the pretense of business, playing the role of a man under the considerable pressures of worldly responsibilities, taking endless phone calls and holding meetings about projects that in fact would never get off the ground.

He looked into an alchemic process that would make it easier to mine for gold, and made calls to anyone he thought could help get Ten-Net going. He even became involved in an improbable campaign to draft the heavyweight champion Muhammad Ali into a run for the U.S. Senate. (Hartford announced his support for Ali's bid, even though it was never determined in which state the boxer would be running—Ali owned homes in New York, New Jersey, Pennsylvania, Kentucky, and California. The campaign never materialized.)

After dark, Hartford's life became a parody of Don Juanism. He was an old man darting from party to party, driven less by desire than by the fear of waning passion. "I remember spotting him in some loud, awful place, looking like the old man of the mountains," recalled the society writer Joseph Dever. "There he was, bloodhounding different girls at random. 'Oh God, does it never stop?' I thought." Dever exchanged pleasantries with the heir for a few minutes, and then Hartford was off again. "It was as if the solution of his life hung on the next pick-up."

Instead of legitimate fame, Hartford found a garish tabloid half-life. He personified the historian Daniel Boorstin's definition of celebrity: he was well-known for being well-known. He formed a troika with Andy Warhol and Sylvia Miles, fixtures who certified to the world that a gathering was an Event. "Huntington Hartford would go to the opening of an envelope," the wags used to say. "It was," sneered one chronicler of a particularly marginal evening, "the kind of party where the only person that you recognized was Huntington Hartford."

Hartford would sometimes attend four or five events in the course of an evening. It didn't matter who or what was being honored: he turned up at Mick Jagger's birthday party, at the reopening of El Morocco, and even at a book party for Patricia Bosworth's biography of Montgomery Clift. He made it to the reopening of the Electric Circus discotheque and voiced complaints about the ambience: "The clothes are great," he told a reporter, "but I wish the lights would quit flashing so I could see the girls better."

His celebrity did not necessarily imply social desirability. In the fifties and sixties, Hartford had been on every guest list in town, but by the seventies his popularity had started to wane. Hosts could no longer automatically use the name Hunt Hartford as a draw—indeed, his presence often produced quite the opposite effect. According to Jonathan Michaels, the bow-tied impresario responsible for orchestrating much of the New York social scene in the late sixties and early seventies, as Hartford aged he became more and more of a social liability. "He got to be known as the classic dirty old man," said Michaels.

"He always did the same thing, no matter who it was," recalled Norma Jeans, a young woman who met Hartford on the party circuit in the mid-seventies. "You'd be sitting there talking to him, it didn't matter about what, and he'd reach over and start feeling you up." Usually, said Jeans, the object of Hartford's attentions could dissuade him simply by placing his hand back on his own knee. "He never pushed it much beyond that." Passive though Hartford's pursuit may have been, for New York hosts trying to retain a modicum of gentility it was unacceptable behavior for a man in his sixties.

Hartford might have been rebuffed in his overtly amorous pursuits, but if he wanted to go to a party it was not easy to keep him out. As many a Manhattan host discovered, leaving Hartford's name off the guest list was by no means a guarantee he would stay away. "The flash bulbs would pop because it was Huntington Hartford," said Michaels. Then the lights would stop popping, and if Hartford's name wasn't on the list, the guard would take his name to the host. More often than not the host would say Hartford was not welcome.

Hartford seemed to revel in the face of that rejection; he brazenly elbowed his way into parties where clearly he was not wanted. "If there was a party Hartford wanted to go to, he would call me and ask if I could get him on the list," said Michaels. "A lot of times I would call up the hosts and they would say, 'I'm sorry, I don't want him there.' Then I'd call and tell him he couldn't go—but the more I told him he couldn't go, the more he wanted to."

One party Hartford wanted to attend was hosted by Ethel Kennedy at Lincoln Center. He heard about it at the last minute and decided to try his luck at the door. His name, of course, was not on the guest list. As luck would have it, when the guards asked him to leave, Ethel Kennedy emerged; she knew Hartford from his days in Palm Beach. "Hunt, what's going on here?" she asked. "Well, I guess I'm not invited," he replied. "You are absolutely invited," she said, steering him away from the guard and into the party.

Other Kennedy family members were less enthralled with their uninvited guest. Later in the evening, Ethel's brother-in-law Stephen Smith approached the heir. "Do you always go around crashing parties?" he demanded. Hartford just looked away.

▲

On those occasions when Hartford was an invited guest, he often used the gatherings as a public confessional. He answered personal questions before reporters asked, instinctively knowing that by divulging the more intimate details of his life he was guaranteed a place in print. He turned up at one Junior League benefit at Bloomingdale's, marking the opening of the department store's model rooms—eighteen designer specials, each assigned a different dream theme. He stayed close to the bar, telling anyone who would listen that he had to have surgery on his right heel, which he had cut recently on a shower door, and that Elaine had vanished the previous night. "I think she took off when she heard I had to have surgery," he announced. "If anybody knows where she is, please let me know."

Wherever the early part of the evening took him, there was the mandatory late-night appearance at Studio 54, the locus of New York bacchanalias during the mid-to-late seventies. Steve Rubell, one of the owners, remembered Hartford as a constant, quiet presence who went around collecting women, generally those under twenty-five. "He looked old to me, like he was trying to play a game that had passed him by." Elaine was also a regular, but she was rarely at the disco with her husband. "Hartford used to come and ask if I'd seen her," remembered a woman who worked there. "He always seemed to be looking for something."

Evenings at Studio 54 would inevitably be followed by later evenings at Beekman Place. As one transient in the New York City night circuit said, "It was the sort of place you went if you were very brave." The gatherings were informal and druggy, ten to twenty people collapsed on the couches trying to avoid the dawn. "The crowd reminded me of what the Playboy mansion must be like," said Linda Never, who was a door guard at Studio 54 besides being a regular at Beekman Place. "There were a lot of old men and very young girls."

There were, of course, young women who did respond to Hartford's advances; a battalion of underage waifs meandered in and out of Hartford's bedroom, those who would entertain an old man's attentions knowing that they could hit him up for a month's rent—or at worst fifty dollars, ostensibly for the taxi ride home. As Anita Brooks, the public-relations woman who organized Hartford and Elaine's wedding, put it, "These girls weren't aspiring actresses, they weren't even aspiring secretaries."

Scores of assorted urchins coursed through Hartford's Beekman Place triplex in the middle to late seventies. Cathy was in and out, as were

Elaine and her group of hoodlum friends. "They were young, fascinat-
ing—they seemed intelligent," said Hartford. "You didn't ask what kind
of business they were in. . . . I never asked about their addresses or
anything." Another resident, tucked away in a far corner known as "the
drug-free zone," was Timothy Dickinson, an Oxford-educated poly-
math given to homburgs and spencer jackets who made his living supplying appropriate literary allusions, obscure facts, and little-remembered
quotations to the likes of George Plimpton, Lewis Lapham, and Tom
Wolfe. Dickinson even claimed credit for furnishing an obscure reference about Pope Urban IV that George Will once used in a *Washington
Post* column on power-hungry politicians. Literary rather than libidi-
nous, Dickinson was an island of Victorian asceticism in this vortex of
prurience, the last whisper of Hartford's past.

Hartford's was not a household suited for children, but Juliet Hartford
was a regular visitor. "I had to go over there, otherwise we didn't get
our alimony," said Juliet. "Sometimes I would go over with a girlfriend,
and then I didn't mind, because my girlfriend was always so shocked
and devastated and overwhelmed by the house that we'd sort of have
fun."
And if she came alone, there was always Elaine. "If I didn't have
anyone to talk to when I was over there, I'd just sit in her room. Elaine
was gorgeous, and she would be running around in these tight leather
pants—her Sid Vicious clothes. I'd sit on the bed and talk with her and
play dress-up."
Juliet was sent to see her father one Christmas Day in the mid-
seventies. "Elaine kept telling me not to go into the library. I kept
saying, 'I won't, I won't.' " But she could not resist. When Elaine
finally left her alone, she ran in. "There were these glossies of models
all over the table," said Juliet. "I picked up one glossy with a huge
mountain of cocaine on it; I thought it was sugar. I threw it on the floor
because I wanted to see the model's face. My father made fun of me for
that."
In this house where decadence reigned, there were a few last relics
of gentility. "It would be three in the afternoon and they've just woken
up," recalled Juliet. "The paint is peeling off the wall, there are cartoons on television, and there are bottles and joints all over the place.
And here's my father; he sits down with me, and the maid brings a tray
out for breakfast, a silver dome covering the plate. There was milk,
toast, scrambled eggs and bacon, and a beautiful teacup, in the midst of

this holocaust. He always had that. Even when all the furniture was out
the window.''

He didn't smoke and he didn't drink, but if it could be swallowed or
inhaled Hunt Hartford would likely be interested. By the end of the
seventies, his drug use had escalated to an alarming degree; no one,
probably not even Hartford himself, knew just how much he was taking.
But on February 3, 1978, it became clear that it was too much. That
afternoon at about three—his usual wake-up hour—one of the housekeepers went to serve him breakfast. She knocked and knocked. There
was no answer; she went in and found Hartford unconscious on his bed.

An ambulance was called; it delivered Hartford to New York Hospital.
Newspapers picked up the story, although they never published the rea-
son for his hospitalization. A spokesman for the hospital refused to dis-
close anything except the fact that Hartford was ''resting comfortably.''
Those who lived in the house did, however, offer a simple explanation:
It was a drug overdose.

Hartford was out of the hospital within the week. The near miss had
virtually no effect on the household. The flow of drugs—cocaine, Quaa-
ludes, heroin—continued unabated. ''This household operates on one
premise,'' Elaine used to say. ''Anybody that enters can have as much
rope as they want until they hang themselves.''

The scene at Beekman Place recalled the last days of Henry VIII; the
palace was rife with intrigue and petty jealousies. Elaine even commissioned a series of drawings to chronicle the fall of the House of Hartford;
they look like Bosch on LSD. The two dominant figures are a full-
breasted blonde (Elaine) and a craggy-faced old man in rumpled pajama
bottoms (Hartford). In one drawing, he is being attacked by maggotlike
masses of humanity; in another, Hartford and Elaine are bound at the
genitals by an asp. The last in the series is a skyline of Manhattan,
balanced on the back of a clawed reptile. One Beekman Place is silhou-
etted in front. The drawing was the only one in the series that bore a
title: ''Witch Hunt / Last Days Beekman One.''

20

"*I* KNOW what it is that makes my
father work," explained Juliet
Hartford. "He did all of it, and then
he sort of gave up and just wanted to self-destruct. As long as he was
self-destructing in the public eye it was okay, as long as he got the
publicity, as long as everybody knew about it. I think he wanted to get
to where he had nothing, and when he finally did reach the bottom, so
low, maybe he could do it all over again and do it by himself."

Huntington Hartford expected the contradictory and the impossible: he wanted to spend all his money and still have some left. But by
the time he hit bottom, he no longer had the inner resources for the
climb up.

Throughout his life, high drama made Hartford come alive, and as he
aged he required overstimulation in an ever-increasing supply. The relationship with Elaine went a long way to providing those histrionics.
In the first year of their marriage, she knocked out one of his teeth in
the course of an argument; the papers later reported that she had it gilded
and attached to a gold neck chain, then gave it to him as a present for
their second anniversary. According to various houseguests, Hartford
kept a snapshot of the two of them on his bedstand; Elaine was pictured
with a knife to her husband's neck.

Hartford was still trying to get Ten-Net going. Toward that end, he
called an old tennis teammate from Harvard, Germaine Glidden, founder
and president of the National Art Museum of Sport, and invited him to
discuss what might be done about launching the sport.

Glidden went to Hartford's home about a week later. "Some Filipino
maid let me in; it was clear he had no idea I was coming," Glidden

remembered. The phone rang downstairs; the maid picked it up and told Glidden it was Hartford calling from upstairs. "You came at the worst possible time," Hartford told him. Glidden could hear Hartford arguing with Elaine. "She was being worse than a harridan. I won't repeat what he called her; it's not the kind of language you use in polite company." Still, Glidden persisted. "Can't you come downstairs?" he pressed Hartford.

"This is a bad time," Hartford replied. "She has a gun out."

"I was worried that the next day I would read something about it in the papers," recalled Glidden, who had no interest in waiting around for the headlines. "I left pretty quickly after that."

In 1981, to almost no one's surprise, Hartford filed for divorce. Elaine's alimony was inconsequential, just $20,000 a year for five years. But for the Hartfords, the threats and the guns and now the divorce were mostly just their modus operandi. Even though they had papers sealing the divorce, the marriage was hardly over. Elaine Kay Hartford never moved out of the triplex.

The former Mrs. Hartford retained her place in the retinue of Beekman Place regulars, along with some of the motley crew from the seventies. Cathy Hartford stayed with her father occasionally; her younger brother had permanently decamped. Timothy Dickinson still kept his quarters, unsuccessfully trying to maintain some sense of order. There were a few new additions, most notably Ariana Adereth, a seventeen-year-old who described herself as Elaine's best friend, and an eighteen-year-old Bronx-born high school dropout named Sheila Dowling, whom Hartford paid $200 a week to be his "secretary," though her duties were never quite clear.

Elaine and Sheila had a fractious relationship, and by Christmas 1981, the stage was set for a confrontation. Before leaving on a trip to Florida, Ariana and Elaine told the teenager they expected her to be gone by the time they returned.

"You're a rat," Ariana told her, "and you know what happens to rats, don't you?"

"Yes," Sheila answered, "they die."

"You'd better remember that," Ariana replied.

On January 18, Sheila arrived home at about six in the morning after a night out at Studio 54. Elaine and Ariana were waiting for her in her bedroom, armed with knives.

"I ran to try to grab something to protect myself," Sheila recounted later, "and screamed loudly. We started fighting. . . . I went to the bathroom and they knocked me to the floor and my hands were tied behind my back.'' They stripped her, Sheila said, and then Elaine left the room and came back brandishing a pair of scissors. "They dragged me out of the bathroom and started cutting my hair. While one of them held me down, the other one shaved my head. Elaine held a knife at my throat and theatened to disfigure my face.''

The ordeal over, Sheila was left in a chair. She threw on some clothes and ran to the police. Soon after, several police officers stormed into the apartment. Upon surveying the wreckage, one of the policemen commented, "It looks like the butler did it.''

The story made headlines from New York to Los Angeles to London. In big black letters the front page of the *New York Post* promised a sordid tale: "Tycoon's Ex / 'Torture' Rap." Elaine, ever the pouty-faced beauty, was pictured underneath on her way to her arraignment. "You want it,'' she spat at photographers as she sashayed into court. "You're in trouble. You're in my neighborhood now.''

The story got more byzantine at every turn. The next day, the *Post* published a letter from Sheila to Elaine, handwritten on engraved flowery stationery. It was dated the previous September. Sheila apologized for letting her drug use interfere with her friendship with Elaine, and said she would be willing to submit to any punishment (no specifics were named) in order to get back into Elaine's good graces.

Sheila's mother got into the act, telling reporters in her Irish brogue that Elaine and Ariana had kicked her daughter "in her privates and everything. This isn't the first time they beat her up. They tied her to the bed, beat her and cut all her hair off. She's wearing a knit cap now. Her hair was her pride and joy. It wasn't her clothes, it was her hair.''

By the end of the month, Sheila had attracted the attention of the best-known negligence attorney in New York, an elfin lawyer named Harry Lipsig. On February 4, Sheila filed suit against Hartford for $65 million in damages, alleging that he had done nothing to prevent the attack. She later amended the complaint to include charges that Hartford, Elaine, and Ariana had exposed her to "narcotics, weapons, and deviant sexual behavior.'' Hartford, she said, had used her to arrange sexual encounters with other teenage girls, and Elaine had once "arranged'' for a man to have sex with her.

The next week, Elaine and Ariana appeared in court to face charges of assault and criminal possession of a weapon. Elaine knew how to make an entrance: she showed up at the courthouse in an ankle-length ranch mink coat. As she entered the courtroom, she looked over at Lipsig and smiled. "Oh, he's so cute I'd just love to hug and kiss him." Lipsig was not amused. "The charm of these ladies is hardly in keeping with what happened," he told a reporter. "These gals are dangerous."

The scandal rocked the staid residents of One Beekman Place. Calling Hartford's tenancy "undesirable" and in violation of a house rule forbidding persons of "dissolute, loose or immoral character" from entering the premises, the board of directors commenced eviction proceedings.

The Dowling affair was "only the latest" in a series of "serious problems," according to the board's president, Raymond Larsen, one of the founders of *Time* magazine. The trouble with Hartford had begun in May 1981, when the board president at the time, Donald Petrie, sent Hartford the first of a number of letters complaining about the stream of noisy visitors heading up to his triplex at odd hours of the night.

For six months, missives flew back and forth between Hartford and the Beekman Place board. Then Hartford sent a note to the superintendent indicating that no one was to be admitted to his apartment without his personal approval. Two days later, though, he sent another note, countermanding the first. Apparently Mrs. Hartford had learned that she was no longer entitled to admit guests on her own—and she was not happy about it. This time, Hartford indicated that his ex-wife could have whomever she wanted in the apartment. Scrawled across the bottom, in red ink, Elaine added her own message:

Take note!
  Mrs. H—
  (The boss)
Money talks, bullshit walks

It took five more months, but Hartford and the Beekman Place board finally managed to smooth over their differences. A letter from Hartford sealed the agreement. He reported that he had instructed his ex-wife to comply with the building rules and promised to avoid inconveniencing the other tenants in the future.

But six weeks later, Elaine and Ariana put a razor to Sheila Dowling's scalp, and the ceasefire was over.

When the eviction notice was filed, Hartford was, predictably, furious. "Come-lately social climbers," he called his neighbors, adding,

"I lived there for twenty-eight years." He sued the co-op board to prevent his eviction and obtained a temporary injunction while the co-op's residents voted on whether to oust their most notorious tenant. By May, the votes were tallied, and the injunction was overturned. Hartford was on the way out.

In July 1982, Elaine and Ariana pleaded guilty to misdemeanor charges and agreed to pay fines of $500. Hartford, however, didn't get off quite so easily. In September, on the eve of a court-ordered deposition, he settled Dowling's civil suit for $117,000. "Sheila is living a beautiful life," Harry Lipsig said. "It's a good price for a haircut." And, he added with a smirk, "you would be surprised what homeowners' will cover."

Hartford sold the triplex in mid-1983, and by November, he and his entourage had finally started to "evacuate," in the words of one of the Hartford crew. The movers came and went, packing boxes, carting away furniture, until all twenty-one rooms were empty, save the master bedroom. And there, Huntington Hartford maintained an absurd sense of decorum until the very end, king of an empty palace.

Richard Savage, an on-again, off-again Hartford retainer, returned to Beekman in the middle of the move. "I went up to Hartford's bedroom. There [he] was, standing in the bathroom in his underwear, brushing his teeth. I walked in, said hello, and he said, 'Why don't you wait in the bedroom. I'll be in in a minute.' It was the most insane situation imaginable—and he was enjoying it. [He] enjoyed the unpredictable and the ridiculous. If things simmered down to normal, he had ingenious ways of making them abnormal again."

Finally, the boxes, the beds, and the other furniture were moved to a four-story townhouse on East Thirtieth Street. Hartford spent his days sleeping and his nights on wild scavenger hunts, looking for pieces of manuscript, scraps of his life that had been misplaced in the move. Something was missing, Hartford would tell Savage, "and we would have to find it. It might have been the smallest piece of paper, [one] he could barely describe, but it was important that everyone begin looking for it immediately."

Savage was paid $250 a week to attend to Hartford's bizarre demands. "One night he insisted that we go through all the file cabinets," Savage remembered. "He showed me what he wanted to accomplish, by picking up a key from a coffee can full of keys and holding it, then kind of staring at the cabinet and aiming for it. [Savage mimed Hartford standing, key clutched at chest level, then stumbling toward imaginary files, his key never quite making contact with the lock.] He would come back and try again and again. I told him I wasn't going to help him. He told me a story about Napoleon and one of his lieutenants who had just been wounded and asked if he might fall out of rank and attend to his injury. Napoleon refused the request. Hartford said I was supposed to follow his orders and stay up all night until we got the job done.''

In 1985, Hartford threw what was likely to be his last big bash. As Savage told it, Hartford became obsessed by the invitations; he wrote and rewrote the cards. Finally time ran out, and guests were invited by phone.

Savage's stay at the Hartfords' ended just before the party. Elaine told him that she wanted him out of the house—immediately. ''There was a security guard downstairs demanding I leave,'' recalled Savage. ''A gate surrounded the front yard, and I left my things there so I could go across the street and make a phone call and figure out where to go.'' When he returned, his possessions were gone. (Not long after, Savage notified Hartford's attorney that he wanted to be reimbursed for his lost property. Savage implied that unless he received a settlement he would take the sordid story of the Hartford household to the press. ''I told the lawyer that the scales must be balanced,'' said Savage. Within weeks, he received a few thousand dollars from Hartford for past services rendered.)

Savage may have gone, but a hundred or so guests turned up for the party—the usual Hartford crowd, with a few unusual exceptions. One was his sister. Josephine still made occasional society-column appearances during the racing season in Saratoga, but her fortune too was largely diminished. In her case, though, it had less to do with feckless spending than the decline of the A&P. Ever the dutiful Hartford, she had held onto her stock as it drifted down to less than $10 per share.

Hartford's son came down from his home in Connecticut. Jackie had grown into a quiet, lanky musician who lived reclusively in the New England countryside, composing works that were rarely performed. A few months earlier, he had married an outspoken stockbroker named Kathleen Lischko. His father had a hard time adjusting to the union and told anyone who would listen that she had been his girlfriend first; people wondered what he meant, exactly. ''At first I was against the marriage,'' Hartford said a couple of years after the wedding, ''because I figured Jackie could do better. But now I think she's good for him.''

▲

The party marked a quiet end to an era of decadent festivity at the Hartfords'. Although visitors still trooped in and out of the house, the gold-chained mobsters vanished; a Thirtieth Street townhouse where the liquor was kept under lock and key didn't have the same appeal as a Beekman Place penthouse. Two housekeepers attended Hartford during the daylight hours: Stella, a sturdy middle-aged Hispanic woman who came for the early shift, and Paulette, an ebullient West Indian married to a Baptist minister. The two women provided what little order there was in the household. The last bastion of propriety, Timothy Dickinson, never made the move from Beekman Place to Thirtieth Street; he had long since left for Washington, D.C.

Hartford occupied the third-floor bedroom, the largest in the house. Elaine was in one of the fourth-floor bedrooms; Richard Sanchez (not his real name), a sort of houseboy who took out the garbage and made the beds and helped ensure a regular drug supply, was in another; Cathy Hartford was holed up in the third.

"Poor Cathy," said one friend, "she never quite managed to cope." Cathy had been a beautiful teenager, a long-limbed brunette. Her father kept Richard Avedon photographs of her in a minidress, every inch the sixties model. By the early eighties, though, that image was all artifact: Cathy had ballooned to nearly two hundred pounds and was addicted to cocaine, heroin, and alcohol. In 1983, there had been a brief marriage to a mad inventor, a union arranged by her father. But within months of the wedding, her husband died of acute alcoholism and Cathy landed back on Thirtieth Street.

Cathy and Elaine would make regular forays from the townhouse to the grimy streets of Manhattan's Lower East Side, desperate searches for hypodermic needles and $10 bags of heroin. When Cathy's own supply ran out, she would go into her father's room; while he slept, she would look under his bed and behind tables for used glassine packets of the drug, and then scrape off whatever residue remained.

While the Hartford family foundered, the A&P, which had provided the fortune that helped create their indolence, at long last began to show signs of recovery. Through the seventies, the grocery chain had declined. In 1974, William Kane, the chief executive who had fended off Gulf + Western, was replaced by Jonathan Scott, the first outsider to take over the A&P. Scott tried to pare down the company's operations in hopes of returning it to profitability, but his strategy was all wrong. He closed inner-city stores while maintaining the distribution network that supplied them, and as a result, the majority of the few profitable stores that remained became losers. By 1978, the stock was down to $8 a share. Finally Henry Adams, who headed the John Hartford Foundation, was convinced that his organization should sell.

In January 1979, the Tenglemann Group, a privately held German retailer headed by Erivan K. Haub, announced it would be buying a forty-two-percent controlling interest in the company for $8 a share; the purchase included shares belonging to the Hartford family as well as the John Hartford Foundation.

A year later, Haub installed a new chief executive at the A&P, a Scot named James Wood. The consensus was that there was little chance for recovery—according to one reporter, it would take a "miracle man" to turn the A&P around.

That was precisely what James Wood turned out to be. In his first two years, he closed more than five hundred stores, eliminated 20,000 employees, shut down the A&P's food-manufacturing business, and terminated the company's pension plan. He pulled back to twenty-five states from thirty-two and announced that the A&P would no longer be national. "We took ourselves out of environments where we had damaged our image beyond repair," he explained. By the end of the 1984 fiscal year (February 1985), the A&P was in better shape than it had been in for decades; it had pulled in a net income of $215 million. In June 1985, *The New York Times* called James Wood the "Supermarket Savior."

Huntington Hartford had spent forty years and tens of millions of dollars trying to create a legacy worthy of the empire his uncles had built. When that empire teetered, Hartford, a most improbable and inept corporate soldier, had nonetheless rushed to its defense. And when he learned of its rescue, he telephoned to offer Wood his congratulations.

But the A&P's savior apparently had little interest in the heir of the men who had built the grocery empire. According to Hartford, Wood never returned his call.

21

BY THE WINTER OF 1984, Elaine's drug problem had escalated into a drug crisis. Just before New Year's Day 1985, while on a visit to Melody Farm, Elaine had her first seizure, most likely caused by cocaine. She was taken to the emergency room of the nearest public hospital, where the doctors urged that instead of being discharged she be admitted into a drug detoxification program.

Hartford never visited her in the hospital, but he did agree to pay for her to go to Fair Oaks, a drug rehabilitation center in New Jersey. He was torn about his ex-wife's recovery. On the one hand, he knew that her addiction endangered her life; on the other, he was frightened that if she ever freed herself from drugs she might leave him. He telephoned constantly. "I miss you, I need you here," he would beg. With its endless supply of drugs, East Thirtieth Street was the worst place Elaine could be.

For six months, she resisted Hartford's pleading and stayed in New Jersey, dividing her time between the drug center and Melody Farm, where she was cared for by a former radio executive named Bill Raphael and a private investigator named Margaret Clemons.

Clemons, a sharp-tongued thirty-one-year-old given to raw-silk suits and spiked heels, had met Elaine when she was hired by Hartford to look into the Sheila Dowling incident. Unlike most of the people who passed through the Hartford townhouse, Clemons didn't do drugs and had her own place to live—an immaculate apartment in an East Side high-rise. "All of the people that know Hunt and Elaine, the people that go to that house, are there for a reason: drugs, alcohol, or a free place to stay,'' Clemons explained. ''In the odd instance where someone at the house didn't have an ulterior motive, Elaine could be charming.''

The two struck up an unlikely friendship, and Clemons was determined to get Elaine off drugs. Elaine was an intelligent woman, she explained, and without drugs she was transformed from a tabloid harpy into a creature of childlike sweetness. Elaine would give gifts of hand-made gingham sachets, with satin ribbons and dried flowers tied around the top. But she was a hard, hard case: having spent her twenties and much of her thirties addled by opiates, she was virtually incapable of functioning in the world. When asked how she thought she might support herself, Elaine suggested that she could set up a stand outside the gates of Melody Farm and sell painted pine cones.

While Elaine dreamed of her cottage arts-and-crafts industry, the Manhattan townhouse turned into an all-purpose crash pad. No one was quite sure who lived there, or just how anyone had gotten in. If nothing else, Elaine had acted as gatekeeper, intimidating weaker-willed indigents. Once she was out of the house, they huddled back in, eager for a meal and a bed.

Each weekday morning, one of the housekeepers would collect $200 in cash from Hartford's attorney (she would get three times that amount on Fridays so there would be enough to get her employer through the weekend). As much as half of the allowance went to a courier for his runs to the pushers. The rest of the funds kept the refrigerator stocked with six-packs of Coca-Cola and Heineken and the freezer full of chicken breasts.

A locked second-floor closet served as the liquor cabinet; it was full of Baileys Irish cream. After years as a teetotaler, Hartford had taken a liking to the cloyingly sweet liqueur. With the exception of the Baileys, the kitchen supplies were considered fair game for anyone in the house.

With its full larder and dark corridors, the townhouse provided sustenance and anonymity, ideal elements for the sort of transients it attracted. But those dimly lit hallways also made the house increasingly perilous for an old man of unsteady step. In April 1985, during one of his late-night perambulations, the seventy-four-year-old Hartford tripped on a staircase between the second and third floors, skidded to the bottom, and stayed there, contorted and moaning, until morning, when he was discovered by the housekeeper and rushed to the hospital. He had broken his hip, and the doctors warned that he might not survive the trauma. But Hartford made it back to consciousness, and when he did, he began demanding drugs—and not the sorts his doctors would supply. The hospital did its best to limit Hartford's access to those illicit narcotics; nurses kept guard over his room and chased his suppliers away.

Hartford was back at East Thirtieth Street within the month, presiding over his motley court from a hospital bed. Ginger Fleming, an erstwhile photographer staked out in the first-floor bedroom, served as chief greeter. The fourth-floor bedrooms became a dormitory for those with little to say about their occupations or their last names. There was a textile designer named Suzanne, along with Flynn, a redhead from New Jersey. Then there was Ginger's best friend, Melanie, who, Ginger said, had just been released from a mental institution. Melanie was a fixture at the dining room table, where she would stare off into space and hum. Sam Kimbrell was the only one who was even superficially presentable; he affected the mien of a southern gentleman. With Kimbrell came a traveling companion who purported to be a tennis pro.

The chief attendant to this mix was a psychiatrist named Joseph Gross, an affable, scattered sort, given to safari hats and seersucker suits. He prescribed Tranxene and Thorazine to help Hartford's mood and tried to minister to an increasingly desperate Cathy Hartford.

"I have depended on my father for years for a place to live whenever I needed it," Cathy wrote in her journals. "This way I didn't need to pay rent, and I could get free food and all the money I had I could use to buy drugs and alcohol. [My father] would often express his disappointment that I was doing nothing with my life. . . . His anger grew until, in the summer of 1984, he would treat me on a daily basis like a most insignificant human being, worse than the sleaziest hanger-on."

When it came to intoxicants, Cathy was a gourmand. Her drug of choice was freebase cocaine, a smokable and combustible form of the drug. "I ended up with 12 free-base pipes," Cathy wrote, "and I used 151 proof rum to light them. . . . Occasionally the little cotton balls soaked in rum would alight and start an impressive fire."

Cathy was drinking the rum as well, much to her father's chagrin. "My father knew I was doing cocaine, which he didn't mind, but he still did not approve of my drinking," she wrote. Cathy was a sloppy drunk, and one night, when Hartford heard her stumbling home, he had her locked out of the house for several hours. Finally, one of the house's residents, tired of the relentless knocking, let Cathy in. The hours on the doorstep had not sobered her up; worse, they had pushed her into a drunken rage. She took a knife to two of her mother's paintings—one of Hartford, the other of an African prince in full tribal regalia.

Cathy was two years older than Elaine, and she decided that her own experience made her the one who could get her father's fourth ex-wife off drugs. If she started doing drugs with Elaine, then stopped, she figured, Elaine could follow her lead and come clean.

The theory was flimsy to begin with; the practice was outright lunacy. "After shooting for several days [Elaine] indicated I wasn't yet a junkie, so I kept going thinking I was strong enough to quit," Cathy recounted. "It got out of control and I could only get dull needles. Within three months I had destroyed all my veins. I had done to myself what had taken her three and a half years."

One night in early June 1985, Cathy left a message threatening suicide on Joe Gross's answering machine. Gross rushed to the house and called the police. When they arrived, they found Cathy hysterical. She was admitted to Bellevue, then taken to Hazelden, a rehabilitation center in Minnesota.

Her father, meanwhile, passed the summer in bed. Although he could walk with a cane, he had little interest in crossing from his torpid rooms to the sidewalks of Manhattan. "This is really like a prison, you know," Hartford said of his house. "All you need are a few more bars on the windows."

Hartford had managed to maintain amicable relationships with his first two ex-wives. Mary Lee regarded him with fond regret, and he still insisted that Marjorie was a genius and called her in Ireland at least twice a week. But his third wife was another matter altogether. The troubles that had characterized their marriage drifted into their divorce. Diane, the woman who said it would be a long time before she ever remarried, never did.

In the years since their divorce, Hartford periodically tried to cut off her alimony. Once he accused her of living with a man; another time he charged that Diane had prohibited their daughter, Juliet, from seeing him. In the first instance, a judge ruled against Hartford. "A husband may be a lover," he ruled, "but a lover is not perforce a husband." In the second, Diane agreed to make sure Juliet paid regular visits to her father's house, however unsavory his circumstances.

In August 1985, Hartford called his youngest child, and Diane insisted that her daughter take the call. "Your father wants to go to dinner with you," she told Juliet. "This might be the last time you'll ever see him— you'll regret it if he dies."

Juliet agreed to the date, and a few days later she and her mother went to collect the old man for dinner at the "21" Club. "It was the first time the three of us ever went out together," said Juliet. "We went over there. My mother told me that he was so excited that he had spent two days getting ready. He was dressed like I had never seen him before. He always went out with his pants rumpled. This time they were perfect. His shoes were perfect. He was standing there, and he looked so old and so sad. And he looked like he really cared. We went, we sat down on the bed, me and him, and everybody stood outside and we were alone for the first time ever. I showed him my yearbook, the French play that I had starred in, to impress him, and it was just like incredible."

Three weeks later, Juliet returned. "He had forgotten all about '21,' all about everything. He was a wreck, people were smoking pot. It was the old scenario all over again. I went over to him, and he forgot who I was. Then this eighteen-year-old girl walks in and sits down. . . . I won't be around that. I refuse to be sitting around some girl he's making a pass at who's my age."

Hartford walked into the bathroom and Juliet spotted him snorting lines of cocaine. "She came running in, crying, 'I'm never coming back, he's killing himself,' " said Hartford's nurse. "She was a little girl who wanted her father to be someone other than who he was."

Elaine returned to East Thirtieth Street at the beginning of October. The doctors at Fair Oaks warned that she wasn't ready to return to the city, but she was of a different mind. She was back on drugs within days. Still, her reappearance was not without its benefits; she purged the townhouse of its ne'er-do-well guests. By the end of the month, only Richard Sanchez remained.

Hunt and Elaine immediately reestablished their shrill symbiosis, an interdependency defined by mutual desperation and hysteria. Hartford reverted to Victoriana, using a few stanzas from a Kipling poem to describe Elaine. The poem was "The Vampire."

The thirty-three-year-old woman who returned from the drug treatment center in New Jersey to live with her ex-husband was no longer a beauty. Her body was bloated from the weight she had gained trying to kick her drug habit, and her hands were swollen like baseball mitts, her veins engorged from too many needles. But none of that mattered to Huntington Hartford. Elaine was still his Paradise Island beauty, his spent youth—never mind the tracks. And he still hungered after her company. But the drugs had robbed her of any interest in human companionship. Most of the time she stayed alone on the fourth floor. She preferred the bathtub to her bed; she spent hours lolling in the warm water, drifting off in a stupor.

Just about the only thing that could rouse Elaine's passion was drugs—and making sure she had enough money to stay high. One evening, not long after she returned, she summoned Hartford to her room to find out where the funds were for that day's drug supply. Hartford informed her that he had given the money to his drug courier that afternoon; he had promised to be back by morning.

Elaine's screams could be heard two floors below. "You stupid fool. I don't want it tomorrow, I want it today. I don't want any of your stupid asshole stories."

Hartford tried to calm Elaine, but to no avail: she was hurling obscenities as he hobbled down the stairs to his own bedroom.

Two days after Elaine returned from Fair Oaks, I visited the Hartford townhouse, preparing an article for *Forbes* magazine, the first profile of the heir in more than ten years. Hartford, his hunger for publicity still not sated, wanted Elaine to come downstairs to meet me. He ventured to the banister of the stairway leading to the fourth floor. "Elaine, come down, baby," he called out. "Please come down, say hello, as a favor to me. Just come down to say hello. . . . That's all you have to do."

There was no response. Perhaps she might respond to a visitor's knock? "She might throw you off the balcony," Hartford warned. "I wouldn't want to try it out." He called up again. Still no answer.

I ignored Hartford's warnings and ventured upstairs, gingerly weaving around the fossils of Hartford legitimacy. In the third-floor hallway, bound volumes of *Show* and scores of film canisters—reels of *Face to Face* and the Murrow interview—teetered in lopsided piles on the patchy, stained carpeting. The fourth floor, by contrast, was barren, more like a hotel than a home. The hallway was lined with doors, each studded with multiple locks. A knock on the door to one room went unanswered. Turning the doorknob proved futile; the locks did their job.

Only the bathroom door was open. An addict's grim still life was neatly laid out on the counter next to the sink; a flowered cloth knotted as a tourniquet, a spoon, and an unlit candle with a charred wick.

Elaine never emerged from her room.

At seventeen, Juliet Hartford was a beauty. She had her father's dark features, framed by a mass of ebony curls. In looks she was the twin of the teenaged Ed Barton; in spirit she had the gumption of her iron-willed grandmother, Henrietta. Home from her Swiss boarding school over Christmas break in 1985, Juliet decided it was up to her to take charge of her father's condition.

She was still a minor, too young to go to court herself, so she asked her mother to request that the State of New York appoint a conservator for her father's affairs. Two months later, Diane Hartford filed the papers, charging that her ex-husband had suffered mental and physical degeneration because of old age, alcohol, and improper nutrition and medical care. The agent of the corruption, she said, was Elaine, "who has usurped control of his business affairs, social life and household management."

Juliet filed her own affidavit describing that August evening when she had seen her father snorting cocaine. She wanted to do something, she testified, so that her father "would not become another John Belushi or Elvis Presley."

As they had so often in Hartford's life, the tabloids made hay. The *New York Post* headlined: "Ex-Wife: A&P Heir's a Dope Fiend." When the *Post* reporter called the Hartford home in search of comment, a maid replied: "He did not lose his mind. He doesn't even smoke. He's not an alcoholic. He doesn't take dope."

In his own affidavit, Hartford admitted using cocaine, but only sporadically. "While most people would not approve of my life-style . . . that is my concern and not theirs. If I choose to spend my money in what some people believe is a frivolous manner, or if I choose to give it away, that is my affair."

Diane's interests, he charged, had more to do with the well-being of his bank account than his health. Of his expenses, by far the largest single outlay was the $100,000 or so he paid her annually in alimony and child support.

In truth, although Hartford's spendthrift ways might have jeopardized Diane's alimony and child-support checks, there was not much of an estate left. Hartford's only major assets, the townhouse and Melody Farm, were both heavily mortgaged. While the trust still produced $600,000 a year, there was no principal to fight over: that would revert to charity when Hartford died. And since none of the projects it was created to fund existed anymore, Hartford was not sure just who would end up with the last of his A&P millions.

What Juliet wanted was a lot harder to attain than her father's money. "I thought, Wouldn't it be nice if he could just get his act together," she said. "I wanted to get him straight, put him in a beautiful apartment with a lot of books and let him write all the stuff he said he was going to write. He could do a thousand million things. Then he could have his money and be able to be a father—someone who could be a figure in my life and not this pathetic old man.''

Her half brother, Jackie, saw it differently, and he jumped to his father's defense. ''To take away control from my father and his finances . . . would crush him [and] would affect his spirit and his will to live,'' he wrote. ''It would, in fact, be the final act of humiliation, a final blow I am afraid he would not survive.''

Diane and Juliet's case was buttressed by the report of a court-appointed guardian. ''It is my opinion that Mr. Hartford's abuse of drugs has persisted over the years without being addressed by those close to him,'' wrote the guardian, Lynne Terrelonge.

Over the next months, psychiatrists paraded in and out of Hartford's house, charged with determining whether the old man was capable of handling his own affairs. They concluded he was. In one test, Hartford was asked to draw a picture of himself. The figure had facial features and pants, but was missing parts of its arms, hands, and legs. From that, the psychiatrist concluded Hartford had an exceedingly low opinion of himself. As one report put it, the patient was depressed, but not without reason. While he needed psychological help, Hartford was most certainly sane.

As the conservatorship papers volleyed between attorneys, Hartford received word that his old Paradise Island nemesis, Jim Crosby, was dead. The ten or so years since Hartford had been squeezed out of Resorts had been extraordinarily profitable for Crosby's company, which was the first to get a gambling license in Atlantic City. Bits of the company's past did come out in the licensing hearings before the New Jersey Gaming Commission, though. Ironically, it was Sy Alter, Hartford's onetime aide-de-camp, who was sacrificed, in part because he had been charged with bribing a judge to approve the license for the New York City liquor store Hartford had bought him more than twenty years before.

''Maybe now they'll believe me about the conspiracy,'' Hartford said when he heard Crosby had died after surgery. ''Now they'll have to believe I know what I'm talking about.''

Of course no one ever did. Paradise Island changed hands twice in the next two years; it went first to Donald Trump, then to Merv Griffin, who paid $250 million for those eight hundred Caribbean acres that Huntington Hartford had reclaimed and renamed Paradise. (As it turned out, Hartford wasn't the only investor to get taken on Paradise. Griffin borrowed too much money to buy the Caribbean property, and at the end of 1989, his operation filed for bankruptcy.)

Thanks to the conservatorship battle, Huntington Hartford, a man who, in the words of Thomas Hoving, could hear a camera going at five hundred yards, had his chance to go public once more. After reporters for *Forbes, Vanity Fair,* and *People* came to call, photographers Harry Benson and Annie Leibovitz were dispatched to document the heir's decline.

Judge Albert Tyler ignored the garish portraits of the heir and stuck to the psychologists' reports. On January 7, 1987, he ruled that Hartford was capable of handling his own affairs, that Diane's petition "fail[ed] abysmally" to substantiate her claims. Hartford never showed up in court to speak for himself; Judge Tyler never saw the man he ruled capable of handling his own affairs.

Four months later, there would be reason to wonder if the judge had acted precipitately. On May 6, the *New York Post* ran a story that asked: Why does Huntington Hartford live in fear? The piece was the result of an interview Hartford had consented to in April with one of the *Post*'s gossip columnists, Cindy Adams; he had agreed to appear on her segment of the television show *A Current Affair.* She arrived at the door late one afternoon, camera crew in tow. As she walked in, she heard a woman shrieking on the floor above; the insistent ringing of the first-floor phone added to the din.

Adams picked up the phone; Hartford was on the other end, asking to talk to Paulette, the housekeeper. Adams responded that she was there for the interview. Why wasn't he coming downstairs? "I can't," he whispered in a hoarse voice. "She won't let me. Please, Cindy, please understand."

"What are you talking about?" Adams replied. "Who is 'she'?"

"She's my former wife," he said.

Then came a shout from two floors above. "I am not your former wife," Elaine yelled. "I am your wife."

Adams and her crew inched up to the living room on the second floor; from there, she called to Hartford on the floor above. Finally, Elaine tore past Adams and her crew, shouting at them to get out of the house.

Adams told Elaine that she was a friend of her husband's.

"That's what they all say," Elaine said, then left and slammed the front door behind her.

Adams chased Elaine as she ran down the street, but quickly lost her.

She returned to the house to find Hartford walking slowly down the stairs. "Please," he told her, his hands shaking, "I can't do the interview. She'll take it out on me. It will be terrible for me if I do. She won't let me. You can see that, can't you?"

Huntington Hartford had long since stopped keeping track of time; he lived from one desultory crisis to the next. Most of his waking hours were spent sorting through papers, working on endless revisions of *Art or Anarchy?* He wanted to republish it, he said, this time as "The Violence of Genius." He made a study of artists who had died poor.

"There's Balzac and Dickens," he reflected. "Sir Walter Scott went bankrupt. Bizet was booed and hissed at the opening of *Carmen* in Paris. He was poverty-stricken and died a few months later. He never saw a successful *Carmen*. People in the arts want to give, and they're not particularly concerned how they're going to pay for it. That's my excuse, anyway."

The pharmacology of East Thirtieth Street was considerably more restrained than it had been at One Beekman Place. There were no open caches of cocaine; indeed, Hartford apparently was often given placebos instead of the real thing. According to Margaret Clemons, it was Elaine who wanted to keep her ex-husband clean of heroin and cocaine, and she instructed Richard Sanchez to give him lactose, the powdery milk sugar used to dilute the drugs. Even as a drug addict, Hartford ended up the victim of a scam.

While Hartford may have been inadvertently clean at times, his last ex-wife was not. Elaine generally saved the genuine article for herself— a dangerous habit. On an early February morning in 1988, Sanchez discovered Elaine having a seizure, thrashing about uncontrollably. The police arrived to find her in bed, semiconscious and surrounded by crack pipes and syringes. As she came to consciousness, she was arrested and taken to Central Booking in downtown Manhattan, charged with possession of a controlled substance. After pleading guilty, Elaine was released on her own recognizance; she never made it to court for her final sentencing hearing, and a judge put out a bench warrant for her arrest.

In November, New York police received a call that a drug ring was operating out of the Hartford townhouse. A posse of officers broke down virtually every door in the house. They didn't find much evidence of serious drug-trafficking, but they did turn up a groggy septuagenarian and one very strung-out blonde. When they called her name into headquarters, they discovered the bench warrant. The police left the old man alone, cowering in his bedroom, but Elaine was carted off to jail on Rikers Island, where she languished for nearly two months. Finally, she received a conditional discharge, based on time served, and was released with the hope that she would once again enroll in a drug rehabilitation program.

There was no indication in her criminal record that she ever did. By the middle of January 1989, Elaine was back at East Thirtieth, and back on drugs. The townhouse drama was down to a cast of three: Elaine, Hartford, and Paulette, an island of optimism in the midst of those extraordinarily bleak circumstances. "Mr. Hartford, he has nine lives," she would say, smiling, whenever anyone asked how her employer was faring.

Cathy Hartford did not share her father's fortitude. After her stint in Hazelden, she managed to stay clear of drugs and liquor for about a year. She returned briefly to her father's house, then went off to Ireland, where her mother had a cottage and studio just outside Dublin. Eventually she decided to settle on the Hawaiian island of Maui. It was like the sixties there, she said, artistic and spiritual. The island held true to that decade in other respects as well; drugs and alcohol were abundant, and Cathy didn't have the discipline to resist. She started to drink again and fell in with a bad crowd; no one even knew she had taken a new husband until it was all over.

During the first week of June 1988, Cathy was found on the beach, bruised and suffering from exposure. Her father was informed of her condition; he said he wasn't well enough to fly over. Before the week was out, Cathy Hartford was dead at thirty-seven.

Cathy's husband made it to the mortuary and took possession of her body. He had her cremated and disposed of the ashes. There was talk of holding a memorial service, but the plans remained just that.

A few days after Cathy died, an old friend of the family visited the East Thirtieth Street house. "I was sorry to hear about Cathy," she told Hartford.

He brushed by her to get to his ex-wife. "Elaine," he pleaded, "do you have any drugs?"

Hartford might not have been well enough to go to Maui to attend to his daughter, but he still managed the occasional party. New York's more fashionable hosts had long since scratched his name off their guest lists, but it still carried enough curiosity value to be on lists for a few marginal events. Hartford was regularly invited to parties thrown by Baird Jones, a Wally Cox look-alike and peripatetic keeper of Andy Warhol's flame, who had made a career of filling discos on the downslide with parties that attracted crowds (though never quite the *right* crowd).

On June 16, 1988, Jones threw a party at Casey's, a waning Upper East Side discotheque. The occasion: a show of Warhol prints (a small Marilyn Monroe and a large pink-and-blue cow's head among them) and a few paintings by Allan Midgette, the Warhol impersonator whom Andy had once sent out on tour in his place. The invitations, printed on yellow index cards, billed Huntington Hartford as the host, and small print promised complimentary admission and mixed drinks.

Jones stood guard by the dance-hall door, greeting guests and affixing small orange stickers to their lapels; these served as coupons for the free drinks. The "host" came through the door just before midnight, leaning heavily on the arm of a young Hispanic man. Hartford wore a heavy black-and-white tweed jacket, inappropriate for the warm evening. He stood in the corner for an hour or so, propped up by the side of the bar. He wasn't conversing much; he seemed barely aware of the guests. Huntington Hartford seemed less a celebrity than an artifact, a wax-museum dummy from a bygone age.

A few survivors of the Warhol era turned up. Taylor Mead (star of Warhol's *Taylor Mead's Ass*) was there, along with Isabelle Dufresne, whom Warhol had christened Ultra Violet. She came sheathed in a floor-length satin gown that she had painted in red and gold chinoiserie. She glanced over at Hartford and surveyed the shadows of his past.

"I've seen him go through many wives and many fortunes and many drinks and many drugs," Dufresne said. "I just wish he had taken better care of himself. He was the number-one millionaire, you know, but times change. . . . The American Dream is not only the dollar in the bank, it's the quality of the soul . . . and if you indulge in drink, the soul gets cloudy."

In the months that followed, Hartford rarely ventured out of his squalid townhouse. But Juliet, undaunted by her failures with the New York judiciary, remained convinced she should draw her father out of seclusion. A few weeks before Christmas, she invited him out for the holidays. She wanted to make sure he was presentable, so she asked his housekeeper to buy him a new suit for the occasion.

On Christmas Eve, a chauffeur-driven limousine delivered Juliet to her father's house. He was still in bed when she arrived; he had forgotten the invitation. "I don't even think he knew what day it was," Juliet said later.

After the housekeeper had Hartford dressed, Juliet presented him two choices: They could go to services at the Church of St. James, or to dinner at the Pierre Hotel, where she had made reservations. (Juliet first had tried to make reservations at the River Club, where her father had had a membership for nearly a half-century. When she called she was informed that her father was no longer welcome; apparently he had appeared at a party there in some state of disarray. "They told me they couldn't have him showing up like that," Juliet explained. "It came as quite a surprise.")

Her father rejected church and the Pierre, and then Juliet gave him a final alternative. She had been dating one of Adnan Khashoggi's sons; Khashoggi had invited her to his apartment at the Olympic Tower for both Christmas Eve and Christmas dinner. "I wanted to go to church," said Juliet. "My father wanted to go to Adnan's." And so father and daughter ended up at the apartment of the Arab magnate, who was out of jail on $1 million bail, as he awaited trial on charges of helping Ferdinand and Imelda Marcos smuggle money out of the Philippines.

It was an awkward entrance. There was already a crowd when the two arrived: Nikki Haskell, an aging New York hostess, was there with her entourage, along with assorted Iranian émigrés. Juliet left her father at the door with Lamia, Khashoggi's thirty-five-year-old wife. "I couldn't take it," Juliet explained later. "Nobody talked about it, but it wasn't hard to tell what they were thinking. They just kept watching him and wondering how he could be in such bad shape." She brought him along to Christmas dinner the next day, a much smaller affair; only Khashoggi, his wife, three sons, and two retainers—a live-in chiropractor and a live-in fortune-teller—were at the table. Afterward, Lamia took Juliet aside. "You must be strong," she told her, "you must do something about him."

But Juliet was not sure she could muster the resources to wage another war.

In February 1989, I paid a final visit to the Hartford townhouse. The appointment had been made days in advance and confirmed that morning.

I arrived at three in the afternoon. The courtyard was cluttered with half-open bags of garbage; their stink suffused the air. A notice from the City was jammed in the door: the house's owner, it warned, was in violation of various Health Department ordinances.

I pounded on the door for five minutes before Hartford, clad in a stained oxford-cloth shirt and boxer shorts, finally appeared. He said nothing as he opened the door; he turned and silently limped back up the stairs.

The rooms he led me past were all empty; in the living room, a television game show played to no one. Each doorway was framed by jagged shards of wood, evidence of the police raid two months before.

I followed Hartford up to his bedroom, watched as he lay down on the bed. "I'm so tired, I'm just so tired." He sighed and curled into fetal position. "Do you know where Elaine is?" he asked, then drifted off into unconsciousness without waiting for an answer.

Moans, presumably Elaine's, were audible from the floor above.

I walked down the stairs and let myself out. An unkempt man in a tattered plaid fleece coat crouched just outside the gate.

"Do you live in that house?" he demanded.

"No," I responded.

"Strange people live in that house," he mumbled as he wandered down the street. "Strange people."

Years and years before, Huntington Hartford had crafted his own epitaph in one of the early versions of *Show* magazine. "I have tried to use my millions creatively," he wrote. "The golden bird, coming to life, has sometimes wriggled out of my hand and flown away."

SOURCE NOTES

More than two hundred interviews were conducted in the course of researching this book, including more than twenty sessions with Huntington Hartford. These sessions with Hartford, and his writings, were major fonts of information. Material provided by Avis Anderson and Olivia Switz of The Hartford Family Foundation was invaluable as well. Hundreds of articles about Hartford were supplied by the morgues of newspapers in New York, Los Angeles, Miami, Nassau, and London. The most substantive of those interviews and articles (with the exception of several sources who requested confidentiality in return for cooperation), as well as various magazine articles, court documents, and personal journals and letters, are cited below.

List of Abbreviations

DN	New York *Daily News*
JA	New York *Journal-American*
LAHE	*Los Angeles Herald and Express*
NYHT	*New York Herald Tribune*
NYP	*New York Post*
NYT	*The New York Times*
WSJ	*The Wall Street Journal*
WT	New York *World-Telegram*

1

Interviews: Norma Jeans, Herbert Smokler.

Lisa Gubernick, "Poor Little Rich Man," *Forbes,* October 28, 1985.

2

Interviews: Josephine Hartford Bryce, Claire Booker Crosbie, Columbus O'Donnell, Nuala Pell, Emily Steele, Olivia Switz, Mary Weisse.

Anne Rittenhouse, "America's Social House of Peers," *Ainslee's Magazine,* October 1905.

Roy J. Bullock, "The Early History of The Great Atlantic & Pacific Tea Company," *Harvard Business Review,* April 1933.

Edward Hartford, undated letter to Josephine Hartford.

Edward Hartford, last will and testament, December 7, 1907, and related documents.

3

Interviews: Cleveland Amory, Louis Babbitt, Jack Barnaby, William Blanc, Henry Bogert, Beekman Cox Cannon, Mary Lee Fairbanks, William Foulke, Arthur Gordon, Richard Heath, John Lockwood, Mrs. John H. G. Pell, Edward Rollins, Morgan Smith, Francis Lund Van Dusen, Mrs. John Walker, Steven Whitney, Malcolm Wister.

"Mrs. Hartford's Social Ambition Is Topic for Conjecture in Newport," *JA,* April 3, 1928.

"Mrs. Hartford Is Now a Vital Factor in the Gay Social Whirl of Newport," *JA,* June 30, 1928.

"500 Will Attend Hartford Tennis Ball at Newport," *JA,* July 16, 1928.

George Huntington Hartford, "On Conventional Vacations," *Horae Scholasticae* (Concord: St. Paul's School), December 1930.

"Mrs. Edward V. Hartford Adds Plantation in South Carolina to Her Residences; Son, Now at Harvard, One of the Greatest Matrimonial

'Catches' Newport Has Known," *JA,* April 9, 1931.

"Girl 'Guard' of Boy's Morals Sues for Fee," *JA,* September 9, 1931.

"Glass House Fails to Guard 'Richest Boy' from Temptress," *DN,* September 10, 1931.

"Mayfair Chuckles over Rumor re: H. Hartford," *JA,* September 13, 1931.

"Hartford Heir to 200 Million Secretly Wed," *WT,* September 15, 1931.

"Mother Tows Heir on Trip," *JA,* September 16, 1931.

"Apron Strings Guide $200 Million Heir to Altar," *DN,* September 16, 1931.

"Mystery Romance of the Chain Store Heir," *EveryWeek Magazine,* November 29, 1931.

Harvard University, *Harvard Class of 1934: 25th Anniversary Report.* Cambridge, MA: Harvard University Press, 1959.

Daniel Snydacker, "The Great Depression in Newport," *Bulletin of the Newport Historical Society,* Spring 1985.

Henrietta Hartford, Documents relating to the estate of George Huntington Hartford II, minor.

Bronson Winthrop, letter to Henrietta Hartford, December 15, 1931.

4

Interviews: Mary Lee Fairbanks, Michael McIntosh, John Rentz, Jules Seligson, William X. Shields, William Walsh.

"The *Joseph Conrad*—Famous Old Square Rigger Sails in Quest of

Pirate Lore,'' *Coastal Topics,* February 1937.

''Sailing off to a New Treasure Island,'' *WT,* August 28, 1937.

Huntington Hartford, ''Gone Without the Wind,'' *Esquire,* October 1938.

Rich Girls,'' *Forbes,* October 26, 1987.

General release of claims by Mary Barton and George Huntington Hartford II, April 3, 1939.

Original trust agreement for Edward Barton Colt, April 3, 1939.

5

Interviews: James McKinley Bryant, Timothy Dickinson, Janet Edwards, Nelda Hitchcock, Penn Kimball, Jules Seligson, Herbert Smokler, Rae Weimer, Rico Zermeno.

Le Carnet Mondain, September 1937.

''Pignatelli's Ex-Wife Says She Paid the Bills,'' *NYHT,* December 17, 1937.

''Spotlight Hits the Hartfords,'' *DN,* January 9, 1938.

''Liberal Divorce Law Would End Pretense,'' *WT,* January 13, 1938.

''Not Wed After All,'' *DN,* January 13, 1938.

''What Ended Princess Pignatelli's Wifely Tolerance?'' *The American Weekly,* January 30, 1938.

''Heir to A&P Millions Loses Bride to Doug,'' *New York Sun News,* April 15, 1939.

''Prince Pignatelli Had Paid Court to Various U.S. Heiresses,'' *JA,* April 27, 1939.

''A&P Heir to Be No. 3 for Arline,'' *DN,* August 3, 1940.

''Consumers' Nickels and Dimes Pay for the $65,000 Diamond A&P Heir Gave Hollywood Cutie Pie: 'Where Economy Rules' Is No Slogan for Private Life,'' *WT,* August 9, 1940.

Carol McD. Wallace, ''Poor Little

6

Interviews: Gregson Bautzer, Dick Cowell, Janet Edwards, Stephen Elliot, Marjorie Steele Fitzgibbon, Jerry Ford, Nelda Hitchcock, Herman Hover, Murray Lerner, Robert Neal, Joseph Perrin, Bruce Pfeiffer, Michael Sher, Phyllis Sher, Mrs. Benjamin Van Raalte, Rico Zermeno.

''13 U.S. Families Hold Control of $2,700,574,000 Securities,'' *NYHT,* October 14, 1940.

''A&P Heir Named as 'Love Child's' $500,000 'Friend,' '' *DN,* January 12, 1943.

''The Strange Case of Mary Barton,'' *DN,* January 17, 1943.

''Jeers at Club Fail to Alter Hartford Plan,'' *DN,* August 12, 1947.

''Princess Pignatelli, One of Wealthiest Women in U.S., Dies,'' *NYHT,* June 4, 1948.

''So the Chain Store Heir Peddles Pretties,'' New York *Mirror,* February 6, 1949.

''Push 'im Around—Like the Poor Working Girl Did Huntington Hartford,'' *DN,* October 19, 1949.

'' 'Confirmed' Bachelor Goes to Hollywood,'' *DN,* October 30, 1949.

''Film Preview: *Tough Assignment,*'' *Variety,* November 8, 1949.

"Offbeat Millionaire: Rich Mama's Boy Grew Up to Be a Rich Ladies' Man," *DN,* March 2, 1961.

Ron McCrea, "Wright Intentions: Homes in Los Angeles Wright Might Have Built," *LA Style,* June 1988.

William Grundhoefer, application as administrator to the estate of Mary Chastain Grundhoefer, and related documents (including depositions of Virginia Caserta and Benjamin Van Raalte).

Henrietta Hartford, last will and testament, and related documents.

Personnel records of George H. Hartford, U.S. Naval Service–Coast Guard, February 14, 1942, through January 30, 1946.

7

Interviews: Marjorie Steele Fitzgibbon, Herman Hover, Seymour Krim, Harry Morgan, Rulon Neilson, Charles Rogers, Morton Winston.

"It Thinks in Tons Rather than Dollars," *Fortune,* November 1947.

"Real Refuge for Budding Genius," *Philadelphia Inquirer,* April 3, 1949.

"The Great A&P Muddle," *Fortune,* December 1949.

"Red Circle & Gold Leaf," *Time,* November 13, 1950.

"Art Trouble in Paradise," *Life,* February 4, 1952.

"What's Art?" *Fortnight,* February 4, 1952.

"Where the Versatile Cigaret Cinderella Led the Millionaire Grocer Boy," New York *Mirror,* December 21, 1952.

"The Handicap of Wealth," *DN,* January 25, 1953.

"Millionaire's Wife at Work," *Look,* February 24, 1953.

"The Most Magnetic Men," *JA,* March 13, 1960.

Tom Wolfe, "The Luther of Columbus Circle," *NYHT,* February 23, 1964.

Wendell Berge, letter to George Huntington Hartford, February 19, 1945.

Prospectus for The Oil Shale Corporation (Tosco), May 14, 1959.

8

Interviews: Seymour Alter, Roland Balaÿ, Marjorie Steele Fitzgibbon, Catherine Hartford, Thomas Hoving, Rico Zermeno.

"Face to Face," *NYT,* January 5, 1953.

"The Current Cinema," *The New Yorker,* January 24, 1953.

"Marjorie Hartford," *Art Digest,* February 15, 1953.

"Marjorie Hartford," *ARTnews,* March 1953.

"Statement," *Reality: A Journal of Artists' Opinions,* Spring 1953.

"As Actress A&P Wife Knows Her Groceries," *DN,* August 6, 1954.

"Woman Decorator Spends $750,000 'Dressing' a Theater," *Los Angeles Times,* August 24, 1954.

"Helen Hayes Speaks and Drama Lives," *Los Angeles Times,* September 28, 1954.

"2000 in Stands Watch Premiere of LA's First Playhouse in 27 Yrs.," *Los Angeles Examiner,* September 28, 1954.

Cobina Wright, "Society As I Find It," *LAHE*, September 30, 1954.

"A Stage for Screen Capital," *Theatre Arts*, February 1955.

Arthur Millier, "Attack on Art Held Illogical," *Los Angeles Times*, April 24, 1955.

Huntington Hartford, "The Public Be Damned" (paid advertisement), *NYT*, May 16, 1955.

"Battlefronts," *Time*, June 20, 1955.

Eleanor Roosevelt, "The Case of Mr. Hartford and His Ad Against Art," *WT*, July 30, 1955.

9

Interviews: Seymour Alter, Benjamin Buttenweiser, Dick Cowell, Paul DeGives, Eddie Dodds, Roger Donoghue, Janet Edwards, Marjorie Steele Fitzgibbon, Catherine Hartford, Nelda Hitchcock, Robin Moore, Robert Neal, Richard Schickel, Budd Schulberg, Rico Zermeno.

"Name Huntington Hartford in Boy's Paternity Suit," *LAHE*, August 31, 1955.

"Suit Names Food Chain Heir as Father of Actress' Son, 17," *NYP*, August 31, 1955.

"Process Servers Hunt A&P Heir," *JA*, September 1, 1955.

Cobina Wright, "An Insight into the Case of Huntington Hartford," *LAHE*, September 9, 1955.

Florabel Muir, "The Love Child Who May Win a Fortune," *DN*, October 23, 1955.

10

Interviews: Marjorie Steele Fitzgibbon, John Ireland, Michael McIntosh, Thor Ramsing, Olivia Switz.

"A&P Wealth Warms a Hearth but Chills a Career," *NYP*, November 29, 1955.

"Errol Flynn Walks Out on Role in His Old Friend's Play," *NYP*, February 19, 1958.

Brooks Atkinson, "The Theater: *Jane Eyre*," *NYT*, May 2, 1958.

"Art Museum at Columbus Circle Planned by Huntington Hartford," *NYT*, June 1, 1958.

"Huntington Hartford and the English Starlet," *NYP*, August 13, 1958.

"Hermit Kingdom," *WSJ*, December 12, 1958.

"Errol Flynn's Pretty Baby," *People*, October 17, 1988.

Huntington Hartford Enterprises v. Regal Shoe Store, assorted documents.

Documents relating to the establishment of A&P voting trust.

11

Interviews: Brett Adams, Seymour Alter, Marjorie Steele Fitzgibbon, Jerry Ford, Wayne Headrick, Thomas Hoving, John Ireland, Sandy Lee, Thor Ramsing, Robert Wool.

"More Than Modern: Edward Durell Stone," *Time*, March 31, 1958.

"Modern Art in a 'Marble Monolith,'" *NYHT*, May 29, 1959.

"No Honky Tonks on Hog Island," *NYHT*, June 22, 1959.

"How to Be Happy Though Rich," *Playbill*, November 16, 1959.

"Hartford Gives City a Café for Central Park," *NYT*, March 14, 1960.

"In Central Park—No," *NYT,* March 17, 1960.

"Moses Adamant on Café in Park," *NYT,* May 2, 1960.

"The Hartfords Split over Skin Diver," New York *Mirror,* August 17, 1960.

"Art-and-Park Man," *NYT,* August 31, 1960.

"Mrs. Hartford Asks All the $ From A to P," *DN,* October 20, 1960.

"Mrs. A&P Asks $1,000 Daily for Groceries and Other Bills," *DN,* November 8, 1960.

"What This Millionaire Wants for Christmas," *Daily Sketch* (London), November 30, 1960.

"Hartford Must Pay—Plenty," New York *Mirror,* January 10, 1961.

"An Urge to Do Good Fills Hartford Heart," *DN,* February 28, 1961.

"Chariot Racing for Nassau," *The Miami Herald,* March 5, 1961.

"Marjorie Steele Marries, Costs Her $60,000 a Year," *NYHT,* November 17, 1961.

"The Benefactor," *Time,* March 2, 1962.

"The Park Café Sales Pitch," *NYT,* March 14, 1962.

"A Millionaire Brings 7th Century to Paradise," *Miami News,* August 12, 1962.

"Huntington Hartford: A Most Unusual Client," *Architectural Forum,* March 1964.

Ada Louise Huxtable, "More on How to Kill a City," *NYT,* March 21, 1965.

"That Expendable Park Café," *NYT,* November 18, 1965.

"Hartford Gets $22,000 Profit on Café Failure," *NYHT,* March 2, 1966.

Ralph King, "There Goes the Neighborhood," *Forbes,* October 26, 1987.

Edward Barton, release of paternity suit against Huntington Hartford, and related documents.

795 Fifth Ave. Corp. et al. v. City of New York, assorted documents.

12

Interviews: Winslow Ames, Edward Collins, Frank Gibney, Catherine Hartford, Diane Hartford, Phyllis Sher, Henry Wolf, Robert Wool.

Show, vols. 1–4.

" 'Ideal' Man Departs," *Newsweek,* May 29, 1961.

"Boom Town in the Tropics," *JA,* January 30, 1962.

"Hartford's Party the Most," *JA,* February 20, 1962.

"The Creative Urge," *Newsweek,* March 5, 1962.

"Paradise Regained," *Town & Country,* May 1962.

"A&P Millions Create a Profit-less Paradise," *The Miami Herald,* July 8, 1962.

"Glamour & Simplicity Won Hunt Hartford," *DN,* October 8, 1962.

"Hartford's Cinderella—No Coal in Her Shoes," *NYP,* October 8, 1962.

"How to Marry a Millionaire," *Evening News* (London), October 11, 1962.

"Town and Around," *The Nassau Guardian,* November 8, 1963.

13

Interviews: Seymour Alter, Benjamin Buttenweiser, William Cross, Marjorie Steele Fitzgibbon, Michael McIntosh, Margaret Potter, Howard Schneider, Phyllis Sher, Henry Wolf.

Tom Morgan, "George Huntington Hartford II, Peripatetic Patron," *Esquire,* March 1963.

"The Man Who Owns Paradise," *The Saturday Evening Post,* April 27, 1963.

"Hartford Pulls Out Stops for Permit," *The Miami Herald,* December 5, 1963.

Tom Wolfe, "The Luther of Columbus Circle," *NYHT,* February 23, 1964.

Ada Louise Huxtable, "Columbus Circle Gallery Will Open Mid-March," *NYT,* February 25, 1964.

Alfred Frankfurter, "Caviare? New York's Newest Museum," *ART-news,* March 1964.

"Huntington Hartford and His Museum," *NYP,* March 14, 1964.

John Canaday, "Art: Hartford Collection," *NYT,* March 17, 1964.

"Dalí Says It's a Dilly," *NYHT,* March 17, 1964.

"Hartford's Gallery," *The New Yorker,* March 21, 1964.

"Hartford Modern: What's in a Name?" *Newsweek,* March 23, 1964.

"Philanthropic Philistine," *The Christian Century,* May 27, 1964.

"Huntington Hartford: Where the Money Went," *NYP,* August 13, 1966.

"Kingdom in the Sun," *WSJ,* October 19, 1966.

Richard Nixon, letter to author, January 21, 1987.

14

Interviews: Selig Adler, Bernard Cornfeld, James Doolittle, Frank Gibney, Allan Hughes, Gilbert Kraft, Charles Murphy, Richard Olsen, Howard Schneider.

Daily Mirror (London), July 19, 1963.

"Hartford Acts to Sell His Liquor Store," *NYT,* December 11, 1963.

Tom Wolfe, "A Sale Near for *Show,* Hartford's Magazine," *NYHT,* March 31, 1964.

"A Dreamer with Checkbook in Hand," *Business Week,* May 2, 1964.

"*Show* Must Go On: Hartford Drops Plan to Sell the Magazine," *WSJ,* May 20, 1964.

"Reprieve for *Show* Magazine," *NYT,* August 6, 1964.

"Huntington Hartford Seeks Buyer for Paradise Island," *WSJ,* October 5, 1964.

"Paradise Island Rumors Flying," *The Miami Herald,* October 6, 1964.

"A Millionaire Art Buff Takes on the Bad Guys," *Life,* November 27, 1964.

"*Show* Magazine Sold," *NYT,* December 3, 1964.

"Got It? Use It," *The Miami Herald,* February 15, 1965.

"Hartford Plans to Shut Down Artists' Retreat," *Los Angeles Times,* May 2, 1965.

"Hartford Seeks Aid for Gallery," *NYT,* May 15, 1965.

"Hartford on the Rocks?" *Newsweek,* June 7, 1965.

Joshua Hammer, "Last Resorts," *Manhattan, inc.,* February 1987.

15

Interviews: Harry Brown, Jack Davis, China Gerard, Robert Peloquin, Howard Schneider, Phyllis Sher, Herbert Smokler, James Vanderpol.

"Hidden Money: Bahamas Called Way Station to Swiss Banks," *NYT*, February 17, 1965.

"Hartfords Make Scene," *NYP*, November 6, 1965.

"Advertising," *NYT*, November 9, 1965.

"Hartford to Diane: Take Me Back," *NYP*, November 22, 1965.

"Hartford Will Sell A&P Shares," *NYT*, June 8, 1966.

"Hunt for Success," *Time*, June 17, 1966.

"Kingdom in the Sun," *WSJ*, October 19, 1966.

"The Bahamas: Bad News for the Boys," *Time*, January 20, 1967.

"Black Day on Bay Street," *Newsweek*, January 23, 1967.

"The Scandal in the Bahamas," *Life*, February 3, 1967.

"The Mafia at Work," *The Saturday Evening Post*, February 25, 1967.

"Chesler Concedes Paying Huge Sums for Gambling Permission in Bahamas," *WSJ*, April 19, 1967.

"Gamblers' Ties Traced in Nassau," *NYT*, April 22, 1967.

Huntington Hartford, "Why the A&P Doesn't Care!" *Show*, October 1967.

"Heir Attack on A&P," *NYT*, October 5, 1967.

"Sands Sold His Influence to Bring Gambling to Bahamas," *WSJ*, November 21, 1967.

"A&P Meeting Faces Hard Questions," *NYT*, June 18, 1968.

"Changes in Paradise," *Holiday*, November 1968.

16

Interviews: Harry Brown, Marjorie Steele Fitzgibbon, Catherine Hartford, Diane Hartford, Herta Headrick, Wayne Headrick, Burton Monasch, Dallas Pell, Nuala Pell, Charles Rumsey, Phyllis Sher, Herbert Smokler, Demetrius Vilan.

"Diane Sues Huntington for Divorce," *DN*, September 5, 1967.

"How Darin Met Diane," *DN*, September 24, 1967.

"Hunt, Diane Together Like A&P at a Show," *DN*, October 11, 1967.

"Was This Suicide Heir's Son?" *Los Angeles Herald-Examiner*, November 9, 1967.

"Hartfords Patch Their Nest with $1.5 Million Egg for Baby," *DN*, December 15, 1967.

Catherine Hartford, unpublished journals.

Wayne Headrick, unpublished writings.

17

Interviews: Dick Adler, Mario Amaya, Marilyn Chambers, Digby Diehl, Art Ford, William Hitchcock, Robin Moore, Peter Sammartino, Sally Sammartino, Donna Wilson, Morton Winston.

"Huntington Hartford Tells Me How the Cookie Crumbles," *The Daily Express* (London), January 21, 1966.

"Hartford: Millionaire Moralist," *DN*, July 19, 1968.

"Hartford Planning Oil Shale Lawsuit," *NYT*, July 20, 1968.

"So What Went On? Diane Won't Tell," *DN*, April 25, 1969.

"New Image for an Aging Playboy," *Tropic*, April 27, 1969.

"Huntington Hartford Gives His Museum to Fairleigh Dickinson," *NYT*, July 16, 1969.

"Mexican Divorce for Hartfords Today," *DN*, July 7, 1970.

"Free Advice," *Forbes*, April 1, 1971.

Enid Nemy, "Huntington Hartford's Club Open with a Throng, *NYT*, October 27, 1972.

"The Grocery Bills Don't Bother A&P Heir," *The Miami Herald*, November 19, 1972.

"Hartford Believes You Sign Your Life Away," *DN*, November 5, 1973.

"Hartford Paddles His Own Game," *DN*, November 24, 1974.

Resorts International, Others," *WSJ*, August 15, 1973.

"Rebozo Banking and Gambling in Bahamas Attract Investigators," *NYT*, January 21, 1974.

"Court Lets Bank Sell Collateral," *DN*, February 7, 1974.

"Hartford Marrying Again," *NYP*, February 26, 1974.

Linda Christmas, "Fortune and the Teller," *The Guardian* (London), July 6, 1974.

"Resorts International, Huntington Hartford Settle Long Dispute," *WSJ*, October 16, 1974.

"Dinner with a Friend from Southeast Asia," *The Washington Post*, May 9, 1975.

Huntington Hartford v. Resorts International, James M. Crosby, and Bank of Commerce, complaint, affidavits, and settlement papers.

United States v. Victor Danenza, complaint, conviction papers, and related documents.

18

Interviews: Seymour Alter, Anita Helen Brooks, Jack Davis, Timothy Dickinson, Marjorie Steele Fitzgibbon, Catherine Hartford, Jonathan Michaels, William Perlmuth, Thor Ramsing, Howard Schneider, Henry Williams, Donna Wilson.

"Huntington Hartford Has Devoted a Lifetime to Spending a Fortune," *WSJ*, February 6, 1973.

"Hartford Accuses Vesco, Charges Casino Plot," *DN*, June 24, 1973.

"Court Grants Order Asked Against

19

Interviews: Earl Blackwell, Anita Helen Brooks, Joseph Dever, Timothy Dickinson, James Doolittle, Anthony Haden-Guest, Catherine Hartford, Juliet Hartford, R. Couri Hay, Norma Jeans, Mary Kirby, Jonathan Michaels, Linda Never, Joseph Perrin, Bill Raphael, Steve Rubell, Henry Williams.

"House Tour: Perfect Chance to Poke Around," *NYT*, May 30, 1971.

"Trustees Are Seeking a Buyer for New York Cultural Center," *NYT*, November 22, 1974.

"Days Are Numbered for a White Elephant," *NYT,* September 10, 1975.

"Cocktail Danse Macabre Marks the Demise of Cultural Center," *NYT,* September 26, 1975.

"Buddhas and Spilled Ice Cream Catch the Eye in Model Rooms," *NYT,* October 2, 1975.

"A&P Heir Hospitalized," *DN,* February 4, 1978.

"Timothy Dickinson Is a Secret Weapon in Authors' Arsenal," *WSJ,* December 21, 1982.

20

Interviews: Timothy Dickinson, Germaine Glidden, Juliet Hartford, Ted Kerin, Harry Lipsig, Dallas Pell, Richard Savage, Herbert Smokler, Olivia Switz.

"Heir Now, All's Well That . . . ," *NYP,* June 9, 1976.

"Playboy Tycoon's Ex Accused of Torture," *NYP,* January 21, 1982.

"Victim's Mom Up in Arms over Assault," *NYP,* January 22, 1982.

"Hartford Ex Faces 'Torture' and Giggles," *NYP,* February 12, 1982.

"He Finds Court Is Very Cooperative," *DN,* February 24, 1982.

"Hartford Loses Eviction Fight," *NYT,* May 29, 1982.

"A&P Heir's Ex-Wife Pleads Guilty," *DN,* July 9, 1982.

"Bringing A&P Back from the Brink," *NYT,* June 23, 1985.

Hal Davis, "Ex-Wife: A&P Heir's a Dope Fiend," *NYP,* March 27, 1986.

Catherine Hartford, unpublished journals.

Sheila Dowling v. Huntington Hartford, complaint, affidavits, and related documents.

Huntington Hartford v. One Beekman Place, Inc., complaint, affidavits, settlement papers, and related documents.

21

Interviews: Margaret Clemons, Linda Donoghue, Raoul Lionel Felder, Diane Hartford, Juliet Hartford, Bill Raphael, Mary Weisse.

Gioia Diliberto, "Family Feud," *People,* June 9, 1986.

Marie Brenner, "Whatever Happened to Huntington Hartford?" *Vanity Fair,* July 1986.

Cindy Adams, "The Mystery of A&P Heir Huntington Hartford: Why Does He Live in Fear?" *NYP,* May 6, 1987.

"A&P Heir's Daughter Dies," *NYP,* June 8, 1988.

Michael Gross, "The Deb of the Minute," *New York,* August 28, 1989.

Diane Hartford, individually and on behalf of Juliet Hartford, a minor, for the appointment of a conservator of the property of George Huntington Hartford II, complaint, affidavits, settlement papers, and related documents.

The People of New York v. Elaine Hartford, complaint and related documents.

SELECTED BIBLIOGRAPHY

Albury, Paul. *Paradise Island Story.* London: Macmillan, 1984.
—— . *The Story of the Bahamas.* London: Macmillan, 1975.
Amory, Cleveland. *The Last Resorts.* New York: Harper & Brothers, 1958.
—— . *Who Killed Society?* New York: Harper & Brothers, 1960.
Baltzell, E. Digby. *The Protestant Establishment: Aristocracy and Caste in America.* New York: Random House, 1964.
Balzac, Honoré de. *The Physiology of Marriage.* Philadelphia: Avil, 1901.
Bartlett, Donald L., and James B. Steele. *Empire: The Life, Legend and Madness of Howard Hughes.* New York: W. W. Norton, 1975.
Bergreen, Laurence. *James Agee: A Life.* New York: E. P. Dutton, 1984.
Boorstin, Daniel. *The Image, or, What Happened to the American Dream.* New York: Atheneum, 1962.
Braudy, Leo. *The Frenzy of Renown.* New York: Oxford University Press, 1986.
Carr, J. Russell. *The* Joseph Conrad, *1882–1982.* Mystic, CT: Mystic Seaport Museum, 1982.
Connell, Brian. *Knight Errant.* Garden City, NY: Doubleday, 1955.
Cowles, Virginia. *The Astors.* New York: Alfred A. Knopf, 1979.
Demaris, Ovid. *The Boardwalk Jungle.* New York: Bantam, 1987.
Epstein, Joseph. *Ambition.* New York: Random House, 1962.
Fairbanks, Douglas, Jr. *The Salad Days.* New York: Doubleday, 1988.
Flynn, Errol. *My Wicked, Wicked Ways.* New York: G. P. Putnam's Sons, 1959.
Freedland, Michael. *The Two Lives of Errol Flynn.* New York: Bantam, 1980.
Friedrich, Otto. *City of Nets—A Portrait of Hollywood in the 1940's.* New York: Harper & Row, 1986.
Gabler, Neal. *An Empire of Their Own: How the Jews Invented Hollywood.* New York: Crown, 1988.
Gates, John D. *The Astor Family.* New York: Doubleday, 1981.

Hartford, Huntington. *Art or Anarchy?* New York: Doubleday, 1964.

——— . *Has God Been Insulted Here?* New York: Privately printed, 1951.

——— . *You Are What You Write.* New York: Macmillan, 1973.

Hecksher, August. *St. Paul's: The Life of a New England School.* New York: Charles Scribner's Sons, 1978.

Heimann, Jim. *Out with the Stars: Hollywood Nightlife in the Golden Era.* New York: Abbeville, 1985.

Herzog, Arthur. *Vesco.* New York: Doubleday, 1987.

Higham, Charles. *Errol Flynn: The Untold Story.* New York: Doubleday, 1980.

Hoopes, Roy. *Ralph Ingersoll: A Biography.* New York: Atheneum, 1985.

Hougan, Jim. *Spooks.* New York: Bantam, 1979.

Hoyt, Edwin P. *That Wonderful A&P!* New York: Hawthorn, 1969.

Jacobson, Judith S. *The Greatest Good: A History of the John A. Hartford Foundation.* New York: Danbar, 1984.

Lawrenson, Helen. *Whistling Girl.* New York: Doubleday, 1978.

Mahon, Gigi. *The Company That Bought the Boardwalk.* New York: Random House, 1980.

Miller, Russell. *Bunny: The Real Story of* Playboy. New York: Henry Holt, 1984.

Morella, Joe, and Edward Z. Epstein. *Lana: The Public and Private Lives of Miss Turner.* New York: Dell, 1971.

Moses, Robert. *Public Works: A Dangerous Trade.* New York: McGraw-Hill, 1970.

Moskowitz, Milton, et al. *Everybody's Business.* New York: Harper & Row, 1980.

Pierson, David Lawrence. *History of The Oranges to 1921.* New York: Lewis Historical, 1922.

Plagens, Peter. *Sunshine Muse: Contemporary Art on the West Coast.* New York: Praeger, 1974.

Podhoretz, Norman. *Making It.* New York: Random House, 1967.

Reid, Ed. *The Grim Reapers.* New York: Bantam, 1970.

Sammartino, Peter. *Of Colleges and Kings.* Cranbury, NJ: Cornwall, 1985.

Secrest, Meryle. *Salvador Dalí: A Biography.* New York: E. P. Dutton, 1986.

Shields, William X. *Bigger than Life: A Biography of Francis X. Shields.* New York: Freundlich, 1986.

Turner, Lana. *Lana: The Lady, The Legend, The Truth.* New York: E. P. Dutton, 1982.

Veblen, Thorstein. *The Theory of the Leisure Class.* New York: Macmillan, 1899.

Walsh, William I. *The Rise and Decline of The Great Atlantic & Pacific Tea Company.* New Jersey: Lyle Stuart, 1986.

Wolfe, Tom. *From Bauhaus to Our House.* New York: Pocket Books, 1981.

ACKNOWLEDGMENTS

I am grateful to all the people who took the time to answer my questions; their contributions made this book possible.

My mother, Grace Gubernick, has been a source of inspiration throughout. Friends on both coasts provided much wisdom and good humor, especially Sunny Bates, Mary Billard, Richard Cardran, Bairj Donabedian, Deirdre Fanning, Sherry Fuqua Gilson, Ellen Hamilton, Joanne Hart, Michael Hughes, Tricia Joyce, Steve Kling, Nancy Miller, Deborah Mitchell, Deborah Rosen, Jinny St. Goar, Sue Steinberg, Jeffrey Trachtenberg, and David Weitz. Martha Trachtenberg contributed extraordinary research and indefatigable enthusiasm. Tom Tisch pointed out that how fortunes are lost is just as interesting as how they are made.

I would also like to express my appreciation to my agents, Eric Ashworth and Candida Donadio, who believed in the project from the beginning; my editor, Faith Sale, who asked the questions needed to make the book better; and Anna Jardine, whose relentless copyediting improved the text in both style and substance.

Thanks to the editors at *Forbes,* Jim Michaels, Laury Minard, and Steve Lawrence, who provided safe berth while the book was completed; and most of all to Shelly Zalaznick, who shepherded me through the article that got me started.

None of this would have been possible without the wit and support (and editing) of my husband, Paul Fishleder.

INDEX